STILL STANDING

Also by Paul O'Grady

AT MY MOTHER'S KNEE . . .
AND OTHER LOW JOINTS

THE DEVIL RIDES OUT

and published by Bantam Books

STILL STANDING
The Savage Years

Paul O'Grady

BANTAM BOOKS

LONDON • TORONTO • SYDNEY • AUCKLAND • JOHANNESBURG

TRANSWORLD PUBLISHERS
61–63 Uxbridge Road, London W5 5SA
A Random House Group Company
www.transworldbooks.co.uk

STILL STANDING
A BANTAM BOOK: 9780857501028

First published in Great Britain
in 2012 by Bantam Press
an imprint of Transworld Publishers
Bantam edition published 2013

This book is a work of non-fiction based on the life, experiences and
recollections of Paul O'Grady. In some limited cases names of people,
places, dates, sequences or the detail of events have been changed solely to
protect the privacy of others. The author has stated to the publishers that,
except in such minor respects not affecting the substantial accuracy of the
work, the contents of this book are true.

Every effort has been made to obtain the necessary permissions with
reference to copyright material, both illustrative and quoted. We apologize
for any omissions in this respect and will be pleased to make the
appropriate acknowledgements in any future edition.

A CIP catalogue record for this book
is available from the British Library.

Addresses for Random House Group Ltd companies outside the UK
can be found at: www.randomhouse.co.uk
The Random House Group Ltd Reg. No. 954009

The Random House Group Limited supports The Forest Stewardship
Council® (FSC®), the leading international forest-certification
organisation. Our books carrying the FSC label are printed on
FSC®-certified paper. FSC is the only forest-certification scheme
supported by the leading environmental organisations, including
Greenpeace. Our paper procurement policy can be found at
www.randomhouse.co.uk/environment

Typeset in 11/14pt Sabon by Falcon Oast Graphic Art Ltd.
Printed and bound by CPI Group (UK) Ltd, Croydon CR0 4YY.

2 4 6 8 10 9 7 5 3 1

For all those London cabbies who have ever asked,
'How did you get started in this game, then?'

ACKNOWLEDGEMENTS

Thanks to all the people who helped jog my memory in the writing of this book.

David Dale, Vera, my sister Sheila and cousin Marje, Joan Marshrons, the late Peter Searle, and everyone else who received a phone call with me asking, 'Do you remember when . . .' And also thanks to Doug Young at Transworld for his patience.

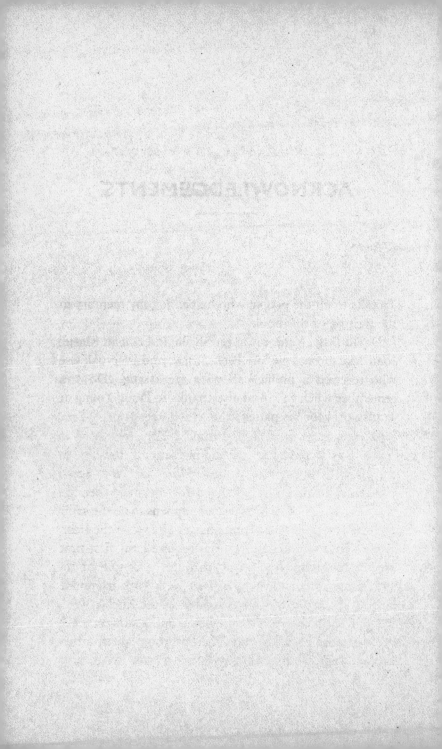

PROLOGUE

JANUARY 2011. SOUTHAMPTON. IT'S BEEN FIVE YEARS since I swore I'd never do panto again yet here I am, staggering against a biting, icy wind down the small lane that leads from my rented digs to the Mayflower Theatre for a matinee performance as the Widow Twankey in *Aladdin*.

I like Southampton and the Mayflower is one of my favourite theatres. The last time I appeared here in panto was ten years ago, stomping around the stage as the Wicked Queen in *Snow White and the Seven Dwarves*. So much has changed for me since then yet the flat I've rented, which just so happens to be the same one that I stayed in last time, hasn't altered in the least. Same telly and video player that required any first-time viewer to plough their way through a couple of instruction manuals the size of two New York telephone directories, same washing machine in the kitchen with but one temperature setting – boil – and a slowest wash cycle of nine hours, and on the bathroom shelf, a tiny ceramic half-moon that had fallen off the front of a

9

pottery oil burner I'd bought for want of something to buy at a local craft fair and left on the shelf a decade ago. Walking into this flat again, I felt as if I'd never been away and for a brief moment I experienced a rush of affection for the old place as I surveyed the living room, over-crowded with the same familiar furniture. I forgot that last time I was here I'd lost my deposit, and a susbstantial one at that, to pay for what the landlord had described as 'damages to the furniture, appliances, carpets, walls and ceiling'. I'll admit to throwing a few parties during my stay but to the best of my knowledge I can't recall anyone sticking to the ceiling. We were a particularly lively com-pany, it's true: David Langham, the actor who played the Queen's henchman, aptly summed it up after another night of carnage in the pubs of Southampton when he wryly described us as 'the Rolling Stones do *Snow White*'.

Sherrie Hewson, playing the part of Ms White's nurse, had conveniently rented the flat next door to mine. I've known Sherrie for years and our combined flats quickly became the gathering place for those cast, crew and band members who were still raring to go and fancied a drink after the pubs had closed.

One night – or should I say early morning – after a particularly rowdy shindig that might just possibly still be going on today, Sherrie, in a rare display of sensibility, reminded us all that we had a matinee that afternoon and that we needed to get some sleep. Just as I was drifting off into a drunken coma in my bed I felt something tugging on my duvet. I opened one eye but couldn't see anyone. Buster, my dog, was flat on his back with his legs in the air fast asleep so I knew it couldn't be him, yet the mysterious tugging continued. Eventually I peered over the side of the bed and, attempting to focus in the gloom without my specs, I encountered what appeared to be a naked dwarf hanging on to the duvet. Was this what they called the DTs? If so I was never touching anything stronger than tea again.

A few of the cast had stayed over as the hour was late and it was easier to crash on the floor and sofa than trek back to their digs. Among the seven actors who played the dwarves were a few real party animals and it wasn't an uncommon sight to find them kipping on our floor after an impromptu post-show party.

I really enjoyed working with the dwarves: they were a lot of fun and, even though it was my name that was above the title on the posters outside the theatre, as far as I was concerned the seven dwarves were the undisputed stars of the show. Now here was one of them naked in my bedroom and seemingly trying to pull the duvet off me. Had he been consumed by an overwhelming urge to ravish me? And if so, was I up for it?

'I wanna pee and I can't get in the bathroom,' he said politely, scotching any thoughts I had about a sexual proposition.

'Why not?' I asked, for it seemed the only appropriate response at the time.

'Because Snow White has collapsed behind the bathroom door,' came the answer – a line you don't hear in panto, kiddies, delivered in a tone that implied Snow White's demise somehow might have been my responsibility.

'What do you mean, Snow White's collapsed?' The

11

edges were starting to blur. Was our fantasy life on stage somehow bleeding across into real life?

I fell out of bed and, putting my glasses on, made my way to the bathroom, and gave the door a good push. Somebody was indeed lying against it. I pushed again, only harder this time, until I managed to open it just enough to get my head inside. Lying on the floor and sleeping contentedly was Andrew, our Prince, curled up on a pile of towels, with the pedestal mat substituting for a pillow.

'It's not Snow White, it's Prince Charming,' I snorted matter-of-factly, as if sleeping princes on bathroom floors were a common occurrence in the O'Grady household. 'Go back to bed.'

'But I wanna pee,' the naked one beside me pleaded.

'Then use the lav in my bathroom, or pee over the balcony,' I snapped, making my wobbly way back to bed. 'I don't care where you do it.'

He took advantage of my ensuite in the end. But during the night someone did pee over the balcony, because the resident of the ground-floor flat told me the next day as I was leaving for the theatre that she thought the overflow pipe from my toilet wasn't working properly as she'd heard it pouring outside her bedroom window at around 4 a.m.

Typically, the landlord turned up unexpectedly the next morning to find the front door wide open and a hopeful Buster wagging his tail at him in the hall, despite the contract firmly stating that pets were not allowed. Neither was smoking, yet here he was, surrounded by overflowing ashtrays, empty bottles and bodies sprawled

12

across the living-room floor. To make matters worse, Buster took this opportunity to express his displeasure at our landlord's attitude towards all things canine by contemptuously cocking his leg and weeing up the leg of the coffee table. On reflection I'm not surprised I lost my deposit.

That's panto. You work hard and play hard, or at least for every production I've ever appeared in we have. I'm usually the instigator of any outside-work activities, quick to winkle out the cast, crew and band members who enjoy a good time.

I'm not suggesting for one minute that panto is an excuse to party, because it isn't. I take it very seriously, giving it one hundred and ten per cent at every performance regardless, whether I've been tucked up in bed at midnight or out on the razz until 2 a.m. the night before. The same can be said for every other cast member I've ever worked with – it's a matter of pride and a respect for your audience that when you're out there on stage you give it your all however you may be feeling. There's a myth that in panto you make the script up as you go along and can do and say any old thing that takes your fancy. Nothing could be further from the truth. A certain amount of ad-libbing is expected, of course, but for the best part I always try not to stray too far from the script. Pantos are long enough as it is without a self-indulgent performer hogging the stage and putting extra time on the show instead of getting on with it and moving the story along.

I had naively assumed that after having two heart attacks and years working solely in the cosseted world of television, I'd have found a stint back in panto completely exhausting. However, from the first day of rehearsal it was as if I'd never given it up and I took to being Lily again with gusto. Even after two shows I still had enough energy to go out with members of the cast and didn't, as I'd anticipated, find myself wearily dragging my poor worn-out carcass back to the digs to an early night.

I rarely drink these days (I've got witnesses) and surprisingly I found getting back into the saddle on the tipsy pony remarkably easy, just as it was equally painless to slip out of it once the panto season was over and return to my mostly abstemious ways again.

I didn't give up drinking for health reasons, I simply went off it. My village pub is sadly neglected, as are, apart from the odd occasion, the West End clubs and bars that I used to live in.

The hangover is an effective deterrent. I've found as I've got older that hangovers can no longer be shaken off by partaking of that age-old restorative, a healthy serving of chips smothered in gravy and washed down with a nice big bottle of Lucozade. Now, at the ripe old age of fifty-five, a decent hangover feels akin to a near-death experience and requires a couple of days lying prostrate in a darkened room with a bucket by the bed, just in case, and a label on my toe saying 'Do not attempt life-sustaining measures.'

My dad always used to say that if you wanted a drink then you went out for one to the pub; drinking was all about socializing. Sitting at home boozing on your own was frowned upon, an anti-social habit only an alcoholic would indulge in. Consequently I've never enjoyed drinking at home, though parties and Christmas are different, naturally. Then the booze flows, and at a do or an evening in a pub with a group of lively companions I can sink it with the best of them, even though these days I'm a bit of a part-timer as it only takes a couple of glasses of wine or a pint or two of cider and I'm well on my way.

At home I drink tea and I'd never consider opening a bottle of wine to accompany a meal. My parents, even if they could've afforded it, never drank wine with a meal at home, and as far as I know nor did anybody else. Mary next door would often have a bottle of Mackeson with her dinner but then she was known to have one with her breakfast as well so she doesn't count, but nobody drank wine. According to my mother, people who drank wine were winos, miserable drunks who haunted Yates's Wine Lodge getting paralytic on tumblers of Aussie white.

It was a different matter, however, if you happened to be my mother's idea of posh. Then it was perfectly acceptable to drink as much wine as you liked, as that was the sort of behaviour she expected of toffs, but it was not something us working classes did.

On the very rare occasions when we went posh and my dad treated us to a meal at the Berni Inn in New Brighton, my mother and my aunty Annie would have a glass of the house white, the only time I ever saw them drinking wine, followed by an Irish coffee each after their dessert of Black Forest gateau. My dad would stick to his pint and I'd drink pop and read the I-Spy book that they gave away to children to keep them quiet.

Anyway, as my creed is now more or less 'abstinence

makes the heart grow stronger', I naturally assumed that this season at the Mayflower would be a more genteel affair with less inclination on my part to party. However, I hadn't reckoned on the dark magic of panto to weave its spell and awaken like the Sleeping Beauty the dormant hell-raiser inside me. I started off with good intentions: a quiet drink after the show and then home to cheese on toast, a bit of telly and early to bed. I'd even bought a blender online from Amazon so I could set myself up for the day with a vitamin-rich smoothie, but after two days I rinsed the glass jug out with boiling water and the damn thing cracked, putting paid to my healthy aspirations.

Vera, a person you'll already be aware of if you've read *The Devil Rides Out* (if you haven't, then in a nutshell Vera is a lifelong friend whose real name is Alan and who I've shared many scrapes and misadventures with along life's highway), anyway Vera insisted I send it back, but I'd thrown the box out and couldn't be bothered with the hassle of finding a replacement, wrapping it up, etc., so it was consigned to the back of a kitchen cupboard and for all I know it's still there, keeping the half-moon in the bathroom company.

Nutrition can be a problem when you're doing two shows a day. After the matinee you ask yourself, is it worth taking all the make-up off, getting dressed and then going out in lousy weather to find somewhere half decent to eat? It isn't, it's far simpler to stay in your dressing room and rely on your dresser or a member of the cast or crew who are going out to bring you back something to eat, after which if you're sensible you'll get your head down and try to catch some sleep. If you're lucky enough to have a dressing room with a decent-sized sofa or, in rare cases – the ultimate luxury – a bed, then you can have quite a good sleep. If not, then you make the best of the floor with your coat or sports bag acting as a pillow. Luckily I can sleep on either, although I prefer the bed. I can sleep anywhere, any time and have frequently done so. On tour with *Annie* the musical I used to push the orphans' beds together on stage and catch half an hour's solid kip. I should mention I only did this between shows and not during a performance – well, hardly ever – and one wet December afternoon in the dressing room of the Victoria Palace in London I once lay scrunched up on a tiny two-seater sofa in full Wicked Queen slap watching three mice on the floor fight over a Malteser.

The Mayflower is fortunate in having a very good restaurant and, even though I'm not very good at eating when I'm working, I'd order some food which the staff would obligingly bring to the dressing room. Then I'd eat a proper meal with fresh veg and fruit instead of the usual diet of sarnies, crisps and pasties. I was very happy with myself, eating properly, getting enough sleep, not finding the schedule tiring – until I was un-expectedly felled, bloody unfairly as well in my opinion, by the flu. No, not what you women mockingly refer to as man flu: this, in spite of taking the precaution of having a flu jab, was the real McCoy. I'd had a slight cold to begin with, nothing bad, but by the time I got home to Kent after the second show on Christmas Eve I was feeling dog rough. Christmas Day and Boxing Day

I spent in bed, unable to move apart from the violent tremors that occurred intermittently as I alternated between freezing cold and hotter than walking through hell in a pair of gasoline drawers, if I can quote my aunty Chris. On the 27th I dragged myself out of bed into the car and back to Southampton in time for the 1.30 matinee. I went on and got through it but was sent home for the second show.

Quite rightly a lot of the audience were more than a little pissed off at my absence, despite being offered a refund or the option to come back when I was better. The front-of-house staff unfairly received the brunt of all the abuse. One woman said that the only reason she'd accept for my no-show was if I was dead, which I thought was a bit extreme. Another, who claimed she was a psychic, threatened the woman behind the merchandise counter with all manner of vile retributions, screaming that she'd come all the way from Shirley, a distance of a few miles. Had I been the member of staff she was abusing, I'd have had trouble resisting the urge to snap back that if she was as psychic as she claimed then she should've seen this coming in her soddin' crystal ball, thus saving herself the bus fare from Shirley.

I hate having to miss a show, it's so bloody depressing lying ill in a strange bed, fretting because you know you should be on stage yet are unable to do anything about it. Although my understudy, Rob, one of the young dancers, did an admirable job in my absence and even though the doctor blithely told me to take a week off, I only missed two shows. Despite a cough that shook the foundations of the theatre I soon felt a lot better and, having missed out on the Christmas celebrations, for the rest of the run I resumed my rightful title as party animal of panto and had a bloody good time.

We had a couple of days off but none of the cast, myself and Vera included, could get home due to a heavy fall of snow. ('The worst weather since records began', the papers delighted in telling us, as they are wont to do every time it snows.) I now live in a village in a rural part of Kent that was completely cut off; getting to Siberia would've been easier than trying to get home to the Romney Marshes. When the weather is as bad as this I worry for my animals: Blanche the pig, Billy and Olive the goats, Minerva the owl, my flock of sheep and assorted chickens and ducks. The poor old ducks I worry about the most as a frozen pond allows easy access to their island home for any hungry fox who might happen to be on the prowl. Thankfully my concerns were unfounded as Sean, Bob and his son Tim who work for me had somehow managed to get in, despite six-foot snowdrifts, and seen to the needs of my menagerie.

The show came down at seven o'clock and the majority of the cast gathered in the Encore, the pub next to the theatre, for a 'quick one'. By midnight quite a few of us were in the pub over the road and at 2 a.m. the musical director, Vera and I were flat on our backs in the lane that led to the flat.

Vera started it. He'd no sooner set an unsteady foot down in the lane than the next moment he's shooting across it with all the speed of the puck in a vigorous game of all-girls' ice hockey on the thick layer of ice and snow that had transformed the lane into a picturesque but deadly winter landscape. The amount that Vera had consumed in lager and vodka and tonics in the course of the evening had nothing to do with his loss of balance, of course. He lay on his back waving one arm, shouting that he thought he'd broken a hip. I tottered back to help him and being, as the Irish like to call it, 'with drink' myself I fell on top of him and lay there helpless with laughter amid screams of 'Gerrof me.' It was Adrian the musical director's turn next. Coming to our aid, he also hit the deck and as we lay there in a heap I was suddenly aware that a small group had gathered at the end of the lane, watching us with some amusement as we writhed around on the ice like the Human Centipede.

'That's Paul O'Grady,' one of them said and proceeded to film us on his mobile. I believe the result is or was somewhere on YouTube.

I'm smiling as I remember that night days later as I totter down the lane towards the theatre, avoiding the hard rocks of impacted snow and trails of ice, laughing to myself as I picture Vera flat on his back waving one arm with all the gusto of one of the Railway Children. It really is cold, the wind feels like shards of glass as it attacks my nostrils, red raw and sore to the touch – not from the ravages of cocaine, I hasten to add, but from the continuous nasal drip I've been cursed with as an aftermath of the flu.

Surely there'll be nobody waiting for a picture or an autograph in this weather, I silently hope as I approach the theatre, but already I can see a couple waiting for me under the awning. They turn out to be mother and son and they both look as if they're freezing to death, the son in particular. His only protection from the weather is the short biker's jacket he's wearing.

'Where've you been?' he asks accusingly, standing on the theatre steps close to the wall in a vain attempt to escape the elements, his shoulders hunched with his blue hands half wedged into the pockets of his overtight jeans. 'We've been waiting here for bloody ages. This is me mother.'

Me mother seems blissfully unaware of the arctic elements that whip around her sensible fur-lined bootees and play havoc with the voluminous pink plastic rain mac she's wearing over her big brown coat. She is happily showing me creased photographs of her two cats, explaining their quirky nature, sleeping habits and dietary needs as she tries to hang on to this clutch of photos in the gale-force wind. I'm paralysed with the cold and I'm really in no mood for this but even so I smile and make appreciative noises as I gaze adoringly at the photo of Sonny stretched across a windowsill against a background of net curtains and geraniums.

'D'ya want a picture, Mother?' The son scowls as he pulls his mobile phone out of his jacket packet. 'Put your arm around her,' he orders, 'and pose for a photo with her, she's one of your biggest fans.'

He fiddles with his phone while I throw my arm around Mother, who comes up to my waist and feels like a damp horsehair armchair that still has its plastic covering on.

'I've told her,' he adds, 'I remember you from years

21

ago when you were working down the Elephant and Castle, rough as arseholes that pub was and so were you. Smile!'

I resist the overwhelming urge to retort that while his looks have obviously faded over the years, remarkably his feeble mind still seems to be intact, and I smile passively into his mobile phone instead. The mother finally releases me from her vice-like grip and I escape the baleful glare of the son and into the theatre.

I'm supposed to use the stage door, but the front of house is quicker. Besides, I prefer to walk through the empty auditorium and across the stage to my dressing room; there's a nice feel to it that makes you aware you're earning your living in a very special way. I still view working in the theatre with a slightly romantic eye. I like to sit in the empty stalls in the older houses before the show and imagine the great names who've appeared there on the stage. The Mayflower was built in the twenties, Tallulah Bankhead has trod these boards as has Gypsy Rose Lee and, in later years, Bill Haley, the Beatles and the Rolling Stones have all played here and now it's my turn to have my name outside the theatre. If I sit and dwell on it I find the notion of such responsibility extremely daunting and a mild panic can set in if I allow it to, believing that one day the jig will be up and I'll be caught out, exposed as a talentless fraud and sent back to Birkenhead to work in the children's home.

I'm early today as I've agreed to an interview over the phone with a local newspaper. The ensemble are already in and on stage warming up for the show. I don't know how they do it. They can do two strenuous shows a day

22

and still go out afterwards and dance all night, then present themselves the next morning fresh as daisies to do the whole thing over again. I resignedly put it down to youth as I watch them enviously from the stalls manoeuvring their lithe bodies into crippling positions that I couldn't get into for cash up front. They catch sight of me and wave, in return I let out a low wolf whistle as they lie on their backs and splay their legs apart. I flirt with some of them for fun but they know that they're dealing with the burnt-out wreck of a once glorious disco and have no reason to worry.

Vera's already in the dressing room. He was up early this morning and sat in Southampton General because something was wrong with his eye. He's had lots of trouble with his eyes over the years and numerous operations to repair detached retinas and various other ocular ailments. This morning when he woke up the eye was kicking off again. He said his eye felt like it had a broken milk bottle in it, although how he knows what that feels like is anyone's guess. Nevertheless he took himself off to the hospital where a doctor told him that the eye had 'dried out' as he'd obviously gone to sleep with one eye open. I laugh now as he tells me the doctor's diagnosis as I can visualize him lying in the dark like a snoring Cyclops, his one dehydrated eyeball staring blankly up at the bedroom ceiling.

'And d'ya know what he said to me?' Vera squawks indignantly.

'No, what?' I reply.

'He said, "Have you been drinking?"'

'And what did you say?'

'I said I'd had a couple of pints after work but nothing that would cause me eyeball to shrivel up.'

I try to ignore the image of him sprawled across the hall floor at 2 a.m., with me, equally inebriated, attempting to pull him up but failing miserably and ending up on top of him instead, incapable with laughter – but I can't, so I remind him of it.

'Oh, well the jury's still out on that one,' he sniffs, sitting down and flipping open the *Daily Mirror*. 'I don't remember anything like that.'

Vera's reaction to the post mortems that inevitably follow a spectacular night out on the lash is to take my side of the story with a sack of salt, as his creed has always been thus: if he can't remember the event then it obviously didn't happen and if by some chance an incident did take place then my account is a highly exaggerated version and not to be believed.

The fibre-optic Christmas tree that has made numerous appearances in dressing rooms up and down the country over the years is switched on, as are the lights around the mirror. In the background Jeremy Vine is on the radio, chairing an angry debate about wheelie bins, of all things. Vera, unconcerned with such mundane affairs, has turned his full attention to the *Daily Mirror*'s crossword and is hunched over it, sucking the end of his biro and sniffing as he tries to work out the answer to ten across.

I take my coat and sweater off and put my dressing gown on in preparation for the tedious business of 'slapping up'.

One of Jeremy's callers is having a heated argument with a woman from the council. They're getting on my nerves. How could anyone get into such a state over a bloody wheelie bin?

'Is there nothing else on, Vera?' I moan.

'They've fixed your hat,' he sighs, slowly getting up from the chair, folding up the *Daily Mirror* and shoving it behind the pot containing the orchid that Cilla had sent me as a first-night present. It's a plant that obviously thrives in the artificial light of the dressing room, if the way it keeps producing blooms is anything to go by. Cilla is appearing in Aylesbury as Cinderella's Fairy Godmother while Barbara Windsor is at Bristol giving her Fairy of the Bow Bells in *Dick Whittington*.

We compare notes regularly by phone. Cilla's back is killing her from the pressure of the flying harness but she is carrying on regardless, while in Bristol Barbara is also flying thirty feet across the stage at the end of a wire. In any other civilized country, if two ladies of an age when they are eligible for a bus pass were swung across a stage on the end of a wire twice daily for the amusement of the general public, there would be outrage. It's commonplace, however, in the UK. The practice breaks out over the Christmas period in towns and cities all around the country. Meanwhile, up in Birmingham, Julian Clary is in bed with a lime-green duck called Orville. There really is no business like show business.

'Did you hear me?' Vera sparked up again, switching the radio over to Classic FM. 'I said they've fixed your hat.' He is referring to the enormous piece of millinery in the shape of a cartwheel draped in reams of black chiffon that I have to wear for the opening scene, set in a Birkenhead graveyard at the funeral of Mustapha Twankey. Unusual opening for a panto, I know, but it was my idea and I claim all responsibility in the face of any detractors. Luckily the audience loved it, especially the reveal when I lifted the veils and showed my face, or rather the visage of Lily Savage, for the first time and I was genuinely gratified to hear by the cheers that the old scrubber still has a few fans out there.

The hat, however, is my bête noire. It's extremely heavy, vision is limited once the veils are down, it's uncomfortable to wear and has to be virtually nailed to my head to keep it on.

'D'ya want a cup of tea, Lily?' Vera asks, predicting my reply by switching the kettle on. He always calls me Lily, just as I've always called him Vera, and we think nothing of it and so far neither does anyone else.

A couple of the dancers knock on the door. They've come to have a look at Vera's many bruises, which are fast achieving legend status.

'This one is where I fell on the ice,' he says proudly, rolling up the sleeve of his jumper to reveal a purple mass on his upper arm. 'And this one on me other arm looks suspiciously like a pinch mark.' He directs this statement at me. 'I wonder how I got that then?'

'I didn't pinch you.'

'No, you never do, yet how come after a night on the bevvy with you I wake up black and fucking blue?'

The dancers are lapping up this private cabaret like kittens with a bowl of milk.

'He pushed me down a dirty big hole in Church Street once, y'know,' Vera went on, warming to his theme. 'Six foot deep – six foot! I could've been killed, and this one roaring with laughter in Woolie's doorway.'

This tale has been told to everyone we've come in contact with since the incident originally occurred thirty-five or so years ago. The depth of the hole, I have to say in my defence, has increased dramatically over the years.

'Show them the bruise on your back, Vera,' I chip in to try to change the subject, with not much success.

'The workmen came rushing out of their hut and shouted, "Don't worry, lad, we'll get your girlfriend out,"' he went on. 'You see, I was very slim in those days – I had a beautiful figure and was often mistaken for a girl. They used to call me Tits when I worked behind the bar in the Triton.'

The dancers are much amused by this last bit of information.

'Why? Did you have tits when you were a teenager, Vera?' one of them asks.

'No, but she has now.' I get in quick with this as it's an opportunity not to be missed. 'They're those things hanging around her knees.'

'Cheeky cow.'

Jon Lee, the remarkable young actor and singer playing Aladdin, comes in from his dressing room next door to see what all the laughter is about. Vera is now bent over with his jumper rolled up to reveal a whopper of a bruise on his back. He puts me in mind of Lydia the

Tattooed Lady showing off her prize tattoos, only in Vera's case it's bruises.

'And this one,' he says dramatically, twisting his body round and squinting to see if he can catch a glimpse of his gold-medal-winning contusion in the dressing-room mirror. 'I got this one when I fell on the ice as well.'

'What about that nice fresh one on your side?' I chip in again. 'There's no ice on the floor of the flat, is there? And that looks suspiciously like the result of the early hours of this morning's carry-on when you fell in the hall and banged your back on a doorknob.'

'I was pushed.'

'Who by? There was only me in the flat at the time and I was on the lav. I heard the thud as you fell, I had to come out and help you up. The evidence is conclusive. I rest my case, your honour.'

'Haven't you got an interview to do?' he says, smartly changing the subject. 'You'd better get a move on, you haven't got your make-up on yet and it's nearly twenty past. You know what you're like if you have to rush.'

This is a cue for everyone to leave the dressing room. I root around on the make-up shelf for the bit of paper with the journalist's phone number on it, which is buried somewhere under a mountain of beads, bangles and packets of spare eyelashes.

'I'll fly round to Coleman's and get a couple of sarnies, eh?' Vera says, pouring the hot water from the kettle into a mug with lipstick stains around the rim. 'What d'ya fancy? Corned beef and tomato? Or ham salad?'

Usually I opt for the corned beef but today I fancy the

ham salad on white with a good dollop of Heinz salad cream. Coleman's is a shop close to the theatre that at first glance appears to be nothing more than a newsagent, yet on closer inspection reveals a small back room where a couple of cheery ladies turn out an array of spectacular and extremely tasty sandwiches and rolls of the type rarely found in a British shop today. Cheese and pickle, ham rolls, beef and onion and my favourite, the *spécialité de la maison*, corned beef and tomato on white bread that has been gently caressed by a knife bearing a layer of Daddies sauce. Heaven, especially when accompanied by a polystyrene cup of their piping hot tomato soup. Those chains of coffee houses can keep their walnut, avocado and Brie on ciabatta and soggy BLTs, give me the comfort food of Coleman's any day.

'Get me a cup of soup, Vera, as well, will you,' I shout after him as he leaves for Coleman's wrapped up in enough scarves and gloves for an Arctic expedition.

Dusty, my dresser, comes in with the aforementioned hat and lays it carefully on the bed. She's worked at the Mayflower for years and is everything a good dresser should be. She's also a lot of fun and extremely likeable.

'I'll be outside if you need me,' she says quietly in the manner of a dresser in an old Hollywood black and white movie, closing the door behind her.

I drink my tea and ring the journalist. She sounds very young and slightly nervous. After the initial small talk about Christmas and New Year resolutions we get down to business.

'So how have you enjoyed being in Southampton

then?' she asks, suddenly adopting a brisk manner.

I was glad to be able to answer truthfully that I'd had a ball, had thoroughly enjoyed being back in the insanity of panto again and would be genuinely sorry to pack up and say goodbye to the cast when the show closed at the end of the week.

'I remember watching you as Lily on *The Big Breakfast* when I was getting ready for school,' she chirps down the line, instantly making me feel as old as Methuselah.

'Yes . . .' I reply, my voice tailing off as I make a half-hearted attempt at a laugh.

'Tell me,' she asks after a little pause, 'how did you get started?'

Now if there's a question I've been asked a million times it's that one, by every interviewer, chat show host, cab driver and bloke in the pub.

I give her the old tried and true reply which gets shorter with every telling, trying to sound enthusiastic as I rattle it off, but to my own ears my voice has automatically taken on the monotonous tone of the robot you hear in talking lifts that tells you when the doors are closing and what floor you're on.

Obviously not totally satisfied with my answer, she tries another angle.

'But how did you make the transition from social services to pub drag act to where you are now?'

I look around and apart from wigs and costumes I see a vase of dead flowers that has sat on the shelf since we opened, a bunch of bananas still enclosed in their plastic bag but now mottled with age and slowly decomposing, bits of broken jewellery, make-up, hair clips, elastic bands, old Christmas cards and next to a bottle of Sanderson's Specific a slightly battered tin of Fray Bentos corned beef sent to me by Malcolm Prince, my Radio 2 producer, as part of an emergency food hamper in case I forget to eat. The detritus of a dressing room, or mine anyway. The Land of Corned Beef and Panstick.

I explain to her that as we've only got fifteen minutes I'd find myself hard pushed to tell her exactly what happened over the last three decades, but I give her a potted version anyway as I like her.

'I always secretly wanted to be famous,' she volunteers, comfortable with me now and opening up. 'It must be wonderful.'

'Now look,' I lecture her, 'don't end up as one of those fame-hungry columnists whose ego and photographs are bigger than the crap they write and who would sell their firstborn for two minutes' exposure on daytime telly or one of those awful bloody "list" programmes pontificating on subjects you have no idea about with a load of telly critics and alternative comics that nobody's heard of.'

She laughs at this and assures me that she plans to stay in her chosen profession and she'd never be able to go on stage anyway as she'd be so terrified.

I confess that my first experience in front of a crowd with a mike in my hand was pretty hair-raising.

'Where was that?' she asks.

'Well, the first time I actually spoke and cracked a couple of gags was in a pub in the north but I suppose you could say that it all began in a couple of south London pubs.'

'What were the pubs called? When was it? What did you wear? Did Lily appear fully formed or was she organic?'

'She was never organic,' I tell her. 'She only ate processed foods, believing that the preservatives contained in them were a powerful aid to maintaining her youthful beauty.'

'Oh no, I didn't mean organic food, I—'

'I know what you meant,' I say. 'Lily was like Topsy. She just growed.'

'Pardon?'

'*Uncle Tom's Cabin.*'

Vera reappears armed with soup and sarnies. 'You better get a move on,' he warns me. 'Have you seen the time? You haven't even got your slap on yet.'

'I wish we could talk all afternoon,' the woman from the magazine says, reluctant to hang up. 'I'd love to hear more about the Lily years, the early ones working the clubs.'

'I'll write it down for you,' I tell her, anxious to get off the phone.

And I have. And here it is. My original intention was to go up to the present day and I've finally managed it . . . sort of, even if I have had to skip a few years. Try as I may – and believe me, I have, to the point of dementia on occasions – I can't fit it all into one book. *War and Peace* isn't as long as my trilogy of autobiographies, nor is *The Lord of the* bloody *Rings*, and I feel slightly embarrassed at having stretched it out over three volumes. It's not for reasons of vanity I've done this, nor is it purely for financial gain, it's due to this compulsion I have to write it all down in detail, and if it weren't for those two strapping male nurses entering my ward at this very moment with a hypodermic needle containing the powerful sedative required to enable them to prise the laptop out of my hand, I probably would go on for eternity . . .

CHAPTER 1

1980

'I THOUGHT YOU WERE A COUPLE OF STRIPPERS,' THE landlord of the latest dump we were working in announced, arms folded, across the bar. 'We only have strippers of a lunchtime, not drag.'

'Well, my partner here does a strip,' I said, trying not to sound desperate, which we were, having no money at all, not even enough to buy a gallon of petrol for the clapped-out van parked on the pavement outside to get us home from this crummy run-down pub we'd been booked into on a wet Tuesday afternoon on the out-skirts of Leeds.

'I most certainly do not strip,' Hush said indignantly, his face flushing red.

'You do, what about "Put The Blame On Mame"? You strip to that.' I was determined not to leave this pub without going on and collecting the thirty-quid fee.

'I don't know,' the landlord said, eyeing up the six-foot-two, built like a lumberjack Hush dubiously. 'I don't think a grown man stripping would go down very well with the lads in here.'

Two of the 'lads', leaning on the bar and staring into space over their pints of bitter, slowly turned and glowered at us, as if in affirmation.

'Go on,' I wheedled, trying to mask the desperation in my voice with a forced joviality. 'We're very funny and I do a strip.' I was trying not to sound irritable as I attempted to reason with this oik. 'Look, we're here now, and besides, where are you going to get another act at such short notice?'

'Well, it does leave me two strippers short,' he said, scratching the back of his head and chewing his lower lip. 'I normally have four on of a lunchtime.'

'It'll be a change for the punters,' I added hopefully.

'Go on then, I'll give it a go,' he said, already regretting his decision. 'But what's the odds you die on your bloody arse.'

Hush's face was still burning scarlet and his lips were pursed tighter than a cat's anus.

'Do you have a dressing room?' he asked grandly, picking up a bin-liner stuffed full of wigs on polystyrene heads. 'Or somewhere we can get ready in?' He emphasized the 'somewhere' as if he wasn't expecting too much in the way of facilities.

Surprisingly, not only did this pub have a small 'stage' but behind a ratty curtain leading off it was a room for the acts to change in.

'I'll kill that bloody Phyllis,' Hush muttered, referring to Phil, our driver, landlord and temporary manager, picking up the huge sack that held the costumes and marching towards the dressing room. 'Fancy booking us into this shithole. Why the hell we ever agreed to leave

London and live in the middle of nowhere to work venues like this I'll never know.'

I'd been living in a squat off Camden Square with my two friends, Chrissie and Vera, in the home of a former client, an old lady I'd been looking after when I worked as a peripatetic care officer for Camden Council. The old lady had died and as we needed somewhere to live after our landlord slapped us with a huge bill for the rates and an increase in rent we couldn't afford, we moved into her flat as I still had the key. The council eventually got wind and started asking questions that made me worry that I might lose my job if they were to discover that one of their employees was squatting in one of their properties. Abandoning Camden, we moved into a two-bedroom cottage in Purley, the home of another drag act we'd become friendly with. Stage Three, as they were called, consisted of David, John and Jimmy, alias Hush, Connie and Elsie.

I'd been trailing an act called the Glamazons around the pubs for the last six months with a friend called Paul I'd met in the Black Cap. Hush, who was a wizard with wigs and created gowns out of next to nothing, had been making drag for me and Paul. We'd teamed up for benefit nights at the Nashville pub and as we all got on well and needed somewhere to live Hush invited us to move in, making seven of us, including the odd straggler, sharing a tiny cottage. Vera, Paul and I shared a bed and getting up at 6 a.m. every day to make it to work for eight was a pain in the neck.

We moved again, this time to one room in a grim semi-detached in Streatham, with four of us sharing. At least we had our own beds this time but the downside was having four beds in what was formerly someone's living room didn't leave a lot of room for anything else. It was claustrophobic living on top of each other like this and one evening I returned home from work to find Paul had gone. Tired of being skint and living in one room, he'd gone off to Saudi to work as an agency nurse without any forewarning. I can't say I blamed him. The Glamazons hadn't been getting as much work as we'd wanted and as it was Paul's sole source of income it was time for him to move on.

A northern agent by the name of Avril Barton who booked London acts on the northern pub and club circuit had given us a week's work in pubs in Yorkshire and Lincolnshire. Avril was small and plump and put me in mind physically of Hylda Baker. As well as acting as an agent she was a catering manageress at Leeds University and shared her flat with a collection of parrots and a couple of moggies whom she doted on. Avril's passion was a drag act called Billie Raymond, whom she always spoke of as 'My Billie'. Billie was a very popular and successful act and as far as the adoring Avril was concerned there was no one to touch him. Surprisingly, considering that there was serious unemployment in the north, there was a lot of work for drag acts and Avril claimed that she could guarantee us at least five nights' work a week, plus a couple of lunchtimes if we moved back up there. 'Look at my Billie,' Avril said. 'Never stops.' We agreed to return in a month, this time for a two-week stint, and now here I was in a bedsit in Streatham with no act as my partner preferred earning a fabulous wage taking Arab princes' temperatures to traipsing around the north of England for a pittance.

Hush had fallen out with John and had quit the act. He'd also left the house that they shared, making himself homeless, and so, pooling our losses, I quit my job with Camden, we said goodbye to London and emigrated to Yorkshire. Avril had introduced us to a guy named Phil who put up the acts from London in his flat, driving them around to the different far-flung venues. Phil invited us to move in with him on a permanent basis so he could act as our driver and also as manager.

As both Avril and Phil had promised, there was a lot of work about, providing you didn't mind working the occasional toilet for half the fee we were normally going out for. We weren't fussy, work was work and twenty-five quid was better than nothing but even so, this pub we'd ended up in with its lunchtime strippers won the cigar for being the worst dump in the north-west.

'This is rock bottom, Savage, this is, not even being able to buy a bevvy,' Hush moaned with more than a hint of despair in his voice. 'Since you're so well in with the management, go and ask him if we can have a sub on the fee so we can get a bloody drink. I'm not going on in here sober.' He was unpacking costumes from the huge canvas zip-up sack he'd made to carry them all in and was looking for somewhere to hang them.

'I should've ironed this,' he said, giving his violent

orange satin French maid's outfit a once-over with a critical eye. 'And typically there's nowhere to hang it in here to give the creases a chance to drop out.'

'You think that lot out there are going to care if you've got a crease in your skirt?' I said, bracing myself to go out among 'that lot' to see if I could get a couple of drinks on tick. 'They want filth. Pregnant brides and knicker routines with cucumbers and things.'

'Well there's no way I'm stooping to that kind of behaviour,' Hush snorted indignantly as he attempted to get six costumes on the one solitary rusty nail embedded in the wall. 'And if this is the level of establishment we're going to be working in then I'd better start packing some hooks and a hammer. Knicker routines indeed, the very idea.'

'Go on,' I goaded, 'lift your McNamara's Band frock up and sit on some bloke's head, it'll go down a storm.'

'Certainly not. Now are you going to get the beverage in or what?'

The pub was filling up with a crowd of men who didn't look like they were the type who would enjoy seeing two grown men dressed as Salvationists on a Tuesday afternoon or, for that matter, any other day of the week.

Luckily Phil appeared from behind the curtain. I'd get him to go to the bar.

'And where've you been?' Hush rounded on him. 'Savage had to practically beg to go on, the landlord was expecting a couple of strippers and if it wasn't for Sav here chatting him up we wouldn't be working this afternoon. You took the booking on the phone, did you tell him that we were drag?'

'He never asked, I thought he knew,' Phil said, shrugging his shoulders and not looking in the least bothered.

'Well he obviously didn't know, did he? Now if you don't mind, me and the Sav are gagging for a bevvy so make yourself useful and get us a couple of drinks. Tell him we want a tab.' Hush took a fiery red wig out of the bin-liner and gave it a severe shaking to loosen it up. 'Go on then,' he said, putting the wig back on its polystyrene head. 'A pint of bitter and a pint of cider please, oh and a couple of packets of crisps, I'm starving.'

Against the wall leaned a wardrobe door with a mirror attached to it. Hush gave it a cursory wipe with his towel and after lighting a fag he began to apply a plastic wax to his eyebrows to hide them. I sat on what was left of a sofa and opened the fishing tackle box that I kept my make-up in and proceeded to slap it on. Whereas Hush's make-up box was organized and tidy, mine was a health hazard with strange things lurking among the jumble of lipsticks minus their tops and blunt eyebrow pencils smeared with greasy panstick.

'Have you seen what that sign on the wall says, Sav?' Hush asked, deftly painting clown-white greasepaint over his flattened eyebrows with a brush.

I had. It was written in bold felt-tip on cardboard and read, 'Will all strippers please make sure that they are wearing knickers when collecting their wages from the bar.'

Underneath someone had written in pencil, 'Unless it's a lock-in.'

And below that scribbled in biro it read, 'Dawn and Black Janice, first half – Brenda and Kath, lesbian act second half.'

I'd never met a real-life stripper in the flesh, so to speak, never spent time with one socially and was quite excited at the prospect.

'I don't know what sort of dirty bitches must work here,' Hush said, and as if on cue a wiry little woman with short, badly dyed blonde hair swung the curtain back and hurried into the room. Quick as a flash Hush spun round from the mirror to face her. 'Hello,' he gushed. 'Can we help you?'

She looked at Hush with his gloss-white eyebrows for a moment and then, shaking her head in disbelief, she plonked the carrier bag she was holding on the sofa next to me.

'Well, I'm getting changed in here, love,' she said, taking her denim jacket off. 'I don't know what your excuse is.'

Folding her jacket neatly and putting it on the floor, she stood up and looked around the room.

'Since when did they 'ave drag on in 'ere?' she asked, looking at the various costumes spread about the place. 'They've never had drag on here, never.' She couldn't have been more surprised if she'd walked in and found the English National Ballet warming up for *The Nutcracker*.

'It was a misunderstanding over the phone, we're called the Playgirls and the governor took us for strippers,' I explained.

'Well you would with a name like that,' she said, kicking her trainers off. 'What's your real names then?'

'I'm Paul and this is David.' It always sounded odd calling Hush by his real name.

'I'm Kath.'

'Oh, the one who does the lesbian act with Brenda?'

'How do you know that?' she asked, suddenly on the defensive.

'It's written on that sign over there.'

'Oh I see,' she said, sounding relieved. 'We only do that if there's a lock-in. We pass the hat round first, make sure that they pay up and then writhe about a bit on the floor squeezing each other's tits and sticking our tongues out pretending to go down each other, daft stuff like that. It's a right laugh really, that lot out there think they're watching the real thing, but then what would men know?'

She emptied the carrier bag out on to the sofa. It contained a brush, lipstick, a pair of red patent-leather high heels and a jar of Brylcreem.

'I don't give blow jobs to the punters though, like some of the other girls,' she continued, pulling her T-shirt over her head, 'or let them touch me fanny. A bit of fake lezzy is as far as I'll go.'

From behind me I heard Hush let out a throaty exclamation, the type that Lady Bracknell would employ to register horror at a faux pas made by a socially unsuitable dinner guest.

'I only work this place because it's local, it's right rough,' she said, attacking her hair with the brush with such violence I winced. 'It's only fifteen minutes on the

43

bus and the girl next door minds the kids for me.' She was bending over now, viciously dragging the brush over the back of her head as if her brittle little tufts of hair were a luxurious waist-length mane. 'I can't feed three kids with what I get off the social, y'know, and this is great because the money's not bad and the hours suit.'

'What do you wear?' I asked as there was no obvious sign of a costume in her carrier bag. Where was the evening gown with a zip up the side for easy removal? And the elbow-length white satin gloves that she could slowly peel off? The tassles?

'What I've got on,' she said, scooping out a blob of Brylcreem and running it through her hair.

Hush turned around from the mirror to take a good look at Kath. Her tiny breasts were encased in a cheap black lace bra, and a faded denim miniskirt revealing mottled bare legs and the red patent-leather shoes were the sum total of her ensemble. Hush, who believed everything should have a sequin on it, was far from impressed.

'You haven't given yourself much to take off, have you?' he asked doubtfully.

'That's just it,' she explained, slapping a bit more Brylcreem on. 'There's no point wearing a lovely dress like yours. I'd love to, like, but it'd be a waste of time. The aim of the game is to get your kit off as soon as poss. They only want to see tit and minge.'

Hush made the Lady Bracknell noise again.

Phil, entering with a tray of drinks and complaining of the time it took to get served, felt obliged to ask Kath if she wanted a drink. To his relief Kath said she didn't drink at work as she had to pick her eldest up from school later on and didn't want any of the other mothers smelling booze on her breath. They had a low enough opinion of her as it was.

This image of poverty-stricken domesticity was clashing with the idea of a stripper's life that I had fixed in my consciousness, thanks to their portrayal in the various Hollywood movies I'd watched on the television. If Kath was an example of the modern stripteaser then real life was something very different indeed.

The second stripper arrived, dragging a shopping basket on wheels behind her and asking, just as Kath had done, 'What the hell is drag doing on in here?'

She wasn't as friendly as Kath, glaring at us suspiciously, obviously resenting our presence in the room.

'D'ya mind if I go on first?' she asked Kath ignoring us completely. 'I've got another job at Panama Joe's and I'm a bit pushed for time.'

Her name turned out to be Holly. She was younger than Kath, probably in her late twenties, with long blue-black hair. Her face, which seemed to be set in a permanent scowl, was slathered in bright orange foundation and her wary little eyes were rimmed with thick black eyeliner.

'D'ya want me to move some of our stuff?' I asked her, trying to be friendly.

'Don't bother,' she grunted, 'I won't be in here that long.'

Hush turned from the mirror, took a long drag from his Consulate and hissed as he expelled the plume of smoke. He didn't like her. Neither did I for that matter.

From the shopping trolley she unpacked a pair of thigh-length PVC boots, some dubious PVC underwear and a black plastic mac. Quickly removing her street clothes, she put it all on. Hush and I discreetly busied ourselves with wigs, trying to avert our eyes as she bent over and stepped into the PVC drawers, the tight elasticated waist digging into her flesh and enhancing her plump little belly.

The landlord came in to collect our cassette tapes of music and sort out the running order.

'Here's my tape,' Holly said, producing a cassette from the pocket of her mac. 'It's AC/DC's "Soul Stripper"; you can't get it in the UK,' she added grandly. 'It was only released in Australia. I got a copy when I was working over there last year.'

'Right, I'd best get it played then,' the landlord said, totally uninterested, vanishing behind the curtain and back to the bar to start the show.

After a blast of deafening feedback from the sophisticated sound arrangement and the obligatory two taps with the fingers on the head of the microphone, we heard him introduce Holly.

'One two, one two, testing. Right, shut the fuck up and get your hands together for the first of our strippers today. Let's hear it for a right little cock-stiffener . . . the fabulous Holly!'

A couple of half-hearted cheers and a few wolf whistles were followed by an expectant silence.

'Put the fuckin' tape on,' Holly shouted from behind the curtain, causing Hush to make the Lady B noise for the third time that afternoon.

The music started and Holly stomped out on to the stage in her boots and plastic mac like a stormtrooper, to no audible reaction from her audience.

I watched through the curtain as she went through her routine. Within seconds the mac was off and she was down on all fours, grinding her backside furiously at the men gathered close to the stage. They were staring transfixed by Holly's gyrating posterior as if they'd never seen one before.

After a bout of this bum-grinding she stood up, deftly whipping her bra off to reveal a pair of pendulous breasts that she started to squeeze and play with. It looked a bit painful to me, especially when she pushed them together, but the men leaned forward like dogs on heat to get a better look. You could smell as well as feel the tension in the room.

'She thinks she's somethin', that one,' Kath sniffed, scratching her thigh. 'She might have big tits but have you seen the way they hang? They're like bloodhounds' ears. Mine might be little but they're still as pert as a fifteen-year-old's. Feel them,' she said to Hush, 'they're like little grapefruits.'

Lady B was working overtime today.

Out on stage Holly was on all fours again waving her arse in the air, only this time she was minus her knickers. The men's faces were masks of intense concentration as they focused on Holly's private parts. Absently they took the occasional swig from their pints, seemingly unaware of doing so as their eyes hungrily devoured what they wanted but couldn't have. This wasn't what I considered stripping, this was a grubby sex show in a dirty little pub for the benefit of a gang of sex-hungry men, and I began to regret persuading the landlord to let us go on.

Holly's 'act' lasted no more than twenty minutes, after which she gathered up her discarded bits of costume and strode casually back into the dressing room.

'How did that go?' I asked, trying to show a bit of the supportive camaraderie I imagined should exist among performers flung together in a dressing room.

'I couldn't give a fuck,' she snapped with her back to me, unzipping her boots and slipping into her jeans. 'Why would I?'

Within minutes she was dressed, the shopping trolley packed and out of the dressing room, and at the bar collecting her money.

'She's a miserable cow, that one,' Kath said, watching her leave. 'Now let me get in that mirror for a sec so I can put a bit of lippy on.'

I didn't watch Kath's act, I felt I'd got to know her and it didn't seem right to watch her out there without any clothes on. Instead I went through the elaborate process of putting on my opening outfit.

Our opening number was a recording of 'Who's Sorry Now' sung by an act called the Barry Sisters to an oriental arrangement. Hush had decided that this would be a good excuse to get dragged up as geishas and spent a couple of days on his Singer running up two kimonos complete with a roll of sponge on the back covered in satin to represent the obi. To complete this look, he said, we just had to have the traditional heavily ornamented rolled black wigs. These he'd had made by a company who produced wigs for shop window mannequins; they were rock hard, huge and uncomfortable to wear. Mine was too big for me and kept slipping down my face, and the glittery knitting needles hung with strands of sequins to represent jewelled ornaments constantly fell out. They also stank of powerful fumes from where Hush kept touching them up with spray paint to retain their black lacquered gloss, and after a particularly heavy session with the spray can you'd take the damn thing off and find a black line across your forehead. Under these kimonos we wore cheongsams, tight satin dresses with mandarin collars and splits up either side made popular by Suzie Wong. I did point out to Hush as he was making them that the cheongsam was Chinese, not Japanese, and that we were confusing our cultures somewhat but he said that no one would notice and if they did then tough titty.

My cheongsam was designed as a strip dress and held together with Velcro. Underneath I wore an oversized G-string that I had to pin to my tights to stop them falling down and a matching blue-sequinned padded bra trimmed with a length of white fringing that was also attached by Velcro. The fringing stuck like flies to flypaper until after a while it became frayed and tatty and hung from the bra like the trim on a junk-shop lampshade. Underneath this bra I had two curtain tassels stuck to my nipples with double-sided Sellotape which I would attempt to twirl. Occasionally, much to my amazement, I would actually succeed.

Once I managed to disentangle myself from the mess of Velcro as I stripped to the strains of 'Fan-Tan Fanny', I'd stand there in just the tassels and G-string with no shame at all. I'm grateful that no photographs of me in this tasteful creation exist.

Kath came off stage clutching her skirt and bra to her naked body in an attempt at modesty and gawped at the two six-foot-six geisha girls standing in front of her and taking a slug from their pint pots.

'You look fabulous,' she gasped. 'I'm going to stay and watch you.'

When the landlord announced that there was going to be a drag act on next a groan went up and some of the men began to finish their drinks and drift out. Those that remained were simply not interested and, as predicted, the act died on its proverbial arse. Bored with this pair of nancy boys poncing around when they should be salivating over naked female flesh, a group of lads at a table in the back started to send us up, their heckles neither good-natured nor encouraging.

It was during the 'Saved' number that the normally placid Hush finally cracked. Leaving the stage, he strode purposefully across the pub in full Salvation Army drag, lifted the table they were sat around, which was littered with pint pots both full and empty, and dropped it on them. One of the men, an angry-looking skinhead, lunged at him, his face contorted with rage. Hush stood his ground and quite calmly and with little effort gave the skinhead a punch that sent him crashing into the fruit machine.

'Who's next then, lads?' he asked, rounding on the rest of the group.

Laughing nervously, they escaped from the rubble of broken glass and bar table and slid out through the door muttering threats as they left.

'Right, you,' Hush bellowed, turning his attention to the landlord. 'You can turn that tape off this instant. We won't be going back on and if we don't get paid in full I'm going to put every one of your fucking windows in. Savage, get in there and pack the bags, wench!'

Phil and I hastily packed everything up while Hush continued to tell the landlord in no uncertain terms what would happen if he didn't hand over the fee. Sensible man, having probably never encountered a psychotic six-foot-nine Salvationist hell-bent on ripping his bar apart, he handed over the thirty-quid fee without complaint.

Due to our having to beat such a hasty retreat we travelled home in our Sally Army outfits, stopping at a garage for some much-needed petrol and, as we were in the money again, a late lunch of a cold jumbo sausage roll and a bag of crisps washed down with a can of Coke.

'I've never seen you go off like that before,' I said, through mouthfuls of the dubious pink paste and pastry masquerading as a sausage roll. 'That was some punch you gave that bloke.'

'Serves him right,' Hush replied, daintily picking bits of pastry off his skirt. 'And it's about time Phyllis here got his finger out and started booking us into decent venues, that's if there are any in this godforsaken hole.'

'I've got you the Stone Chair and the Gemini Club tomorrow night,' Phil protested. 'You'll like them, and the money's good.'

'Just as well,' Hush said, shoving the last of the crisps in his mouth. 'Now get your foot down, wench, and let's get home. This girdle is killing me.'

CHAPTER 2

HOME WAS A ONE-BEDROOM FLAT WE SHARED WITH
Phil and Henry, his sparky little cockatiel, in a
small village called Slaithwaite (pronounced either
'Sloughit' or 'Slathwaite' by the locals) that lay in the
Colne Valley five miles outside of Huddersfield. It's a
place that has frequently been used as a location for the
TV shows *Where the Heart Is* and on occasions *Last of
the Summer Wine*, and for the likes of Hush and me
who had got used to living in London Slaithwaite
seemed a grim little backwater inhabited by suspicious
people who twitched their net curtains and kept allotments. Add to this very few amenities (I recall a corner
shop) and a limited transport service and you had a
couple of square pegs who were very much in the wrong
hole.

Many years later, after I'd fallen in love with
Yorkshire and bought a flat in the village of Saltaire, I
revisited Slaithwaite and was amazed to find a re-
vitalized and extremely picturesque village, not at all
how I remembered it. A lot of the buildings had been
cleaned up and stripped of their dirty grey overcoats to
reveal a soft buttery-yellow stone underneath, and the

canal had been cleared out and reopened, as had the railway station. It was a different place with lots of interesting shops and good cafés and a butcher's called E. and R. Grange that sold homemade pork pies and pasties the likes of which could only have been conjured up by angels in the kitchens of heaven.

Back in 1980, Hush and I didn't see it through such rose-tinted glasses. The house we lived in had been split into two flats and we lived in the top-floor one. The flat below was unoccupied apart from the mice, which was just as well as the noise we made on our return home each night from work would've driven any tenant insane.

As our flat only had one single bed, occupied by Phil, we bought lilos from Huddersfield Market to sleep on. They were a bit narrow and made you sweat, squeaking like the plague of mice downstairs when you turned over, but they were certainly preferable to sleeping on the bare floorboards of our loft-conversion bedroom with the sloping ceiling. The three of us shared it with an assortment of wigs on polystyrene heads and costumes reeking of stale cigarette smoke.

Henry would fly up to our eyrie each morning and use our heads as landing pads, pulling our hair and chattering away. Hush didn't like birds very much and wasn't amused by the antics of this flying alarm clock, burying his head under the duvet to get away from him.

Downstairs in the kitchen Phil always had a box or two of Batchelors marrowfat dried peas soaking in a bucket together with a sodium tablet, which he would transform the next day into a grey-green lumpy mass of

'Yorkshire caviar', the humble but delicious mush of peas served with mint sauce and vinegar. It gave us terrible flatulence and made our attic bedroom sound like the Yorkshire Brass Band Championships.

Even though we didn't have a lot of money we always ate at least one good meal a day. Phil was an excellent cook, as was Hush, and both of them were capable of knocking up a three-course meal on a budget of a couple of quid. Between them they'd dish out Desperate Dan-sized portions of shepherd's pies, stews and my favourite, corned beef hash swimming in a lake of velvety onion gravy and accompanied by the ubiquitous mushy peas. Occasionally a good-hearted neighbour would leave us a lettuce or cabbage from his allotment on the front step. One night, arriving home late from a booking, we came across a parcel on the step that looked suspiciously like a human head wrapped in newspaper, which turned out to be nothing more sinister than a snowy-white cauliflower enveloped in a copy of the previous day's *Huddersfield Daily Examiner*.

Our bathroom was probably the most garish in Yorkshire. The walls were covered in a metallic bronze paper tastefully adorned with a pattern of Toulouse-Lautrec images set at odd angles. Strangely enough, considering the bedroom floor was bare, the floor in here was covered in a thick beige shagpile dotted with islands of tatty bath and pedestal mats in a shade of salmon pink that clashed beautifully with the deep scarlet bathroom suite. I doubted if this look was fashionable even way back in the late sixties when the makeover obviously took place but I was grateful that, unlike any other bathroom I'd experienced so far in life, this one was warm and had plenty of hot water on tap.

I'd lie in this bath with a fag and a cup of tea and through the top of the sash window where the glass was clear I could observe the comings and goings of our neighbours, busy in their allotments at the top of the slope. I'd wonder if it was difficult to grow a cabbage and if one day I'd end up proudly tending to an allotment myself. The prospect didn't appeal to me. Reflecting on the future and what it might hold was an activity we rarely indulged in, living as we did a day-to-day, hand-to-mouth existence. Our only care was if we were working that night and for how much. We never turned work down, no matter how poorly paid it was, our philosophy being that it was better to be out working for something than sitting at home earning nothing.

Each night and some afternoons we'd pile into the van and Phil would drive us the length and breadth of the north of England to play in venues, some of which were very pleasant. The others . . . well, as I said, we couldn't afford to be fussy. In one club up on the moors in the middle of nowhere, we got ready and did our quick changes in a freezing caravan at the back of the building, and then had to run across a muddy field and through a fire door to get to the dance floor in the pouring rain. In a working men's club near Bridlington, where we walked on and off the stage to the sound of our own feet, the tape was turned off during one of Hush's big numbers to enable a member of the committee to announce that 'Bingo will be commencing ten minutes after this lot have finished, so make sure you've got your books in.'

In spite of these setbacks and many others like them, I was enjoying myself. There was a sense of recklessness that came with this new lifestyle and I liked the peripatetic existence, travelling around the country visiting previously unexplored territory. I had very little responsibility and for once I was my own boss, not earning a lot, granted, but enough to get by on. I was in a Peter Pan frame of mind, a strangely liberating experience that led me to believe that I could be and do exactly what I liked in this new-found Yorkshire Neverland, answerable to no one, with the exception perhaps of my own personal Captain Hook: my mother.

Her immediate reaction when I rang her up to tell her that I was moving to live in Yorkshire was, not surprisingly, suspicion.

'You're leaving your precious London to go and live in some Yorkshire backwater surrounded by sheep?' she shrieked, highly sceptical at this latest bit of news. 'Well, it doesn't take a Philadelphia lawyer to work out why.'

'Why's that then?' Here it comes.

'There's only one reason why you'd pack up and scarper to somewhere like Yorkshire,' she said with the triumphant finality of Hercule Poirot revealing who dun it at the conclusion of a case. 'And that's because the police are on your tail.'

For once I was able to tell her the truth: that I wasn't Public Enemy Number 1, I didn't have Scotland Yard after me and the reason I was moving back 'oop north' was simply because living conditions were becoming intolerable in London, the unpredictable and lengthy hours that I was expected to commit to working for Camden Council were a bind and I desperately needed a change.

'But why Yorkshire?' she asked, making it sound as if Yorkshire was on the other side of the world.

I told her I had the offer of a job and somewhere to live.

'Doing what?' She was still deeply suspicious.

'Oh, working in pubs and clubs all over the place,' I replied airily. It was after all near to the truth.

'As what?'

'Catering,' I said without missing a beat, ignoring the image that flashed across my mind of me half naked on the dance floor of the Keighley Fun House stripping to 'Fan-Tan-Fanny'.

'Waiting on and working behind a bar, you mean,' she said flatly, unable to hide the disappointment in her voice.

'I'll be able to come and see you more often,' I said optimistically, as if that little drop of oil was going to restore calm to any potentially stormy waters.

'Well, as long as you give me plenty of notice,' she announced grandly. 'I'm hardly ever in these days, if I'm not up at our Sheila's or Brendan's I'm at Mass or the Mothers' Union. I'm an independent woman now, you know. I can go and come as I please, you can't expect me to hang around waiting for a visitation from you.'

I told her I'd ring her secretary and book an appointment.

'You do that. Now you'd better get off the phone, this

must be costing you a small fortune.' My mother still thought in terms of trunk calls and considered the price of a phone call anywhere outside her immediate radius ruinous. 'I'll drop you a line, ta-ra.'

After I'd been living in Slaithwaite for a couple of months and as we had no work booked in for the best part of a week, I took the opportunity to pay my mother a long overdue visit. Hush went down to London to buy wigs and I caught the train to Liverpool, taking the time during the journey to consider the pros and cons of telling her what I was really doing to earn a crust.

I reasoned that turning up and then casually springing on her over a corned beef sandwich that I was part of a drag act might bring on a bit of a 'light blue touchpaper and retire' moment, but diluting it to cabaret act, a more acceptable title, I thought, might just soften the blow and reduce the risk of an explosion. There was no possibility of her ever coming to see me and if she wanted me to go into detail, which she more than likely would, I'd tell her I did comedy sketches and add, just to test the water, a little bit of drag. It might go down well with her, having a cabaret artiste as a son instead of a barman. After all, she hadn't been overjoyed at the news that I was working in catering, showing utter contempt for what she considered to be 'waiting on people', a reminder of her days as an overworked, underpaid slave in domestic service. One thing I was certain of, though, was that breaking the news I was a drag queen would send her apoplectic. It would sound far too *News of the World*, a paper you didn't dare bring into the house as she called it a pornographic rag and said the only thing in it you could believe was the date.

No, if I'm going to say anything then best stick to the less subversive title of cabaret artiste, I told myself, putting it out of my mind for the moment and settling down to a bag of crisps and *Titbits* magazine.

She'd obviously just got in as she was standing in the kitchen waiting for the kettle to boil and still wearing her headscarf.

'Is that you, Paul?' she shouted as I let myself in at the front door. 'You're just in time. D'you want a cup of coffee? And a ham roll?'

It was nice to be home. I still considered this little house in Holly Grove to be 'home', and standing once again in the front room among all the familiar ornaments and furnishings was, as always, comfortably reassuring.

'Jesus, look at the state of you,' she said as I entered the lean-to kitchen, the windows steamed up from the boiling kettle. 'You look like a bloody tramp who hasn't washed or eaten for months.'

I couldn't argue with that. My hair badly needed cutting and I couldn't remember the last time I'd bought anything new to wear, as any spare cash went towards new costumes. I usually slobbed about in a pair of old jeans and a dirty red, white and blue anorak I'd bought as a cheap special offer with petrol at the garage.

'Doing well for yourself then in the catering business,' she sniffed, looking down at my battered pair of trainers as she took out two crusty cobs. 'D'you want mustard on your ham?'

'Actually, I'm not in catering any more,' I said, trying to sound cheerily optimistic and buttering her up for the bombshell I was considering dropping on her. 'I'm doing something else now.'

'You're not that Yorkshire Ripper, are you?' she said, watching me as I poured boiling water on to the Nescafe. 'I always thought it odd that you moved up to Yorkshire. There had to be a good reason.'

'No, I'm not the Yorkshire Ripper.'

'Cos if you are then you know I'm going to have to turn you in,' she said, sounding like the Lone Ranger and making me laugh. 'Here, wait till I tell you this first before I forget.' She was laughing herself now. 'Bring those coffees through to the front and I'll tell you.'

Whipping her headscarf off and making herself comfortable on the sofa, she carefully balanced the plate with the ham roll on the arm and took a sip from the steaming mug.

'Coming home on the bus yesterday from the market I was sat behind this woman and I couldn't help but notice that all her hair was sticking out at the back, a great big tuft of it, like a wire-haired fox terrier's tail.'

I tried to visualize a fox terrier's tail but couldn't bring one to mind.

'Anyway,' she went on, 'it was driving me mad and I wanted to lean forward and tell her, quietly like, not so that the whole bus could hear me, but I suddenly twigged that it was a wig so I didn't say anything.' She paused for a moment to blow on her hot coffee. 'I didn't draw attention to it, you see, because she might have had cancer, the poor woman.'

'What made you think she had cancer?' I asked.

'Well they give you a wig, you see.' She took another tentative sip of the coffee.

'So you go to the doctor and he says, "I'm very sorry you've got cancer but here's a wig to cheer you up"?'

'No, you soft sod,' she roared. 'As a result of the chemo your hair falls out and if you want you can borrow a wig off the National Health. I wouldn't fancy it though as you'd never know who'd had it on before you and I wouldn't want to be walking around in a dead woman's wig.'

I was tempted to say that I'd lend her one of mine if, God forbid, the occasion should ever arise, but didn't think it was quite the right moment for such flippancy.

'So, as we were coming up Whetstone Lane,' she continued, 'I thought to myself, she's got a big back for a woman, and I wondered where she managed to get anything to fit her. Well, it's no good going to C & A's as everything's tiny in there these days and I doubt if even Evans Outsize would've had anything to fit someone with a back that wide. Maybe she got it in George Henry Lee's, it looked dear.'

My mother would've had a field day on an identity parade.

'And then as she was paying her fare I noticed the conductress giving her a funny look. She had hands like great big shovels, huge they were.' She paused to take a bite from her ham roll, attempting to chew the impressive chunk that she'd absently torn off in as polite a manner as possible. This took some time.

'The conductress?' I asked, knowing full well who she meant.

'No, you daft thing, the woman in the mac sat in front of me,' she said eventually, following another bout of prolonged chewing and a hefty slug of coffee to wash the last chunk down.

'It was only when she stood up that I realized,' she said, leaning forward conspiratorially on the sofa.

'Realized what?' I had to play the game even though I was fairly positive I knew what the tag line would be.

'That she was a he. It was a man dressed as a woman,' she crowed, slapping the arm of the sofa to emphasize this shocking revelation. 'What d'ye make of that then, eh? And on a packed number sixty.'

'Well, he's obviously a transvestite,' I offered, slightly embarrassed by the way the conversation was going.

'And how do you know about transvestites then?' she pounced, not missing a trick.

'Cos London's full of them, that's why, they're every-where, the buses are packed with them. This ham roll is gorgeous.' I wanted to change the subject.

'I watched him when he got off, striding across Church Road in his mac, feet the size of a yeti's, poor bugger. I thought, there goes some mother's son, a mother who's probably crippled with shame and broken-hearted and with a bloody big padlock on her wardrobe door. Now what was it you were going to tell me about a new job?'

'Oh, nothing,' I said airily. 'It doesn't really matter, it's just that I've taken a job full time in a pub.' Now didn't seem the right moment to discuss my theatrical career.

'I wish you'd get a decent job and settle down,' she sighed. 'Oh, you're a worry, you really are, all that money wasted sending you to St Anselm's so you could end up working behind a bar.'

'What would you do if I waltzed in one day wearing a frock and wig?' I asked her, eager to get her off the subject of my schooling but also curious to see what her reply would be.

'I'd bloody poison you, that's what.'

No, this was definitely not the time for full disclosures. Best leave sleeping dogs undisturbed for the moment.

The days of the great northern variety clubs were over. Perhaps the most famous club of this genre was the Bartley Variety Club, where for a fiver you could sup your pints of bitter and sip your Cherry Bs in a plush velvet 'pod', dining like a celebrity on chicken and chips served on a red paper serviette inside a wicker basket while watching turns of such calibre as Louis Armstrong, Tom Jones, Shirley Bassey and the Bee Gees.

The clubs were gone and now fun pubs, an oxymoron if ever I've heard one, were the order of the day, springing up like boils in towns and cities all over the north. They were extremely popular even if the punters did sometimes seem a little nonplussed by the antics of the bar staff, who, regardless of age, shape or size, were made to wear a uniform of white T-shirts bearing the name of the pub and white tennis shorts with knee-length socks and pumps. This whiter-than-white ensemble made them glow under the blue fluorescent lighting as if they were coated in luminous paint.

When not pulling pints, these poor buggers were not allowed to stand idle but were expected to bash a tambourine and dance, like people possessed, up and down the bar in time to the ear-splitting music being played by the drag queen DJ, who interspersed his selection of records with pithy put-downs and audience-baiting asides such as 'Look at the arse on her, shame it's got a hole in it.' The end of the evening was usually heralded by a blast of Kim Cordell's 'We're Having A Gang Bang'. This entailed the staff and customers forming a human caterpillar and violently thrusting their hips back and forth to represent mass sexual intercourse. The air of enforced joviality made me withdraw into myself and I seldom got involved, unless I was drunk or found myself unexpectedly caught up in it.

One fun pub that Hush and I both loved was the Stone Chair in Mixenden, just outside Halifax. The management and staff may have worn the obligatory fun-pub uniform but it was friendly, well run and civilized and on a cold winter's night travelling up the lonely Moor End Road in our clapped-out van the rosy glow from the bar windows proved to be a welcoming sight. Action Enterprises was the agency that supplied us with most of our work. Paul, who ran the agency, also ran the Stone Chair with his partner Bob, and when business was slack he'd give us a few extra nights at the pub. When times were really tough he'd frequently feed us or give us an advance on fees not yet earned.

The first time I worked the Stone Chair was with Paul (aka Joyce) in the Glamazons. We'd travelled by train from York to Halifax and then by bus up to the Stone Chair, lugging suitcases and bin-liners full of wigs and arriving at the pub far too early. As the bus pulled away, leaving us alone on this lonely stretch of road, our hearts sank at the sight of what looked like a deserted pub and the prospect of sitting on our cases in the middle of a windy car park until someone showed up.

Fortunately Paul, the landlord, was at home and instead of telling us to come back when they opened – even though we'd rung the bell incessantly and woken him up from a between-shifts nap on the sofa – he invited us in. He showed us to a comfortable back bedroom where we could change and get slapped up, and even gave us our tea. I was fully aware that he'd cottoned on that we were green as grass and took pity on us, and I haven't forgotten the many times he helped us out. Nor do I forget that back bedroom – I still bear scars on my back from that sloping ceiling covered in razor-sharp Anaglypta and whirlpools of vicious little stalactites that I invariably forgot to avoid each time I stood up from the bed to haul up four pairs of supermarket tights over my hairy legs.

The resident drag act at the Stone Chair was a creation called Sid who didn't do an act as such but worked behind the bar. My first encounter with Sid was in the bathroom as I applied my slap in the mirror over the sink.

'Hello, lass,' he shouted cheerily as he breezed into

the room with the force of a tornado. 'Ooh, I've had a right fooking day, look at me fooking nerves,' he said, holding out a trembling hand in demonstration. 'Look at me – I'm shekkin', lass, shekkin'.'

Pulling his miniskirt up and just enough girdle and tights down to allow him access to his tackle, he straddled the toilet bowl and peed.

'Eeh, fook me, lass,' he said, breathing a sigh of relief. 'I've been bursting for that since I got int' car.'

Sid was of an indeterminable age, possibly in his late thirties, tall and slim with a broad Leeds accent. He was wearing a wiry brown wig that had probably started life as a tight curly perm but after years of Sid's ministrations it had surrendered its curl and collapsed, defeated, into a ball of frizz. His taste in drag – a lurex halter-neck top worn with a micro-miniskirt and platform shoes – was strictly Lumb Lane scrubber. Covering his legs, which weren't bad at all, he wore fishnet tights with a hole in them, big enough to drive a hamster through, just above the heel. I could relate to Sid's sense of style though, as mine, in drag, was very much on the same lines.

'D'you think this lippy goes with me complexion?' he asked anxiously, giving himself a good shake, popping it back in the girdle and shoving it between his legs. He could've been juggling red-hot potatoes down there from the way he was hopping about from one foot to the other, gurning and grimacing with the effort of it all.

'It said Burnished Amber on the tube but it don't look like it to me.' He pulled his dress down and wiped his hand down the side of it, satisfied at last that everything was in place. 'Does it look like Burnished Amber to you, lass?'

I wasn't sure what Burnished Amber was meant to look like, but I was damn sure it wasn't the vivid Day-Glo orange sludge that Sid's thin lips were dripping with. His face was caked in a tangerine panstick that ended at the jawline, contrasting sharply with the deathly pale flesh of his razor-burned neck, and there was a blob of kingfisher blue on each eyelid and a dab of carmine rouge on his cheeks. As this look was meant to be au naturel he'd not bothered with false eyelashes, opting instead for a lick with the mascara wand on his own stubby lashes. The evidence of this attempt at beautifying his eyes was written all over his face as there were little flecks of mascara splattered everywhere and you could've been forgiven for thinking that a very small child in a dark room wearing boxing gloves had applied Sid's slap during an earthquake.

'I can't do me make-up like you,' he said, as if reading my mind. 'Me hands shek because of me nerves, you see.' He held his shekkin' hand out again. 'Eeh, I don't know why I put me'sen through it, I really don't.'

'Why don't you ask Miss Hush to do your slap for you?' I offered before I got roped in to assist. I liked Sid, liked him on sight. He was blissfully unaware of just how funny he was and if Fellini had known of Sid he'd have undoubtedly cast him as a tart with a heart in *Nights of Cabiria*.

'Who's Miss 'ush?' he asked.

'Sandra Hush, the one I work with?'

'Why's she called that then?'

'Well, it started out as Sandra Hutchinson and was then shortened to Hush by a friend,' I started to explain.

Sid stared at me blankly.

'Well, originally he was called Sandra Hutchinson after the posh, glamorous one in *The Liver Birds*, y'know? Not that Hush is posh, he's from Wolverhampton, used to be known as Miss Saltley Gas Works in her day.'

'I heard that, Miss Savage,' Hush said, sashaying into the bathroom in full slap and a towering flame-red beehive. 'Never heard of glasshouses and stones on the Birkenhead dock road then?'

'Fookin' 'ell,' Sid gasped, open-mouthed in awe at the vision in front of him. 'You're a big lass.'

Hush liked to take his time putting his slap on so he could enjoy a packet of fags and a few bevvies as he teased and tortured the wigs till they matched his high standards.

'I'm Sid, love,' said Sid, taking a slurp of my pint of cider. 'The bag in drag.'

'And from what I hear you'd like me to do something with your make-up,' Hush said, wincing at the amateur daub smeared over Sid's face.

'Oh, I wouldn't dream of bothering you,' Sid said, putting the toilet seat down quickly and sitting on it, holding his face up to the light in readiness. 'But if you've got a second I wouldn't mind a bit o'spit and polish. If you could try and do me up like Elkie Brooks I'd be right chuffed, lass. Folk say I've already got a bit of a look of her so you've got a head start.'

More like Mel Brooks, I thought, but didn't say anything. I didn't know Sid well enough yet to indulge in a bit of bitchy but friendly banter.

Sid was delighted with Hush's ministrations. 'Eeh, lass,' he kept saying as he preened in the mirror with the enthusiasm of an excited budgie, 'I look fookin' lovely.'

He certainly looked a lot better than when he first came in.

'Here!' he shouted suddenly. 'What time is it? I best get down to that bar before he sends a search party out. You're working the Keighley Fun House after here, aren't you? Her from *Coronation Street* is on, i'n't she?'

She was indeed and I was very excited to be meeting Liz Dawn who played Vera Duckworth as I was a huge fan both of the *Street* and of the lady herself.

'I might come down later,' he said, taking one last glimpse in the mirror at his freshly unearthed loveliness. 'If I hang on in here much longer I'll only want to piss again. I only have to look at a lavvy, me, and it's flying out of me.' And with that little nugget of information he was gone.

I liked working at the Stone Chair. The shows nearly always went well and the crowds were a warm, appreciative audience and even though when we performed there it was usually to pay off the commission we owed – a sensible arrangement – I still always enjoyed it.

Liz Dawn had been working on the *Street* playing factory worker Vera since 1974. Vera's husband Jack had recently been introduced and her role had become more prominent, but even so Liz was still playing dates on the circuit. She had started her career as a club singer.

We arrived at the Keighley Fun House to find a diminutive drag queen berating a couple of strapping youths towering above him in the corridor leading to the dressing room.

'You think you're funny, don't you,' he was shouting. 'You're lucky I don't beat the shit out of you.'

'Classy joint then,' Hush muttered as he struggled to get past them with the costume sack.

'We were only having a bit of a laugh, Diamonds, no offence, like,' one of the lads said in a feeble attempt to mollify this minuscule hell-cat.

'*No offence!*' Diamonds roared. 'You great long streak of piss, go on, bugger off before you get the toe of me shoe up your arse!'

The two lads scarpered, sniggering as they ran.

'And if you're going near that bar then you can get me a large brandy and water as an apology,' he shouted after their retreating backs.

'You having a bit of trouble then?' I asked.

'Do you know what they called me?' he said, flicking his shoulder-length black wig out of his face. 'They said I looked like Tattoo from *Fantasy Island*. Cheeky bastards.'

Fantasy Island, if you remember, was a popular series set on an island somewhere in the Pacific Ocean where those who were able to afford it could go and live out their fantasies. Tattoo was the pint-sized assistant of Ricardo Montalban, who ran the island. I didn't dare look in Hush's direction in case I caught his eye and started laughing as this Diamonds didn't look the type you'd want to offend, so instead I pretended to show great interest in a poster advertising the next week's act.

'For one night only!' it proclaimed. 'Mr Dave Berry!'

And to prove it there was a ten-by-eight photo of the great man peeping mysteriously over the collar of his leather jacket with '"The Crying Game" and other Big Hits!' artfully written underneath in felt-tip pen.

'You must be the Playgirls then,' Diamonds said, unimpressed. He turned his attention to Hush's sack. 'What the hell have you got in there? A dead body?'

Hush explained that it held our costumes.

'And how many costumes have you brought then? They only want a twenty-minute spot, y'know, not the *Ziegfeld* bloody *Follies*. Are you live or mime?'

'Mime.'

'They prefer live in here. Never mind, I'll tell the DJ you're here and you can give him your tape.'

When Liz Dawn arrived she was far more impressed. She was everything I'd hoped she'd be, friendly, warm and very funny.

'Look at these dresses, Don,' she kept saying to her husband, who, like Diamonds, couldn't be less interested. 'You don't get the likes of these off the back of an 'andcart in Salford Market.'

We went on and did our spot and going through my routine I was suddenly aware of just how incongruous our show must seem. An act that was originally conceived and tailored for a gay audience was now being performed to a crowd of mill-workers and miners. I made a mental note that if we were to survive and make a living on this northern pub and club circuit we would have to make the act a little more lairy.

* * *

When the time came for Liz to go on stage she was suddenly gripped by fear.

'I can't do it,' she said to me, grabbing my arm.

'Of course you can, they're gagging for you out there.' I was really surprised she was like this as she'd worked the clubs for years before *Coronation Street*.

'What am I going to say?' She was slowly inching her way back to the dressing room. 'What am I going to do?'

I was genuinely concerned for this lovely lady's distress and tried my best to calm her fears with a few encouraging words. 'They love you, just be yourself, sing a few songs, tell a few gags, you'll be fine.' From behind the curtain we could hear Diamonds out on the dance floor.

'Listen to them,' she gasped, gripping my arm even tighter. 'He's going down a storm, I can't follow that.'

'So, he said to me, "If you can guess what I've got in my hand you can have it," ' Diamonds was saying, the audience loving every minute. 'So I said, "If you can get it in one hand I don't fucking want it." '

Uproar.

'I can't,' Liz said again. 'I really can't go on, honest to God, cross me heart.'

'Come on, Liz,' Don was saying. 'Don't be daft, get out there.'

'Let's hear it,' Diamonds was shouting, 'for our Vera herself. Miss Liz Dawn!'

'I want to go to the lav' were Liz's last words as we pushed her on to the dance floor.

Needless to say, she brought the house down and

you'd never have guessed that the confident, smiling, totally natural performer under the spotlight was the same person who a moment earlier was on the verge of collapse backstage.

As the Fun House was closing, Sid turned up and Diamonds suggested that we all go on to the International Club on Lumb Lane, a notorious thoroughfare in the heart of Bradford's red light district and teeming with ladies of the night of all ages, shapes and sizes, regardless of the fact that Peter Sutcliffe, alias the Yorkshire Ripper, was out looking for his next victim. Diamonds knew the owner of the club and said we'd be OK for a couple of drinks.

'Stay in drag,' Diamonds advised. 'We won't have to pay for our ale that way.'

Diamonds wore a black sequinned dress slit to the hip and a lot of jewellery and I couldn't help feeling concerned at the amount of gold rings, bracelets and diamonds he was wearing, especially in a place like Lumb Lane. Diamonds was nonplussed. 'I'd like to see the one who'd try and take it off me,' he growled. So would I.

Since it was my first trip down Lumb Lane I put my tart's outfit on, the usual ensemble of leopard-skin mini, ten tons of cheap beads and bangles, the platinum blond wig modelled on Vivian Nicholson's hairdo, a tote bag with a tassel hanging off it and a ratty old leopard-skin coat. Dressed like this, a lad could slip into Lumb Lane and blend in with the crowd beautifully. Hush stood out like a sore thumb. He didn't want to go at first but after a few drinks and plenty of encouragement from Diamonds and me he agreed and found himself stepping into the back of Sid's car in an emerald-green-velvet retro swingback coat complete with wicker basket, the type that schoolgirls used to take to their domestic science lessons. To complete this look he wore a red Doris Day-style frock with a green polka dot headband. He wouldn't have looked out of place on the set of *Mad Men* and apart from his height could've easily passed as a well-preserved WASP housewife on her way to a ladies' charity luncheon.

The clientele of the International all looked like they should be helping the police with their enquiries, which on reflection they probably were, and to describe the club, which was in the basement of a house, as a dump would be a gross understatement. It wasn't very busy at first but when word got round that four drag queens were in residence the place soon filled up with working girls popping in and out, curious to have a look at us. We soon got chatting and after a bit of persuasion, not that it took a lot, I was out on the street with them standing alone under a lamp-post sucking on a fag, blowing plumes of smoke up towards the light in a manner I imagined looked glamorously cinematic.

To my surprise and, if I'm honest, horror, a car that had been crawling past at a snail's pace suddenly pulled up alongside me.

'You looking for business then?' the driver asked briskly, leaning out of the open window as if he were ordering a Big Mac and fries at a drive-in McDonald's.

One of the girls who had been sitting on the wall behind me rushed forward to negotiate on my behalf.

'Five quid for a blow job,' she said, much amused.

'Five quid!' I protested in a voice that could be heard in Sheffield. I was only out here on a dare, only pretending to be a hooker, only playing, and certainly had no intention of jumping in a car with what might turn out to be a deranged serial killer for five quid or five thousand. 'Five quid,' I said again, open-mouthed with disbelief, not a good idea when a hooker is negotiating the price of oral sex on your behalf.

'Here, you're not a woman, you're a bloke,' the punter exclaimed, the penny suddenly dropping. 'Not that I mind, like. 'Op in, we'll park up Alice Street.'

'I'm sorry, the shop's closed,' I snapped, mustering what was left of my dignity and turning on my wobbly heels to head back to the relative safety of the club.

'Hang on, luv, I'll go the whole way for fifteen,' I could hear the girl saying. 'Are you on for it or what then?'

They drove off together. I made a mental note of the registration, just in case her body was found on waste ground the next day, but by the time I got back to the club I'd forgotten it.

Thankfully the girl's punter didn't turn out to be the Ripper as within fifteen minutes she was back in the club and stood at the bar enjoying a hard-earned half of lager. I asked her, with a maniac going around killing women, if she wasn't scared each time she got into a car with a strange man.

'Course I am,' she said. 'We all are, but I've got rent

to pay and a baby to feed so I haven't got much choice. I reckon I risk me life each night more times than a lion tamer in a circus.' She studied the bar top for a moment, absently drawing a figure of eight with her finger in a pool of spilled beer. 'I know what you're thinking,' she said.

'What?'

'You're thinking, what a way to earn a living.'

'No, I'm not,' I protested, as I wasn't and besides I could ask myself the same question.

'Well, that's all it is, a livin', and speaking of which standing here won't get the baby fed.' She sighed and draining what was left in her glass she wiped her mouth with the back of her hand and was off.

'See ya,' she said as she strolled up the stairs and out on to the Lane again.

We stayed at Diamonds' flat that night. He set about making a curry as soon as we got in and we demolished it, sitting up till dawn chewing the cud and drinking brandy.

Hush was forever making costumes, and where he went so did his Singer sewing machine. 'I've seen some fabulous fabric in the market, dirt cheap. We'll take twenty quid out of tonight's fee and I'll get it in the morning' became a familiar cry.

We were off to work a club in Denmark for a month and Hush was insistent that we 'needed new'. Almost every afternoon the floor of the flat vibrated violently to the sound of the sewing machine while I sat on the sofa making tassels and watching *Farmhouse Kitchen* on

Yorkshire TV with Henry chattering away and dancing a little jig on my head.

To Hush's frustration his industrious endeavours came to an abrupt halt when, just like a lot of the mills around us, production shut down, although in our case it was because the electricity was cut off. As well as the current bill there were some steep arrears from a previously unpaid bill that Phil had inherited when he took over the flat, and as we couldn't come up with the astronomical sum of three hundred pounds Yorkshire Electricity understandably pulled the plug.

This blip in the proceedings didn't deter Hush for long. He doggedly carried on stitching, setting up camp wherever he could – the back bedroom of the Stone Chair, a garage in Bradford and in the flat above the Amsterdam Bar, home to the resident drag compère Alan Ward. While Hush furiously sewed away, Alan would try to teach me the mystery that was VAT. At first we adopted the spirit of the Blitz and adapted to living a life without electricity but as the nights drew in and the temperature dropped dramatically our gung-ho approach quickly turned to desperation. Without electricity and heating the flat became unbearably grim, particularly as the mice from downstairs had moved in with us.

Slaithwaite seemed to hibernate as winter approached, appearing more foreboding than ever. When I stood alone at the bus stop waiting for the bus into Huddersfield on a cold November night opposite the disconcertingly named Silent Woman pub with its swinging sign bearing the image of a headless woman, it was easy to sink into melancholia and ponder on dark thoughts. When Vera came to visit us one weekend he said standing at that bus stop on a snowy Sunday night was one of the loneliest experiences of his life.

We were glad to be getting out for a while and looked forward to working in Denmark. A Danish agent had seen us in London and had booked us into Madame Arthur's club in Copenhagen for the month of November. The initial plan was for the three of us to travel in the van by boat from Harwich to Esbjerg and then on to Copenhagen. However, the morning we set off from Slaithwaite on our epic journey it became apparent that we'd be lucky to make it as far as Watford Gap in the van, never mind Denmark.

I made a quick phone call to DFDS Seaways to find out if there was anywhere closer to sail from. There was: Newcastle, not exactly round the corner but closer than Harwich. By the time we got to Newcastle Phil had decided not to come with us, so we hastily changed our tickets and boarded the boat with a trolley loaded up with four large sacks containing the costumes, five bin-liners holding wigs and headdresses, four suitcases, two holdalls, a cassette player and the sewing machine. The only thing missing was Henry. We'd intended to bring him with us but he'd gone back to Slaithwaite with Phil in the van instead. I was going to miss him but as Hush had pointed out at the ticket office, 'Getting to Copenhagen with this lot is going to be fun without a bloody bird in a cage to worry about,' and besides, Phil refused to let him go with just us.

As there was a refund on the ticket, we blew some of

it on a cabin. Luckily for us the boat wasn't very busy and we found that we were occupying a four-berth, which meant some heaven-sent extra space for all our gear.

I love sleeping on boats and trains. The last time I'd made an overnight crossing had been as a small boy on the boat from Liverpool to Ireland and lying in the dark of the cabin, the boat rolling on the North Sea beneath us, I felt the same sense of security that I had then. I had no idea what to expect in Copenhagen, nor did I have a clue how we were going to get there from Esbjerg on very little money, but I'd work that one out in the morning. At the moment the most important thing was sleep and with the lullaby of the ship's engines in my ears, I drifted off.

Esbjerg was unremarkable, all I can recall is the dock and the station where we snuck aboard the boat train to Copenhagen and ensconced ourselves in an empty compartment with a sticker bearing the name of a tour group plastered across the window. The entire carriage was occupied by the party travelling with this tour group and all the other compartments were full, yet strangely ours remained empty for the entire journey. We put the luggage on the overhead racks and empty seats and settled in. Since we didn't have a ticket Hush had a nervous breakdown each time the guard walked past our compartment. If he did come in I'd planned to feign ignorance and then attempt to buy two, though just how I was going to achieve this with the few kroner we had between us I had no idea. Looking out of the window at the unfamiliar Jutland landscape, I didn't relish being thrown off bag and baggage at somewhere as alien as a place called Vejle, whatever that might be like.

Miraculously, the guard never once asked to see our tickets. Maybe the tour guide had produced a bunch of them and he'd assumed that ours were among them. Even so, by the time we got to Copenhagen station Hush was a gibbering wreck, having panicked himself to death for the entire journey. We spent the last of our money on a cab, and cramming the luggage into the back and pointedly ignoring the driver's protests at just how much we had we headed to the club, which was on the Lavendelstræde just off the main square and near Copenhagen City Hall.

The club was deserted – not surprising since it was only late afternoon – so we stacked everything up on the step and sat and waited. After about an hour a red-haired woman staggered out of a bar on the other side of the road called the Why Not. She must have taken the question literally as from the way she lurched across the street towards us, attempting to put on a pair of dark glasses and light a cigarette at the same time, she'd obviously been hitting the bottle.

'You must be the cabaret,' she said sleepily in a voice ten octaves deeper than Jeanne Moreau's, swaying back and forth alarmingly as she beckoned us to follow her through the arch at the side of the club. 'Dis vay,' she croaked, weaving across the courtyard towards a door on the opposite side, coughing like a donkey with TB as she carefully negotiated her way around a pile of bins.

Hush opted to stay with the luggage, leaving me to deal with the redhead who was now attempting to climb the many stairs, laughing and coughing and occasionally falling into a heap as she went. Eventually we got to the top of the building and, pointing me towards a room that she muttered was the office, she ricocheted down the corridor to vanish noisily behind a metal door at the end.

Inside, the agent briefly explained the terms of employment and working hours in excellent English, saying that the club would provide a meal each evening from the kitchens that supplied both it and the Prince Arthur restaurant next door. Payday was on a Friday, and as today was Saturday we had six days to exist on absolutely no cash whatsoever. I asked if it might be possible to get a sub on our wages but a curt response informed me that subs were not possible in the first week of employment. Indicating that all business matters were now closed, the agent led me to the door and marched briskly down the hall to our living quarters.

There were two rooms. The larger one had a double bed, a wardrobe minus a door and a small table with a dirty mirror resting on it and a bare bulb hanging above. The other room was much smaller and very narrow with a tiny window set deep in the wall that looked down on to the street. The floor of this room lurched drunkenly one way while the ceiling and walls went the other, as if it had been modelled on the Crazy Cottage at Southport Funfair. There wasn't a right angle or a level surface in the place. In the corner, dominating the room, sat an enormous

ornate safe circa 1910 that could've easily held the Crown
Jewels. The agent proudly told us we could leave our
valuables in it. (What valuables?) Along the sloping wall
there was a beaten-up old leather sofa bed, a small table
and a sink.

I opted for this second room as I knew that Hush
would only sulk if he didn't get the bigger one, and once
the agent had left I sat on the sofa and took a good look
at this grim little garret that was to be home for a
month. I tried to convince myself that the sloping roof
and roughly plastered walls, yellow with age and
nicotine, were actually quite charming and very Hans
Christian Andersen and the creaky old sofa bed was at
least a step up from a lilo. There were added advan-
tages: it was warm, vermin-free and had electricity,
which was more than we had in Slaithwaite.

I went back down to the street to collect Hush and
together we made numerous trips lugging our very heavy
belongings up the seemingly endless flights of stairs. Hush
was philosophical about the accommodation.

'It's a shithole,' he declared, looking around in disbelief. 'But at least we've got leccy.' Since the absence of
electricity from our lives we'd become obsessed with it
and stood gazing like a latter-day pair of Catweazles at
the bare sixty-watt bulb hanging over the mirror, filled
with awe and admiration.

We did two shows a night five nights a week, one at
midnight, the second at 1 a.m. Very acceptable working
hours as far as we were concerned.

In the back of the wardrobe we found an electric kettle

and an ironing board with an iron so ancient it would've been right at home in the Danish Museum of Domestic Appliances if there had been such a place. I pressed the costumes that we would be wearing that night while Hush teased the battered wigs into shape, weaving his magic with a tailcomb and a couple of cans of super-strength lacquer, sculpting waves with a geriatric hairdryer, which as a death trap was right up there with the iron.

We discovered that if we wanted a shower we had to ask the redhead in the flat at the end of the hall if we could use her bathroom. Hush hammered on the door repeatedly, trying to gain access, but gave up in the end as the redhead had obviously passed out and wasn't receiving visitors. It looked like for tonight at least we'd have to make do with what my aunty Chrissie called a 'prostitute's wash', a quick swill in the sink with a flannel.

The club itself was a typical eighties gay disco, all red plush with mirrored pillars on a postage-stamp-sized dance floor overlooked by a shiny chrome DJ console from which the English DJ, a giant of a man with the incongruous moniker of Tiny, surveyed his kingdom. Beside the DJ console was a small space with a curtain in front of it which I recognized from experience as the changing room.

My initial impression of the Danes wasn't favourable. I thought they were a dour lot, lacking in emotion and devoid of any sense of humour whatsoever. I changed my tune after we'd done our two shows as they turned out to be one of the most appreciative and generous audiences that we'd had for a while. They went mad, particularly for the Salvation Army routine, and generously plied us with bottles of the appropriately named Elephant Beer as it was so strong it was probably capable of stunning your average beer-swilling pachyderm.

The redhead turned out to be called Lisa. She worked in the Prince Arthur next door and was the original good-time girl, making Keith Moon look like Ann Widdecombe. Lisa was in her late thirties, an inveterate smoker and drinker and the possessor of a bronchial laugh that seemed to emanate from the very bowels of the earth, shaking the building and making you laugh along with her. It was impossible not to like her. She was a good-natured optimist who on discovery that we had no money lent us some without being asked until payday. She was well travelled and had been around the block so many times she had a season ticket. Naturally I was drawn to her like a moth to a flame. At the moment she was having an on/off casual relationship with a Tom of Finland lookalike she called Horse, due to the generous proportions of a certain part of his anatomy.

'Be careful around Lisa,' one of the barmen whom I didn't much like warned me. 'She'll get you into trouble.'

I thought he was being snide until I found myself one morning after an all-night session with her in various bars sitting on top of a Carlsberg lorry that was making a delivery to the club and trying to crack open a bottle of lager on the side of a crate. Getting up there had been surprisingly easy but making the descent was a little trickier, resulting in Lisa falling and dragging a couple of stacks of crates of lager with her on to the street below. There was a lot of trouble over that one.

On another occasion after a bit of all-night revelry we arrived home to find the gates to the courtyard locked. Lisa, in a dress and high heels, decided that the only option available to us was to climb over it, inevitably getting stuck. The woman who ran the dairy on the corner rang both the police and the fire brigade, who eventually managed, after a lot of fuss, to get her down. She was threatened with the sack over that little contretemps and for the next few days was as contrite as a penitent nun.

Every Sunday morning after the club and restaurant had closed Lisa would make breakfast and a group of us night owls would gather around her big pine table in the dining room. I loved the Danish breakfast with the big bowls of milky coffee served with rye bread and soft white rolls and a selection of cold meats and cheeses. It was a very civilized, leisurely affair after which we'd retire to our respective beds and sleep the day away while Copenhagen went about its business.

Copenhagen in November was very cold and we were unsuitably dressed for temperatures way below freezing, so this vampiric lifestyle suited us. And if we slept all day it meant that we didn't spend money. There didn't seem to be a lot to do anyway. The Tivoli Gardens were closed and we'd made the obligatory visit to the Little Mermaid in the harbour and seen the Louis Tussaud Wax Museum, witnessing the star turn, a somewhat disturbing effigy of Sonja Henie, the Norwegian figure-skating star, spinning around for all eternity on a sheet of fake ice wearing a maniacal grin on her waxen face.

On the nights when we didn't go out after the show and got to bed fairly early, I always found that I woke up the next day at the ungodly hour of 7 a.m. and couldn't get back to sleep. The few people I knew in Copenhagen were nocturnal and therefore asleep, so to pass the boredom of the long solitary days I'd buy milk, bread and cheese from the dairy over the road and spend my time reading. There was a bookshop nearby that carried a few books in English and in the month I spent in Copenhagen I read the entire collection of Miss Read and a dozen Agatha Christies.

Normally our day began around 3 p.m. We'd get up, shower in Lisa's flat and, if she was up and about, she would make breakfast for the three of us. Breakfast for Lisa consisted of very strong coffee, a pack of cigarettes and a large cognac and, if I was in the mood, which I normally was, I'd join her. Hush stuck to his cup of tea, frowning at what he considered to be my 'continental ways'.

When we walked down the Strøget (the high street) in the early hours of a Saturday morning on our way back from a sleazy little hostelry known as the Cosy Bar, it was not unusual to come across a quantity of drunks passed out on the pavement.

'Swedes,' Lisa would sniff disdainfully, trying to maintain her balance as she stepped over them. 'They come over from Malmö to get pissed as the booze is so expensive over there. It's shocking, absolutely appalling.'

She wasn't referring to the sight of so many comatose

drunks littering the street, she meant the outrageous price of the Swedish booze.

'You wouldn't catch me over there, oh, no, no, no.' She went into another of her prolonged coughing fits that echoed down the street. 'C'mon, we'll have a quick drink in the Why Not before we call it a day.'

As it happened, we were asked by the agent if we'd like to work in Malmö on our night off. The money was good and we were curious to see what Sweden had to offer, although after what Lisa had told us we took the precautionary measure of taking our own booze. As the Øresund Bridge had yet to be built we took the ferry over, arriving in Malmö fifty minutes later with Hush as green as a leprechaun's breeches from seasickness.

The Twilight Club we quickly renamed the Twilight Zone, as it had all the good cheer of a Siberian gulag and we had to go on at the curious time of 6.45 to an audience of sullen, sober and predominantly middle-aged couples unimpressed with our efforts. Afterwards we grabbed our fee and got back on that ferry to Copenhagen as quick as we could.

'Well, we won't be going back there again in a hurry, wench,' Hush said as the ferry sailed out of Malmö. 'Never mind, we'll be back in England next week eating decent English jarry food and sleeping in our own beds.'

'On our own lilos you mean,' I corrected him, going in search of a cup of tea.

CHAPTER 3

WE ARRIVED BACK IN SLAITHWAITE AT TWO O'CLOCK on a freezing December morning.

Phil had picked us up from Harwich in the van, which predictably broke down on the motorway. By the time we got the damn thing started again and eventually crawled into the village, tired, hungry and as narky as a trio of mardy children, I just wanted to jump on to my lilo and leave our stuff in the van until we got up again, but Hush insisted that we unload everything and take it up to the flat. Much to our annoyance, the electricity was still disconnected and we had quite a row in the street with Phil over it, causing a few bedroom lights to go on and curtains to twitch in the vicinity. We carted the costume sacks up to the attic bedroom and piled them against the wall, dumping the bin-liners full of wigs on top of them.

It wasn't good to be back and I hankered for the warmth of my Danish garret as the temperature in the flat was below freezing. We didn't bother to undress, just took our shoes off, slipped into the sleeping bags and, despite being back on the lilos, fell into a deep sleep.

We were awoken four hours later by an attic full of police who were very interested to know what was in the suspicious sacks that were propped against the wall. As there were no lights the coppers had to use torches to investigate this possible murderers' bedroom and there was a lot of stumbling around in the dark. Henry added to the chaos. Curious at this unexpected dawn raid, he had flown up the stairs eager to join in the fun and sat happily on top of a none-too-amused policeman's helmet.

It transpired that one of the neighbours had seen us carrying the costume sacks into the flat and in the wake of the current Ripper paranoia had come to the conclusion that something the shape and size of the sacks could only contain one thing. A body.

A young copper picked up a bin-liner and peered inside, his eyes round as saucers as hastily he beckoned one of his colleagues to 'come and have a look at this'. The pair of them stood open-mouthed, staring at the contents of the bin-liner like they were witnessing a war crime. Eventually the older one spoke.

'Do you mind telling us what exactly you have in here, sir?' he asked a semi-conscious Hush.

Despite the hour, Hush was surprisingly eloquent.

'They're wigs, officer,' he announced grandly. 'And those sacks that your friends there are pulling apart contain costumes. We're a cabaret act, you see, and have literally just returned from a four-week tour of Scandinavia.'

'So you weren't smuggling bodies into the house in the middle of the night?' the copper replied, holding up a wig on its polystyrene head.

'No,' I growled, not happy at being woken up from a deep sleep by a copper shining a torch in my face, nor was I concerned that half of the West Yorkshire Constabulary were surrounding my lilo and wondering if they'd finally caught the Yorkshire Ripper. 'We take the bodies of our murder victims straight through to the back and bury them in the allotment, it saves time.'

'Take no notice,' Hush shrieked, laughing nervously and throwing his hands up in the air like a pantomime dame, adding, 'As if' and managing in the process to make those two little words sound like we had something serious to hide.

'We're terribly sorry for disturbing you,' the copper said sarcastically, 'but if we receive a phone call reporting something suspicious you must appreciate that we are obliged to follow it up. We are after all conducting an extensive manhunt.'

'Well, you won't find any men in here,' I snapped, not normally so lippy in the presence of police but still rattled by being woken so early.

'You speak for yourself,' Phil said from the top of the stairs, pulling his beige terry-towelling robe closer and pursing his lips indignantly.

'Oh, shut up, Phyllis, don't you start,' Hush admonished. 'Make yourself useful and put the kettle on,' and turning to one of the coppers he asked, 'Do you think we could get up and get dressed, officer?' forgetting that he was already fully clothed, complete with woollen hat. The police can only have surmised that they'd stumbled across a local dosshouse and as Phil showed them out down the narrow stairs we could hear them muttering and sniggering to themselves as they went.

'God knows what the neighbours will say,' Phil moaned when he came back. 'There's two vanloads of coppers outside.'

'Sod 'em,' I said, from inside my sleeping bag.

'Exactly,' Hush agreed. 'So if you don't mind, Phyllis, we'd like to get back to sleep. We've got a double tonight and I need my kip and then when we wake up, ladies,' he added, sounding like the head girl in an Angela Brazil story, 'we're going to have it out about this electricity bill.'

I couldn't wait.

That night we were working the Stone Chair followed by a gay club called the Gemini. We stayed in drag to make the journey from Halifax to Huddersfield as it wasn't worth the effort getting changed, and as fate would have it we encountered a police roadblock checking all vehicles on a deserted stretch of road.

As we were giving some friends from the pub a lift to the club Hush and I had volunteered to sit in the back of the van instead of up front. We didn't mind, it was comfortable stretched out on the drag sacks, me swigging a bottle of cider and smoking a fag, Hush sipping from 'the baby', a supermarket-sized bottle of Coke mixed with vodka he always took to work with him. Dressed as a couple of hookers, the added advantage of sitting in the back was that we didn't flatten the tops of our gargantuan wigs on the roof of the van.

'What's happening now?' Hush groaned as the van came to a halt and we heard someone talking to Phil.

'Hello again,' we could hear the man saying cheerily. 'Do you remember me, I were in your bedroom this morning.'

'Oh, hello!' Phil gushed, as if greeting a long-lost old flame. 'I thought I recognized you, officer. We're just on our way to work.'

'Well, do you mind if we have a quick look in the back of the van?'

'Oh no,' Hush moaned, squeezing my arm. 'For God's sake, Savage, don't go saying anything to them.'

Phil flung the back doors of the van open and for the second time that day I had a torch shone in my face.

'Well, well, what have we here?' I heard one of the silhouettes say. 'And who are you two young ladies then?'

Without batting an eyelash I slid out of the van with as much dignity as possible when one is wearing dominatrix boots and a leopard-print coat, saluted one of the officers and stated, 'WPC Savage, sir. Ripper bait.'

Returning home from the Gemini Club at 2 a.m., roaring drunk and still in the blond bouffant and thigh-length boots, I took the opportunity to thank the sleeping neighbours for organizing that morning's dawn raid.

'Come out,' I shouted up to the bedroom windows of Crimble Bank. 'Come out from behind your bloody nets and fight like a woman,' a taunt that one of Vera's aunties had once shouted up to his mother during a slight altercation. The good folk lying in their beds sensibly didn't respond and after a bit of a struggle and a few more choice words Phil finally got me indoors, whereupon I upended the ubiquitous plastic bucket of steeping mushy peas over his head. No wonder the neighbours crossed the street to avoid us.

The van finally died a couple of nights later as it attempted to make it up a steep hill in Halifax. We got out and pushed (not easy in high heels), much to the amusement and derision of passing motorists, until we eventually gave it the last rites, abandoned it on the road and called a taxi to take us to the venue.

It was impossible to carry on without transport because of the distances that we covered each night, so we had no option but to flog the van for scrap and buy something else that was not only cheap but hopefully reliable. All the motors we went to look at were way out of our price league until eventually we found a clapped-out old car for ninety quid from someone Phil knew. On our first excursion in it to Birmingham to work the Jug, a club run by a character we loved called Laurie who wore an ill-fitting toupee and called everyone 'me babbie', Phil absently filled it up at the garage with diesel instead of petrol, which meant we had to crawl up the motorway at twenty-five miles an hour and arrived in Birmingham hours late.

We had quite a lot of work on that December and Hush was determined to do a Christmas show. He loved Christmas, and had brought his artificial tree and all the decorations and lights for it with him when we moved up north. Trouble was, there was still no electricity so unless we gave in and paid the bill there would be no lights twinkling on his tree, nor would there be any new costumes made for the proposed Christmas show.

Ever resourceful, Hush took his faithful Singer sewing machine with us to the Green Hammerton Hotel, the next venue we were working at, to make costumes. It was like a holiday with pay at the Hammerton, all the acts enjoyed working there; you did your show three nights on the trot in the cabaret lounge to a very civilized audience, stayed in comfortable rooms and were well fed and watered. The owners, the irascible Sid and his more easy-going partner, Dennis, knew the meaning of the words hard graft, having worked their way up through the pub trade before eventually arriving at their own hotel.

Sid had a temper like a Tasmanian devil and when he lost it, which he frequently did, York Minster shook. He also had a heart of gold and was an excellent cook. His homemade soup, stored on the cool larder floor in a huge pan, was seriously depleted after frequent raids by me throughout the night. It was as addictive as crack cocaine and I couldn't leave it alone, but Sid didn't seem to mind. 'Jewish penicillin, love,' he'd say, being neither Jewish nor medically inclined. 'Put a bit of meat on those tin ribs of yours.'

I was a bit shy with Sid at first but instantly thick as thieves with the manager, Nigel, a smashing Geordie who took upon himself the unenviable task of teaching me to fire-eat. Before going into the hotel trade Nigel had briefly been a stripper, incorporating fire-eating into his act. As I was desperate to learn this impressive feat I eventually, after a lot of pleading, wore him down and got him reluctantly to agree to teach me.

'Go on, pet, shove it in your gob,' he'd say as I stood in the car park holding two rods made from wire coat hangers with blazing tips of cotton wool that had been bound with cotton and then soaked in lighter fuel, the flames seemingly enormous and dancing dangerously in the breeze. 'You wouldn't be so slow if it were a pint of cider.'

Even though my early attempts resulted in frequent blisters on my tongue and an assortment of burns on my arms and hands ranging from first degree to ten, I persevered, determined to master this not surprisingly dying art. He instructed me always to use pure cotton when tying the cotton wool to the rods as polyester would melt, and taught me how to do a 'tongue transfer', moving the flame from one rod to another using your tongue. The very first time I managed a 'blowout' – spitting the petrol through the flame and creating a fireball – I very nearly died of fright as I couldn't quite comprehend how I'd managed to produce such a volcanic emission, worthy of Etna at her angriest.

Nigel was more than a little wary of the force he'd unleashed.

'I can see it now,' he sighed. 'Hotel burns down. Three hundred killed. Drag act and hotel manager arrested.'

While we were doing this three-day stint at the Hammerton, Hush barely left his room except to eat and do the show. Instead he spent his day bent over his machine, running up a succession of amazing costumes with fabrics bought from market stalls and Bradford shops that specialized in materials for saris.

As it was Christmas we thought we should open this show with a suitable number dressed as Cinderella's Ugly Sisters, and for this Hush made me a fat suit.

It was a crude prototype of *Little Britain*'s Bubbles character, only mine, far less sophisticated, was made from thick lining fabric stuffed with a ton of multi-coloured foam chips and an industrial-sized zip running down the back that was an absolute swine to pull up and down once I'd managed to get myself into it. Over this body I wore an enormous tent dress which, after a lot of jumping up and down as any kind of terpsi-chorean movement with my elephantine legs was extremely limited, I stripped out of to the strains of 'The Stripper'. The not-so-body-beautiful underneath had by now taken on such a powerful personality all of its own we'd christened it Biddy. Once out of the frock, there was a bra the size of a hammock containing Biddy's pendulous breasts, each one the size and weight of a large pouffe and complete with an upholstery tassel hanging from the nipple. Underneath the ship's sail that called itself a G-string Hush had stitched a heart-shaped piece of hair cut from an old wig and on one of the buttocks I'd drawn an anchor with a blue marker pen.

I hated Biddy as apart from the prude in me finding it grossly obscene I was forever repairing its bursting seams that spilled foam chips in every venue we worked at. It also took up most of the back seat of the car so that whoever travelled with it, which was invariably me, would have to sit buried underneath the monster.

Unfortunately for me, I couldn't dump it as Biddy went down a storm. Since we got a hell of a lot of bookings out of the bloody thing we had to live with it, even to share the attic bedroom with its all-dominating presence as there was nowhere else to store it. Now, each time I see the Disney animation *The Little Mermaid* and the octopus villainess Ursula, I'm reminded of Biddy and taken back to that Christmas.

While Hush stitched in his room I'd take myself off into York on the bus, mainly to have a mooch around but also to buy zips ('Don't get plastic!'), cottons and all the other accoutrements required for the drag-making factory in room number 3.

I spent the afternoon investigating the antique and curio shops, even though I didn't have a hope in hell of affording anything that I took a shine to, and impressed a party of Americans in The Shambles at the shrine of Margaret Clitheroe with my knowledge of this unfortunate woman. I knew all the gory details of how she'd been stripped, laid under a door and then crushed to death with rocks, thanks to my mother, who knew everything there was to know about the lives of the saints and martyrs and how they'd met their maker.

When I got back to the hotel, a very concerned Sid and Nigel were waiting to greet me.

'I've got a bit of bad news for you, love,' Sid said, busying himself arranging ornaments on the shelves behind the bar. 'There's been a terrible death. We've only just heard, haven't we, Nigel?'

Nigel nodded solemnly in agreement.

My stomach turned over and the room seemed to close in on me. Had Hush stitched himself to death? Had his overworked machine blown up? Or worse, had something happened to my mother? I momentarily went deaf, the only sound the sudden rush of blood pounding in my ears, a tidal wave drowning out what Sid was telling me.

'. . . Shot in the back, right outside the front door,' he was telling me as he gave a glass tankard a good rub with a dishcloth.

'Who?' I asked, now seriously confused. Surely there hadn't been a shootout in the Green Hammerton? It was hardly the Wild West after all. 'Hush?'

'No, you daft cow,' Sid snapped, looking at me as if I was developing early-onset dementia. 'John Lennon.'

We did the Vernons Girls' version of 'We Love The Beatles' that night as a tribute. Dennis, standing in his usual position at the end of the bar as acting MC, said it was very fitting.

The thought of spending a Christmas in that flat without any electricity was untenable and even though the majority of the bill had nothing to do with either Hush or me we capitulated and went into Huddersfield grudgingly to pay it.

Hush was livid at our having to fork out such a substantial amount of money on a bill that was not of our making and vowed revenge on Phil, even though it really wasn't his fault.

'Think of something, Savage,' he said, in his

best Machiavellian tones. 'You've got an evil mind.'

I resented the slight on my good name but even so the retribution Hush was seeking came to me in an old-fashioned chemist one afternoon. In among the jars of dried liquorice root and cinnamon quills I spied a jar of what looked like dried leaves and marked 'senna pods'. Now, I'd learned enough from my mother and aunties over the years, a trio unequalled in their knowledge of bowel movements, or rather the lack of any, to know that senna pods were a powerful laxative.

Buying a large bag of these, I mixed them in a jar of boiling water and left them to steep undisturbed in the back of the cupboard for a week. During this period we waited for the electricity to be turned back on. Christmas was four days away and despite endless phone calls from Phil there was still no sign of any juice. In the end I rang the Yorkshire Electricity Board pretending to be a social worker to ask them if they were aware that there was a seriously ill pensioner and her special needs son who, despite having paid their bill, were living in a state of near hypothermia without electricity in a snow-covered Slaithwaite over Christmas.

The electricity was turned on that afternoon and to celebrate Hush made a magnificent spaghetti Bolognese, with some of the lethal potion hiding under the sink stirred into Phil's portion. Nothing happened at first, much to our disappointment. The following morning the potion took effect, resulting in poor Phil spending the best part of the day sat on the throne and emerging hours later exhausted by the strain of it all.

'Do you think you've overdone the dosage?' Hush asked anxiously as we listened to Phil's moans outside the bathroom door. 'You might've killed him.'

'What d'ya mean "I"?' I said, turning gangster. 'You're as much involved in this as I am. It was you wanted to get your own back in the first place.'

'Yes, but it was your idea to use the senna pods. What if you've poisoned him?'

We listened fearfully at the door for any sounds of a death rattle but all we could hear were a succession of low grunts and wails, until eventually he surfaced from the bathroom three stone lighter and, to coin a crude but apt phrase, the colour of boiled shite.

'Revenge is sweet,' Hush muttered darkly, watching Phil stagger bow-legged into the kitchen. 'But if I ever cross you, remind me never to eat anything you cook.'

Phil went to stay with his parents on Christmas Day, leaving me, Hush and Henry to our own festive devices. We woke late as we'd been working the previous night and after a late breakfast of tea and fags we phoned our respective friends and families to wish them 'all the best'. This brought on a lump in the throat and a melancholia in both of us that required a quick nip of our respective tipples to help banish the blues and restore a sense of festive good cheer, no matter how forced and artificial.

Hush, determined to have a traditional Christmas lunch, pulled out all the stops and produced a meal that could've sustained the entire village during a ten-day siege, should one have occurred. Following this indigestion-inducing blowout we exchanged gifts, a Ben Sherman shirt for me and a red and black lumberjack jacket I'd bought in Huddersfield Market for Hush. Wearing paper hats from the crackers we'd pulled, we sat, bored out of our minds, watching Morecambe and Wise on the black and white telly.

After a while we decided to go for a walk to try to stir ourselves. The village was deserted and covered in a thin layer of frost and ice, Christmas trees twinkled in front-room windows and from somewhere I heard a child imploring her mother to 'Tell him, Mam, I haven't had a turn yet.' A real sense of displacement slowly crept over the pair of us. Everyone in this village belonged here apart from us, they had reasons to be gathered in their front rooms on this Christmas night; Slaithwaite was their home as it had been for generations of families, whereas it certainly wasn't ours. For us it was only transient, before we packed up and moved on to somewhere else.

But to where, I wondered silently, and when?

I was seriously beginning to question this rootless existence with very few responsibilities and if, for once, I was truly honest with myself I knew that we couldn't go on living like this indefinitely. The piper, to quote my ma, would very soon have to be paid.

We wandered over to the canal path. It was eerily silent now by the water and the pang of loneliness in the pit of the stomach we'd experienced earlier in the day started to gnaw again.

'What the hell are we doing here?' Hush suddenly said, breaking the silence, his icy breath mingling with the smoke of his cigarette in the cold night air.

'We were going for a walk,' I said numbly, staring absently into the canal at a shopping trolley that was not fully submerged and had a length of emerald-green tinsel wrapped around the handle.

'No, I mean in bloody Slaithwaite. I miss London, oooh how I miss it so,' Hush literally mooed, the sad and lonely low of a homesick cow who'd suddenly realized it was in the wrong field.

'Well, I don't,' I lied. 'There's a lot more work up here and it's better paid and besides we've got nowhere to live in London. Best hold out here till we've saved a few bob and can afford to go back.'

'I can't stop panicking about the future,' he suddenly blurted out, panicking me in the process. We normally didn't disclose our more personal feelings to each other so I was quite surprised at this unexpected admission, having arrogantly assumed that he had come to accept this strange lifestyle of ours, adapting to it extremely well. On the surface he was quietly confident, even-tempered and sensible, dealing with the pitfalls of life with a philosophical shrug of the shoulder. Hush was Old Reliable, always there to create magic by turning a cheap nylon wig into a towering confection of curls and waves that defied all laws of gravity. He was someone who thought nothing of whipping out his machine and running you up a magnificent creation out of two and a half yards of lurex in under an hour. He was also someone who in all probability was taken for granted.

Still waters run deep, unplumbed, unfathomable depths in Hush's case, so deep there were fish with massive teeth and luminous antennae hanging off their heads swimming about down there.

'I've had enough,' Hush said, finishing the last of his fag. He didn't like smoking in the street, considering it to be 'common', but as it was Christmas and there was no one about to witness this breach of etiquette, it didn't matter.

'I'm going home,' he said, taking one final drag before throwing the butt into the canal. I thought he meant back to the flat.

CHAPTER 4

'WHAT DO YOU MEAN HE'S GONE?' I SHOUTED DOWN the phone, not caring that there was a woman standing outside the phone box hanging on to every word I was saying. It was a pain having to use the public phone outside the block of flats on Kelvin Road but my mother's telephone had a lock on it to prevent anyone (i.e. me) from making any unauthorized calls. She was obsessed with what she described as the 'crippling prices' British Telecom charged and the use of the phone before six o'clock was strictly prohibited.

'Even if I'm having a heart attack and you have to call an ambulance,' she said, making sure the lock preventing the dial going round was good and secure, 'you can get yourself round to that phone box and ring one from there.'

Eventually I learned how to make a call by tapping out the numbers on the little black buttons the handset rested on but as this could be quite a noisy process I only dared do it when she wasn't in residence. It was wiser to make my more private phone calls from the public phone box as my mother possessed an unnatural hearing range that could pick up the sound of a mouse farting across the park, let alone my foghorn voice. The less she knew, the less there was for her to worry and get into a state about. Ignorance was bliss as far as my ma was concerned, although blissful was certainly not how you'd describe my current status quo.

'He went soon as you left. I drove him down. Only got back yesterday,' Phil said casually.

'You mean he's buggered off? Gone back to London?' I couldn't believe that Hush would do such a thing, run off and leave me stranded in Slaithwaite. 'What about the act?' I shouted, making the woman outside forget for the moment that she was pretending not to listen.

'Well, all your drag's here, wigs and everything, but he's taken all his records and all the tapes, so you've got no show.' Phil sounded not in the least bit bothered. 'I don't know what you're going to do for an act.'

'Did you know about this?' I had every intention of killing him for his duplicity.

'No, I knew nowt about it, till ten minutes after you'd left to see your mother,' he whined.

'Then how come you drove him down to London so bloody smartish?' He was going to be found dead after I got hold of him, drowned face down in a plastic bucket of mushy peas.

'Well, I fancied a few days in London and Hush offered to pay me for taking him so I just went. Anyway, you weren't here to stop him.' He sounded like he was eating, which only infuriated me all the more.

'I was at me mother's!' I protested, causing her outside to light a fag and move even closer to the box. At this rate she'd be inside with me if the conversation continued in this heated vein.

'I'm coming back tonight,' I said, more than a little worried at what the hell I was going to do now.

'Suit yourself, I'm going down t' Gemini Club, but you've got your key.' Phil could be maddening at times. Didn't he realize I had a major disaster on my hands? Abandoned, stranded and with me career in tatters? I mentally dramatized everything then, even real dramas that didn't require further embroidery.

'Everything all right?' the woman asked eagerly as I held the door open for her.

'Did you get a good earful then, missus?' I snarled in reply.

'Couldn't help overhearing, love,' she smiled. 'You've got one of those voices that you can't help hearing. Cheer up, there's many a disaster at sea.'

I walked around for a bit to calm down and gather my thoughts as I didn't want to appear agitated in front of my mother. When I got in she was knitting and watching an old black and white film on the telly.

'What's up with you?' she asked suspiciously. 'You look a bit shifty McCoy to me.'

I muttered something in reply, throwing her a look that I hoped she'd interpret as 'Don't be ridiculous' and sat down.

There was no pulling the wool over the eyes of the Madame Defarge of Tranmere, that's for sure. Her response after one glance at me only confirmed that she was more than capable of reading me like a

107

'tuppenny novel', a fact she frequently reminded me of.

'What's this you're watching?' I asked, too distracted by the myriad worries whirling around in my head to show any interest in the film but anxious to change the subject.

'*All About Eve*, an old Bette Davis film,' she said, pronouncing 'film' deliberately as 'fillum' to resurrect the ghost of our old neighbour Mary, an avid fan of fillum, particularly those that starred her beloved Bette Davis. Following an afternoon session with the curtains drawn, matching her chain-smoking heroine fag for fag as she sat glued to her telly, Mary would hold forth from her perch on the back kitchen step.

'I've just watched a marvellous Bette Davis fillum, Molly,' she'd swoon, rolling her ill-fitting top denture in her mouth as my mother brought the washing in. '*A Stolen Life*. Bette played twins. It was marvellous, Molly, marvellous. Ooh, they don't make fillums like that any more.'

I'd always admired Ms Davis's ability to retain smoke. She seemed capable of taking an enormous drag from her cigarette then delivering a lengthy speech without so much as a whiff of smoke escaping from whatever recess deep in her lungs it was lurking in, until just as you wondered where the smoke could have possibly gone she released it, timing it beautifully to coincide with the denouement of her speech. It was Bette Davis, Marlene Dietrich and Dave Allen's fault that I ever took up smoking in the first place: they managed to make it look so . . . interesting.

'He wasn't the genius he was cracked up to be, you

know,' my mother said, suddenly breaking into my daydream.

'Who?' I asked, confused as there were no men in the scene she was watching, just Bette being served breakfast in bed by Thelma Ritter.

'Orson Welles,' she said, holding the sleeve of a pale pink cardigan she was knitting up to the light, scrutinizing it for any dropped stitches or hidden flaws. She was rarely seen without a pair of knitting needles in her hands, having the uncanny ability to read her library book, watch the telly, hold a conversation and keep one eye out for cats invading her garden and the other on a cake baking in the oven all at the same time. Here was a woman who seriously didn't miss a trick.

'He never wrote *Citizen Kane*, you know,' she continued. 'It was really some fellah called Herman Mankiewicz who did all the spadework, though Orson Welles took all the credit. Now shut up while I count these stitches.'

The fact that I hadn't uttered a word apart from 'Who?' was conveniently ignored. However, it was wise to take a vow of silence while stitches were being counted, just as it was to keep it zipped during that period on a Saturday afternoon when my dad checked his pools coupon.

'The Orson Welles who advertises sherry?' I asked.

'He did a lot more than sherry adverts. Twenty-two . . . twenty-three . . .' She considered she counted under her breath but in fact she could probably be heard quite clearly by Dot-Next-Door.

'Twenty-four, twenty-five . . . I read it in the

twenty-six, twenty-seven . . . *Reader's Digest*,' she added in a tone that implied if the information came from the *Reader's Digest*, a publication much revered in our house, as the little piles of them balanced all over the place testified, then it was obviously nothing less than the truth.

'This Herman Mankiewicz was a screenwriter,' she explained, laying her knitting in her lap. 'And it was his brother, Joseph, who directed this film I'm trying to watch. Anyway, as I said, it was Herman who wrote the best part of *Citizen Kane*, not Orson Welles, so there. Now did I say twenty-two or twenty-six? I wish you wouldn't start bloody rabbiting when I'm trying to count – I'll have to start again now.'

Not for the first time I sat in wonderment listening to her prattle on, amazed at the seemingly inexhaustible well of information she was able to draw from, to reel off the facts about the most obscure subjects at any given moment.

'What do you want for your tea?' she asked, giving up for the moment with the knitting and shoving it behind the cushion. 'There's ham in the fridge and some of that steak pie you like from Marks or you could always go over the park to that Chinese you're mad on, though how the bloody hell you eat that prawn curry muck slathered over chips, stinking the house out, is beyond me.'

'Oh, I can't stop, Mam,' I answered in what I hoped sounded a light-hearted and casual manner. 'I've got to go back, there's trouble at work.'

'What?' she replied in tones dry as a martini. 'The police raided the brothel again?'

'No, Mother, we're short of a member of staff. Somebody walked out without warning,' I explained, not speaking a word of a lie no matter which way you looked at it. 'I'll just catch that seven o'clock if I get a move on.'

'I'd need a Philadelphia lawyer to work you out, my lad,' she said, heading for the kitchen. 'I'll make you a little butty before you go.'

At Lime Street Station I rang Paul at the Stone Chair to tell him what had happened. There was a week's work lined up for the Playgirls and if I was going to cancel it was best that I did it now.

Paul was sympathetic but told me not to be too hasty in cancelling.

'Do it yourself,' he said. 'Get a single act together, and in the meantime while you sort yourself out you can do a few nights here behind the bar. Sid's walked out again, it must be in fashion.'

I sat and thought about this proposition on the train to Huddersfield, not really relishing working behind the bar in drag as the resident tranny. I was an act, or at least I thought I was, and pulling pints in drag and having to join in with 'The Gang Bang' at the end of each evening didn't appeal. Still, it was the only offer on the table so far and it was a way of earning some money, a commodity that was, as usual, in short supply.

As for going solo, why not? I encouraged myself with the notion that I couldn't be any worse than some of the other acts knocking about, plus there was the advantage of earning more money as a solo act. I still had all my drag and if I put my mind to it I could easily get a thirty-minute show together. So what, apart from fear, was stopping me?

By the time the train pulled into Huddersfield I'd talked myself into it. I set off for the bus station bursting with enthusiasm and a new-found confidence in the solo career that I was about to launch on the unsuspecting residents of the north.

People were very encouraging about my plan, which only added fuel to my ambition. That night in the Gemini Club, the owner, John Addy, gave me a couple of bookings there and then, act unseen, as did the current managers of the New Penny pub in Leeds. Chris and Steve were a couple of nice lads who did an act themselves called the Dream Girls, and it was Chris who eventually solved the problem of what I should call myself. There had been much debate at the bar of the Gemini, involving me, Phil, John and various members of staff and customers, over what my new stage name should be. Nicky, one of the bar staff who occasionally performed at the club as a member of a trio called the Shagettes (deduce for yourself what sort of act it was), insisted that I call myself Lily Savage – but I remembered Regina Fong saying a lifetime ago in the dressing room of the Black Cap that a name like Lily Savage would never do if I wanted to work professionally. I was determined to find another, less ridiculous name to work under.

'Why not call yourself Paul Monroe?' Chris said. I wasn't exactly crazy about the name, not being a huge fan of Marilyn, and I worried that the punters might expect me to totter out and perform an incredible impersonation of the dead star.

No, I couldn't see myself standing in front of the patrons of Tickles in Wakefield, knee bent, eyes half closed, pouting into the microphone and mouthing the words to 'I Wanna Be Loved By You' and expecting to get out alive.

However, as everyone seemed to think it was a good name I went with it, and so Paul Monroe I became.

On the way home in the car Phil dropped another bombshell on me that day.

'Oh, I forgot to tell you,' he said casually. 'While you were away I told Adrella he could come and stay. I'm picking him up tomorrow.'

Adrella was a well-known act on the London pub circuit and supposedly he'd said something about a number I was doing one night at the Black Cap which was duly misinterpreted and reported back to me by another act desperate to stir up trouble. I didn't disappoint, and predictably went up like a rocket when this supposed bit of slander reached my ears. I threatened to 'have' Adrella the next time I saw him, much to the delight of the other acts who thrived on such fighting talk, praying that they'd be present for the moment of confrontation between us.

Adrella then went off to work in Germany, nothing to do with my threats. He was blissfully unaware that there was any animosity between us, while I moved up north, and to the dismay of a lot of drag queens the showdown between us never took place.

Now here he was, fresh off the plane from Hamburg and running around the kitchen trying to catch a mouse like he owned the place, with me stood on a chair, temporarily defenceless. The mouse broke the ice and, over a pot of tea, it slowly began to dawn on me that we were getting on quite well. There was no need for me to prowl around him in the manner of a territorial tomcat and after clearing the air we became friends.

Avril had promised him a month's work in the north but on his return to the UK he found that she didn't have one single date in the diary for him. Phil had offered to drive him while he was here, and as Peter (for that was Adrella's real name) was finding life with Avril and the parrots untenable Phil offered to put him up with us.

Peter's arrival proved to be a bit of a godsend. Since he had no work and I had over a week's worth of dates booked in but no partner to do them with, we teamed up.

Like me, Peter had worked some rats' nests in his time but he was totally unprepared for a few of the venues we worked in that week. The worst, and it must've been bad because thirty-odd years later we still both remembered the experience vividly, was a pub in Leeds called the Cherry Tree. When presented on a contract, the name made it sound quite pleasant, bucolic even, but arriving on a cold, grey Sunday lunchtime (two spots, fifty quid between us) we found the Cherry Tree was far from the quaint village inn that I'd naively had in mind. It was the kind of pub that sterner members of the SAS would be wary of training in before a stint in Afghanistan, never mind two drag queens, and I later discovered the place was notorious and the mention of its name would make many a hardened act quake in their shoes.

However, we took it all in our stride and were quite philosophical about some of the dumps we ended up in, usually managing to see the funny side and enjoy ourselves. Peter had succeeded in drumming up some work in London and when the time came for him to leave I was sorry to see him go. It also meant that it was time for me to literally get my act together as I had bookings in for 'Paul Monroe' at the end of the month.

I opened with the hated Biddy. I would've preferred to close with Biddy but the time it took for me to get into the fat suit made this idea impractical. I also made more of the fire-eating, finally waking up to the fact that it went down a lot better if I sent it up instead of taking myself so seriously.

Paul Monroe made his debut on a Sunday lunchtime at the New Penny, fortified by cider and my fears muffled by the knowledge that I had a sympathetic audience. To my relief the show went down very well, the evening show even better, and I came away with eighty quid all to myself – a fortune!

I worked at least four nights a week and on weeks when business was slack I'd work behind the bar at the Stone Chair in drag, which I never really enjoyed, feeling stupid and demoralized to be mincing up and down serving pints. On the plus side I got to see some great comics, Dudley Doolittle, Mickey Finn, Stan Richards (a brilliant Yorkshire comic who played Seth in

Emmerdale), Johnnie Casson, and a young Les Dennis who, the manager, Paul, would tell me, was on the brink of big-time stardom.

Paul was always encouraging me to get up on the stage and try my hand at compèring but I was terrified of the microphone. And besides, what would I say?

My baptism of fire as a live act eventually happened one night in a pub in Bradford called the Furnace. The tape broke, and I was left standing in front of a packed pub like a rabbit caught in the glare of car headlights.

'Tell us a joke, Paul,' someone in the audience shouted.

'Yeah, go on,' another joined in. 'Say something.'

Soon the entire pub was baying for me to tell them a joke, and even though I wanted to run off the stage and out of the pub I found myself edging slowly towards the microphone.

Out of desperation I nicked a few gags I'd heard Dudley Doolittle and some of the other comics tell at the Stone Chair but apart from that I have absolutely no recollection of what I said. I do know that after the initial shock of hearing my own voice reverberating around the room and finding that talking into the mike wasn't as bad as I'd imagined, I took to it like a duck to water and stayed up there for over half an hour cracking hoary old gags and having a bit of fun with the audience, who in return gave me a standing ovation at the end.

'Not bad,' the manager said afterwards at the obligatory lock-in. 'This lot are a tough crowd. If I were you I'd ditch the mime act and go live. You're a natural.'

Even Phil was amazed and on the way home he turned into Madame Rose.

'Right, you can start getting a load of jokes together,' he said determinedly. 'Write yourself an act, open with a number and finish with your comedy fire-eating. You'll be able to put your fee up. I'll get on the phone tomorrow. Hush leaving was the best thing that ever happened to you.'

But come the morning I found that the magic had faded. Last night, I told myself as I waited for the kettle to boil, was nothing more than a fluke. I'd been forced to 'go live' out of necessity, driven by a combination of fear and pure undiluted adrenalin, and I doubted that I could repeat that success on a regular basis. By the time I'd made a cup of tea I'd convinced myself that it was easier (and a lot less nerve-racking) to remain a mime act.

Even Paul from the Stone Chair couldn't convince me when he rang later in the day. 'I hear you went live last night,' he said proudly, 'and not before time – how many times have I told you to go live? Played a blinder, I hear, went down a storm. I'll start booking you out as a live act, shall I? You can come and work here on Saturday so I can see if you're any good.'

I turned him down flat. A lack of confidence, I suppose, led me to believe that I wasn't up to scratch as a comic and despite people repeatedly telling me that I should give it a go I returned to the security blanket of the taped voice.

It was to be a few years yet before I picked up a mike again and when I finally did, I couldn't put it down.

* * *

Things were going well and I was slowly getting used to working solo. This was proving to be not just profitable but, if I could only allow myself to admit it, surprisingly enjoyable. I seemed to be going down remarkably well as I did the rounds of the pubs and clubs.

To add to this rare run of good luck, an unexpected bonus landed on the mat one morning from Camden Council in the form of a very tasty cheque. There had been an industrial dispute over back pay and overtime just before I left and it seemed that I was owed a considerable amount of money. I proudly stepped out of the Huddersfield branch of the Halifax Building Society with over fifteen hundred pounds in my account and for the first time in my life felt financially secure.

My happiness was short-lived. A few mornings later Phil threw a spanner in my smoothly operating works.

'I can't drive you any more,' he said. 'I want to earn some decent money so I'm going back as a driving instructor full time.'

I offered him more money but he turned me down flat. I pleaded that without a regular driver I wouldn't be able to work.

'Find another one then,' he said infuriatingly, knowing full well that drivers were as rare as hen's teeth, especially ones like Phil who also acted as a dresser. 'No offence,' he said, 'but I'm getting a bit fed up with driving all over the country and hanging around in naff pubs. I want my life back. I'll drive you till the end of the month and then that's it.'

That certainly was that. The distances a pub and club

act covered were ridiculous: it wasn't unusual to go from Slaithwaite to Pontefract to Hull and back again in one night. Arrogantly I refused to believe that he really meant what he said about returning to civvy street and thought that after a bit of persuasion he would carry on driving me. Wrong again, O'Grady.

The end of the month came and I was due at the Red Lion Music Bar in Mansfield. As I was packing the bags to go to work he asked who was taking me.

'You,' I answered hopefully.

'Not me, I've got a pupil in Holmfirth in half an hour. You'll have to get yourself there, I'm afraid,' he said, straightening his tie in the mirror.

'Pleeease,' I whined but my pleas fell on deaf ears.

'I did warn you,' he answered calmly. 'Gave you plenty of notice.'

I rang the local cab company and they quoted me a price that was twice the fee I'd be earning. Then there was the problem of Biddy – I'd never get the fat suit on the train so I had no alternative but to ring up the pub and cancel.

As he got ready to go out, Phil seemed unconcerned at my panic and frustration at not being able to get to work. I wanted to kill him, even more so when he calmly announced that a friend of his, a girl, would be moving in with us the following week. It was obvious that I was persona non grata and was being squeezed out. But where was I to go? There was no alternative. It was time to throw myself on the mercy of my mother and return to Birkenhead.

* * *

I left early the next morning, telling Phil that someone would be round to collect my records, costumes and books as there was far too much for me to carry. I didn't ring and warn my mother that the prodigal was coming home, preferring an element of surprise that wouldn't give her time to think.

'Hiya, Mam,' I said cheerily as I breezed into the house.

'What the hell are you doing here at ten o'clock in the morning,' she spluttered through a mouthful of toast, 'and as cheerful as a cricket?'

Good start, I thought.

'Up to no bloody good,' she added, shooting me down in flames. 'What exactly is going on?' She leaned forward in my dad's chair like Columbo in a flannelette nightie. 'Something must've happened for you to be up and about at this hour of the morning and so bloody sociable with it, so c'mon, what have you done?'

'Why do you ask that?' I asked, bravely keeping up the Uncle Remus chirpiness in the face of the storm.

'Because, Paul,' she said, pointing at me with a piece of half-eaten toast, 'you know what you're like of a morning – you don't get woken up, you're exhumed.'

I couldn't argue with that so instead I told her the truth, minus a few facts. I told her that without transport I couldn't get to work and that the guy I was living with was moving a girl in.

'So there you have it, Mam, I've nowhere else to go,' I concluded, hoping that my tale had appealed to her better nature.

'And I suppose you haven't got a penny to your name?' She sighed, shaking her head sadly.

'Far from it,' I announced triumphantly, throwing my Halifax book into her lap.

'Jesus, Mary and Joseph,' she gasped, 'where in God's name did you get all this?'

Again I was able to tell the truth – I'd worked for it, and was happy to see her reaction was not one of suspicion but delight.

It was a lovely March morning and to celebrate my successful reinstatement in the family home I offered to take her to Beatties of Birkenhead, a department store on Grange Road, for lunch. Beatties café, sorry, restaurant was where the ladies who considered themselves elegant and refined lunched. My mum wore her new coat and fluffed out her perm and we sat like gentry among the blue rinses and tweed jackets, my mother asking in her best half-crown voice for the 'hem seled plis'.

Afterwards we browsed around the shops and I bought one of the new-fangled Walkmans, considering it the best money I'd ever spent. It was extraordinary, being able to stroll down the street with your favourite music blaring in your ears. The only thing was I found it difficult to walk normally if I was listening to a rousing bit of burlesque music and would frequently find myself unconsciously adopting my version of a stripper's strut.

Like me, Vera was back in town. He had returned from London due to 'circumstances beyond his control' and had moved in with his brother, in a large house in

Prenton, a fifteen-minute walk from my mother's house. It was a very convenient arrangement.

Vera's brother worked abroad and was frequently away for long stretches, leaving Vera in charge of the household and taking care of his two dogs, a large Rottweiler and a Jack Russell. The Rottweiler, Ben, was a beautiful dog with a lovely nature but as soon as Vera took him out for a walk and he spotted another dog Ben would turn into an unstoppable psycho. Vera became quite a familiar sight in Victoria Park, travelling horizontally at great speed as he gamely hung on to Ben's lead.

Times were hard on Merseyside; there was scarcely any work about. In the past I'd usually been able to find some sort of job easily but the vast majority of the independent employment agencies had gone out of business and even the Job Centre in the precinct was in danger of closure.

With all the drag safely transferred from Slaithwaite to Vera's brother's back bedroom I still managed the occasional booking, but without transport getting to venues up to sixty miles away was growing increasingly difficult. Once during a stint at the New Penny in Leeds I spent the long Sunday afternoon between the lunchtime spot and the evening at the pictures, trying to get some sleep during a showing of *Popeye, the Movie* and dining on a cheeseburger in a grimy café afterwards.

I travelled everywhere by train and if I couldn't get home because the last train to Liverpool left at some preposterously early hour I'd be forced to stay overnight in the cheapest bed and breakfast that I could find. You certainly get what you pay for and some of these places were grim beyond imagination. In a hovel in Grimsby there were skid marks on the unwashed bedding and in another dump in a run-down area of Sheffield the curious brown lumps stuck to the rotting lino behind the toilet turned out, on closer inspection, to be a family of decomposing mice.

It was a lonely life trailing around the north on my own and without a driver it was also proving very expensive. After paying my commission, travel and accommodation I'd often wonder if it was worth the effort.

Sometimes Vera came with me on the shorter trips. Much as I appreciated the company, having to pay his fare was yet another drain on my already depleted resources. Painting the slap on one Saturday night in the ladies' lav of a pub in Preston, I declared to Vera and a strange woman who wouldn't leave, preferring instead to lean against the sanitary towel machine swigging from a bottle of beer and hanging on to my every word, that I'd finally had enough. If this was showbiz I was sick to death of it.

'This is it,' I said, more to my reflection in the mirror than the company in the lav. 'No more after tonight. I'm never doing this again.'

Vera said he didn't blame me and the nosy woman asked if she could have my wig, seeing as I was giving it all up.

* * *

123

'Some swine's tried to shoot the Pope,' my mother wailed, her anguished face a mask of concern as she watched the news bulletin on the telly.

'Well it wasn't me,' I shot back.

'God forgive you,' she said, blessing herself with the speed of lightning, 'for being so flippant about His Holiness when the poor man might die.'

'Well, you'd convinced yourself I was the Yorkshire Ripper before they finally caught him,' I replied. 'So it wouldn't surprise me if you accused me of jumping on a plane to Rome and taking a pop at the Pope.'

'Don't talk daft,' she protested. 'I never for once thought you were that Yorkshire Ripper, you're making that up and unless you've got one of those boxes Dr Who's got I can't see you getting to Rome and back in a morning when I know you've been upstairs stinking in your pit. I think I'll just run down to St Werburgh's and light a candle for him.'

'Who for? Dr Who or Stella?'

'You're going to get a thick ear off me in a minute, mate.'

Even though my mother was a devout Catholic whose faith played an important part in her life, she wasn't precious about it and could take a joke, providing she didn't consider it overly irreverent. I always referred to the Pope as 'Stella' after a joke I'd heard Dave Allen tell.

Pope John Paul survived and I grew a moustache. Aunty Chrissie hated it, she said that when I smiled it looked like weeds round tombstones. Nevertheless I liked it and refused to shave it off. This much-chewed moustache of mine was proof that I had finished with dragging up for a living once and for all.

Every day that summer the weather was glorious, halcyon days my mother called them as she pottered around tending to her precious garden in the cool of the late afternoon. I still hadn't found a job and for the moment I was content to be unemployed and live off my savings. What I was going to do when the money ran out was a bridge I'd have to cross later but for the time being I was happy doing nothing. Vera and I went out clubbing at least four nights a week and every Wednesday night without fail we took ourselves off to New Brighton to attend the weekly disco and bingo session at the Empress Ballroom run by the Wirral Campaign for Homosexual Equality, the CHE.

Hi-de-Hi!, that glorious sitcom about a 1950s holiday camp, was very popular at the time, especially with me and Vera, and the Empress Ballroom was very reminiscent of that period. During the evening there would be a break in the dancing for a couple of games of bingo. We thought this was high camp and behaved accordingly, pretending that we were old women and shouting out to the caller, 'Shake your balls, Jack,' and other such ribald remarks. Some of the patrons of the Empress frowned upon such behaviour as they took these bingo sessions very seriously indeed, playing the game with the intense concentration of professional gamblers even though the top prize was only two pounds for a full house.

* * *

Diane and I buried our differences, mine deep in the earth and hers just below the surface, and we started going for the occasional night out together, surprising ourselves by getting along very nicely. She was helping her aunt Flo to run her stall in Birkenhead Market and most afternoons I'd go down and sit with her and even serve a few customers when there was an unexpected rush on. I liked working in the market, enjoying the banter with the customers and the buzz that markets have, even though a lot of stalls were closing and the aisles weren't quite as busy as they used to be. I imagined that working in the market was akin to running a stall in a travelling fairground: lure the customers in with your spiel and then razzle-dazzle them into making a purchase.

Flo's stall specialized in rattan furniture in every shape and size. It was, to quote the great Barry Humphries, 'rattan-infested'. She also sold vases, figurines and prints of the kind that depicted a naked woman posing in front of a swan, its wings outspread against a moonscape background. The front of the stall was stacked high with glass clowns balanced on rattan and wicker tables and a selection of 'genuine' silver-plated items ('Lovely gifts, folks, at a very reasonable price, ideal for wedding presents, christenings and birth-days!'). I've still got a small statue of the Virgin Mary made of cobalt chlorine that was once covered in a glittery paint that changed colour to either pink or blue depending on the weather. Flo, ever the canny business-woman, advertised them as 'Miraculous statues from Lourdes' and within a couple of hours all fifty of them had been cleared off the wicker furniture and into the shopping bags of satisfied customers.

Flo, who was always immaculately groomed and elegantly dressed, seemed to have the instinctive eye of the market trader when it came to buying stock for the stall. Considering her good taste and style I wondered why she didn't go in for something a little more upmarket.

'See that mirror,' she replied, pointing to a little looking glass in a plain wooden frame unadorned by rattan or resin fairies and dumped at the very back of the stall. 'It's nice, isn't it? Well it's sat there for two years, can't give it away. This isn't Harrods, it's the market, flashy and cheap is what sells here. It doesn't matter that the silver tea service is plate. It's only ten quid and will look lovely in some old girl's china cabinet. Give the customer what they want and, more to the point, what they can afford.'

During the school holidays Diane would bring our daughter, Sharon, into work with her and the pair of us would sit at the back of the stall and cautiously try to get to know each other again. She was shy with me at first and sulked at her mother's side, clinging to her leg, progressing after a while to manic bouts of showing off, dancing, shouting and doing just about every trick in her inexhaustible repertoire to get my attention while driving her mother mad in the process. Eventually she calmed down and sidling up to me would slowly climb up on my lap and ask me questions. Where did I live? How old was I? How long was I here for this time?

'Till the wind changes,' I told her in answer to her last

question, a phrase nicked from the Mary Poppins story I'd read Sharon a few nights before. It was the response Miss Poppins had given when asked the very same question by the Banks children. The truth was I had no idea when the wind would change or if it ever would, which for the moment suited me fine. I was happy to be home in Birkenhead.

CHAPTER 5

O N A BALMY JULY NIGHT VERA AND I WERE SITTING IN the Lisbon enjoying a little drink when a couple of queens came charging down the stairs in a state of extreme agitation.

'They're rioting in Toxteth! Every house along Upper Parly is on fire,' one of them screamed in a manner worthy of Scarlett O'Hara describing the burning of Atlanta.

'Anarchy reigns in the city tonight,' the smaller of the two shouted dramatically, determined not to be left out of the limelight. 'We should take to the streets!'

I got caught up in this frenzy and would have been quite happy to take to the streets. Vera, however, was less impressed.

'Don't fuckin' start, Lily,' he said, a little jittery at this rabble-rousing. 'We don't want to be getting involved.'

Fortunately Vera had the keys to the flat of his latest squeeze, who very conveniently happened to be away working in London for the week. This flat was also dangerously close to where the riots were in full swing and to me it seemed foolish not to take advantage and go back there to experience the riot first hand. After a few more drinks Vera was easily persuaded to go back, especially when I reminded him that the bar was about to close, we didn't have much money and this beau of his had an extremely well-stocked wine cellar sitting there sad and neglected.

'This is an historic moment, Vera,' I said excitedly, trying to gee him up. 'We might never see the likes again.'

'And we might never see the light of day again either,' Vera glared balefully at me, 'if someone chucks a petrol bomb at us.'

'That won't bother you, Vera,' I said, dragging him to his feet. 'You'll just mix it with a bit of tonic water and knock it back. C'mon, let's go.'

On the way out of the pub we met Paul, a fairly new acquaintance of ours who had the luxury of a car. Paul was even more reluctant than Vera to go anywhere near the riots but after a bit of the hard sell I managed to coerce him into driving us up there. Paul had only recently come out of the closet and it was all still a bit new to him. He'd never seen the likes of Vera and me before, particularly Vera, and looked at us on our first meeting with the same mixture of terror and awe that I'd experienced on encountering Penny and Francis on my first visit to the Lisbon.

We drove around the streets at first until Paul, concerned for the safety of his car, insisted on getting away from the area. After dropping me and Vera off at the flat he sensibly went home.

We fortified ourselves with a few drinks before

venturing out on to the streets again and when we eventually did I couldn't quite comprehend what I was witnessing. The first thing that hit me, apart from the throngs of people, was the intense heat. It seemed that every single building was alight, blazing furiously and spewing myriad sparks upwards to dance among the swirling plumes of thick black smoke. The effect was satanic.

Standing on the corner of the street, I watched the Rialto, a once famous ballroom that had been reduced to a second-hand furniture shop in the twilight of its life, burn to the ground and felt more than a little sad at witnessing the demise of so familiar a landmark. I'd once bought a slightly battered bamboo bedside table there that wobbled, and a couple I knew had paid ten quid for the wreck of a 1930s three-piece suite that once they'd cleaned it up and repaired it revealed a beauty that wouldn't have looked out of place in Poirot's drawing room.

The noise was deafening, people everywhere, either huddled into groups quietly watching the carnage unfolding before their disbelieving eyes or running around screaming and shouting, hurling missiles at the scores of police chasing after them. I watched a teenage lad make a Molotov cocktail out of a milk bottle filled with petrol. He stuffed the T-shirt he'd torn off his back into the neck of the bottle and after lighting it hurled it across the road, whooping with delight and punching the air in triumph when it hit a wall and exploded.

It was both exciting and terrifying at the same time and a terrific adrenalin rush, being among such total mayhem and madness. That little queen was right, anarchy did indeed reign that night. The anger that had built up over the years as a result of poverty, government apathy, neglect, racial discrimination and the ever-mounting tension between the police and members of this diverse community had finally come to a head. And this was the result.

In Catherine Street we found ourselves caught up in a mob who were facing a group of police officers with riot shields. Someone threw a petrol bomb which thankfully extinguished itself as it flew through the air. The police charged, scattering the mob and sending me and Vera running in the direction of Huskisson Street, where we encountered two women with a shopping trolley filled with cigarettes and booze hurtling down the middle of the road as if they were taking part in a trolley dash.

By the time we got back to the flat dawn was breaking. Our clothes and hair reeked of smoke and our blackened hands and faces made us look as if we were part of a turn-of-the-century travelling minstrel show. We took showers and changed out of our stinking clothes into some very nice towelling dressing gowns and made a fry-up for breakfast, after which we collapsed and went to sleep.

When we awoke it was early afternoon and we assumed that by now the riots would've fizzled out and everyone would've gone back to their homes, those that still had homes standing, that is. Instead the riots seemed to have increased. Looking down into the street below, we could see gangs advancing up the hill, each member carrying an assortment of weapons ranging from pieces of wood to the fender of a car.

Vera put the kettle on while I popped across the street in my towelling dressing gown to borrow a bottle of milk that was miraculously still upright on the step of the house opposite. I also rang home in case my mother was worrying and when she eventually answered the phone – 'I was upstairs, going through the insurance policies' – she told me that at around midnight she'd stood with Dot-Next-Door at the top of Sidney Road and watched Liverpool burn.

'It was like the war all over again, watching the Luftwaffe bomb Liverpool docks, a sight I thought I'd never see again,' she sighed.

I started to tell her what it was like where we were but she cut me short.

'Don't tell me you're looting and rioting,' she roared. 'Jesus, Mary and Joseph, don't be bringing any gear that you've looted into this house.'

I assured her that I had no intention of looting the Kwik Save or torching any buildings.

'Get out of there,' she warned. 'It's not safe, all hell has broken loose.'

Did I heed my mother's advice? Of course not. Instead we rang our friends and acquaintances and invited them round to the flat that night for an impromptu 'riot party'. We had a good idea how Vera's paramour was going to react when he got home and discovered that his supply of booze was seriously diminished, but in the true spirit of the revolution being played out on the streets below we didn't care.

Quite a few people turned up for our riot party and by ten o'clock the place was rocking. The noise attracted the unwelcome attention of a gang outside who started throwing cans and bricks up at the window.

'It'll be a petrol bomb next,' someone shouted, 'or they might kick the door in.' This caused mass panic to sweep through the party.

Hanging on the wall were three antique guns. One of them, a beautifully engraved blunderbuss, I quickly put to good use.

Opening the window I hung out and aimed it at the gang, crying, 'Git off ma land, you varmints!' It was a phrase I'd often wanted to use ever since Granny Clampett of *The Beverly Hillbillies* had said it after telling Jethro to 'Fetch me ma gun, boy.'

'Get that daft cow in, will you,' Vera shouted, panicking at the sight of me with a gun.

The blunderbuss wasn't loaded, or at least I assumed it wasn't, but it had the desired effect and the gang cleared off, running up the street and shouting abuse.

Empowered by my success at driving away the Goths and Vandals with the blunderbuss, not to mention the amount of fine old Irish whiskey I'd put away, I wanted to 'take to the streets again' so a party of us, including Vera, ventured out.

We didn't stay out long as even a drunken fool like me could see that the riots were far worse than the previous night and this was no place to be. It was like a war zone. The mob were feral and very angry, wreaking havoc on the streets. It was as my mother had said: all hell had broken loose. We returned to the flat a slightly more subdued and sober group than when we had left. We sat around for a while drinking and discussing what we had seen until the party dispersed and only Vera and I were left.

'I'm going to bed,' Vera said, staggering towards the gloom of the bedroom like an alcoholic vampire. 'The sun's coming up.'

I looked out of the window. The sky was blood red but it had nothing to do with the sunrise. The heavens that morning owed their crimson hue to the flames below as Liverpool 8 burned to the ground.

'They want hangin',' my mother exclaimed as she read the latest on the aftermath of the riots in the *Liverpool Echo*. 'Shops looted, buildings burned down, over four hundred coppers injured, I've never heard anything like it, and you in the bloody thick of it.'

The morning I returned home from the flat in Liverpool she made me undress in the back yard as I smelt like a burning building. Vera and I only stayed two nights but the riots raged on for nine. We tidied up before we left and collected all the empty bottles in a couple of bin-liners. We had the good sense not to put them out by the bins, where undoubtedly they'd be picked up and thrown as ammunition, but to leave them safely in the hall instead.

As predicted, Vera's gentleman went ballistic on his return home, paying Vera a visit at his brother's. We were in the front room watching the telly and ignored his persistent hammering on the front door. When he started banging on the window and shouting, 'I know you're in there,' we adopted the time-honoured tradition and hit the deck. After a while Vera opened the door. I don't know what was actually said but I do know that the poor fellah went away with a flea in his ear and his spare keys in his pocket and hopefully a lesson well learned, which is that no matter how in-fatuated you are with a one-night stand you don't go giving them the keys to your flat and telling them to help themselves. They may just take you at your word.

My daily visits to the Job Centre were always futile. I applied for what few jobs were advertised in the back of the *Echo* but didn't even receive an acknowledgement from most of them. I even applied to Arrowe Park Hospital to train as a nurse. I was positive I'd sail through the interview but was brought smartly back down to earth when two matronly ladies told me quite bluntly that I wasn't nursing material and turned me down flat.

Apart from a temporary post for a few weeks in a small children's home, it seemed that my luck at landing a job had run out, as had my savings.

'There's nothing for it but to get yourself down to the Brew and sign on,' my mother announced one morning. 'After all, you've paid your stamp so you're entitled to it.' I was amazed my mother had suggested this as she had a loathing of 'living off the parish'. It recalled the old days of her poverty-stricken childhood, and the horrors of the means test and the threat of the workhouse.

Signing on each week was a chore I hated. The

amount they doled out was paltry yet they acted as if it were coming out of their own pocket. My signing-on time was 9.15. I'd drag myself out of bed and down to Hamilton Square and join the queue to give my autograph to a woman who looked like she had a knitting needle shoved up her arse. If you were late they demanded an explanation and then told you off, making you swear you'd never be late again. Sporadically you'd be told that the supervisor wanted to see you, and the queue of people would look at you sympathetically as you slunk off to the end booth to await the inevitable interrogation.

In the end, after a completely unnecessary grilling for being ten minutes late I told them to stuff their money, or words to that effect, and felt all the better for it. Having cut my nose off to spite my face, I needed to find a job, and quickly.

'Why don't you go back to doing drag?' Diane asked me one day as I sat at the back of Flo's market stall, hidden from view by an enormous rattan dressing table.

'Cos it's out of the question,' I told her through a mouthful of bacon sarnie from Betty's Café. 'There's no way I'm going back to that.'

'But why?' Diane persevered.

I chewed on my sandwich for a moment as I tried to think of a good reply.

'Because it's over, that's why' was the best I could come up with. 'I'm finished with all that nonsense. From now on I want to lead a normal life.'

'Normal? You? You don't know the meaning of the word,' Diane snorted, making her way to the front of the stall to serve a tiny old lady. 'Normal? Don't make me laugh.'

All right then, so I was classified abnormal, but even with this extra qualification I still couldn't get a job and if something didn't turn up soon I'd have to seriously consider going back to drag. The prospect didn't appeal to me in the least.

Times were getting so hard I was forced to sell some of the costumes to a second-hand clothes shop on Church Road. I got twenty-five quid for the Japanese kimono and a sequin dress; I knew that they were worth a lot more than that but beggars can't be choosers. The woman proudly displayed them on mannequins in the shop window and it looked strange seeing my old drag in such familiar surroundings. When I walked past the shop with my mother one day, she stopped to have a look in the window.

'Who the hell would wear something like that?' She pointed to the kimono. 'And look at that purple sequin evening dress, cut down to the belly button and slit to the hip. What kind of a trollop would wear that?'

If only she knew, I thought, moving her swiftly on in case the woman in the shop came out and dropped me in it. What would I be doing next to earn some cash?

I was counting out drugs on a kitchen table in a council flat over a betting office on the Prenton Hall Estate while two women hung over me watching my every move like predatory raptors, making sure that I distributed the little yellow pills fairly into two even piles.

'We haven't had any for ages,' one of the women

remarked, taking a long pull on her cigarette. 'I could do with one now and then, takes the edge off.'

She started to cough, exhaling as she did so a dragon's breath of smoke that seemed to fill the room. I couldn't help noticing her emaciated wrist, mottled with bruises, as she wiped her mouth with a crumpled tissue.

A whistle blew in the background. Neither of the women moved. The whistle grew stronger and louder until eventually the smaller of the two gave in.

'Make sure she doesn't nick any of mine,' she warned me as she retreated down the hall. 'I'll just turn this bloody kettle off and I'll be straight back.'

This was no Ken Loach scenario of inner city deprivation, nor had I turned to drugs to make a living, dealing out heroin to a pair of pillheads in a sordid squat. Far from it – I was in the cosy little sitting room of my two aunties, Annie and Chrissie, dividing up half a bottle of Valium between them that my mother had sent up. She had a repeat prescription from her doctor which meant a seemingly endless supply of Valium and Distalgesics at her disposal. She would dole them out in twists of tissue paper to her sisters and anyone else who needed a little balm for their frayed nerves.

Aunty Chris was, to coin her phrase, 'crippled' with duodenal ulcers. Beside her armchair was a little sewing table that played 'The Isle Of Capri' when you opened the lid, not that it was heard very often these days as the surface was covered in a mass of bottles and pots containing the vast amount of medication that she was required to take on a daily basis. It was not uncommon to find her at midday still in her dressing gown, a great

139

quilted job from Brentford Nylons, with a crocheted shawl over her shoulders as further insulation against the cold. Sitting in her armchair hunched over the gas fire, fag in hand, she'd give me a quick lesson in pharmaceuticals.

'See these,' she'd say, proudly holding up a pot of pills, 'one of the most expensive drugs on the market, very few people have been prescribed them, they're liquorice-based and supposedly a miracle cure for ulcers, and do you know what?'

'No, what?'

'They're a pile of shite. Haven't made any bloody difference at all.'

Aunty Chris was a shadow of her former self. She rarely went out except for doctors' appointments, the occasional trip to the Plaza Bingo on Borough Road or if she 'ran down to put a bet on'. She was painfully thin and hid her emaciated frame with layers of cardigans, nighties and scarves, not to mention the all-enveloping housecoat and crocheted shawl. As a reminder of her former glory she kept a sepia photograph of herself as a teenager in a gold frame next to her tablets. She really had been a beauty in her day, with exquisite bone structure and a sly twinkle in her eye. 'Age and illness are cruel taskmasters,' she'd lament as she gazed at the photograph of the lovely girl that she once was. 'Enjoy your youth and good health, lad, while you've still got them.'

Aunty Chrissie died in March 1983. She'd been seriously ill but as always had refused to see a doctor, a throwback I suspect to the crippling poverty of her youth before the National Health Service when a doctor cost money and a spell in hospital might mean that you'd end up in a coffin. Maybe her refusal to seek medical help was because she feared a doctor would make a diagnosis she didn't want to hear. Perhaps she preferred to carry on not making a fuss, convincing herself that there was nothing seriously wrong and that whatever it was would sort itself out.

Her sister, my aunty Anne, deeply concerned at the rate at which she was deteriorating, eventually defied her and after colluding with my mother called the doctor. It was too late for Aunty Chrissie. Her heart gave out and she collapsed in the bathroom and died.

The back-street beauty and pride of the Birkenhead bus fleet who had raised her son in a time when unmarried mothers were looked upon as fallen women was gone for ever, leaving a gaping void that could never be filled. I was truly devastated that this remarkable woman who had left such a lasting impression and been such a huge inspiration to me all my life would never again greet me with the familiar 'What the bloody hell do you want? You're not up to no good, are you?' as she answered the door to that flat above the betting office.

Underneath her tough veneer, cynical eye and scathing wit lay a heart of solid gold and a set of principles that are virtually non-existent today.

She was cremated on a cold morning at Landican Cemetery with no fuss and just a tiny posy of flowers on her coffin lid as she'd requested.

I still miss her.

* * *

As I sat in Liverpool's Masquerade Club, a former Chinese restaurant below Clayton Square, one late November night, Harry, the owner, approached me with a bottle of cider. Harry was supposedly hard of hearing and when you spoke to him he had a habit of tilting his head towards you to enable him to catch every word you were saying. He was also very frugal when it came to handing out free drinks, so I was puzzled as to what I'd done to merit such generosity.

'I believe you used to do a double act,' he said, plonking the bottle of cider down in front of me. 'I hear it was very good. Do you fancy doing a spot here for Christmas?'

I thanked him for the drink but explained that I had retired from drag.

'What was that?' he said, tilting his head forward.

I repeated what I'd just said, only a lot louder this time, but Harry still didn't seem to hear.

'How much do you charge for one half-hour spot?' he asked.

Since I had no intention of performing in the Masquerade or any other club for that matter, I came out with the first figure that entered my head.

'A hundred quid,' I said casually.

'*A hundred quid!*' Harry shouted, nearly having a fit of apoplexy.

He heard that one clear enough, but to my surprise he agreed without question to pay what I considered an exorbitant fee. I couldn't turn down a hundred quid, not in my dire financial circumstances, and before I knew it I'd agreed to appear as the Playgirls the night before Christmas Eve. Now all I had to do was find a partner.

'I'm not doing it,' Vera said when I informed him the next day he was about to appear at the Masquerade Club.

'You bloody well are,' I told him. 'I'm not turning down the chance of earning a hundred quid.'

'I'm going into hospital next week for me operation on me eye, how can I?' he protested.

'We don't go on till the twenty-third, the eye will have healed by then.'

Vera was always having trouble with his eyes. A vicious mugging a few years earlier had left him with a detached retina and he was going into Birkenhead General Hospital for a few days to have it repaired.

'I'll make a tape up and bring the Walkman in and you can learn the show while you're in hospital, give you something to do while you're lying in bed.'

Even though I'd sworn I'd never have anything to do with drag again it was only for this one night, and I wasn't about to turn my nose up at the opportunity of having fifty quid in my pocket over Christmas.

'As soon as you come out of hospital, we'll start rehearsing. You're going to be fabulous, Vera,' I said, refusing to take no for an answer.

'But what about me make-up?' Vera said.

'I'll do it.'

'But I won't be able to see without me glasses.'

'You'll manage.'

'And costumes? What am I going to wear?'

143

'You can wear mine, I've got plenty and I'll take them in to fit you. Now get up them stairs and let's get you into a couple of frocks. By the time I've finished with you, Vera Cheeseman, you're going to be a star.'

Sighing loudly, he took his glasses off and rubbed his eyes. 'Why do I allow myself to be talked into these things by you?' he asked, blinking like an owl. 'Well, if I'm going to do it can I wear that red and white polka-dot dress?'

Vera was in the bag.

I got together a thirty-minute spot from all the old numbers I'd done as a Glamazon and a Playgirl, trying to keep it simple for Vera by giving him numbers that he more or less already knew.

I was more than a little alarmed when I collected him from hospital as he was very unsteady on his feet (a sight not unfamiliar to me over the years) and half of his face was covered by an enormous bandage. Would he be ready for the twenty-third, less than two weeks away? He'd have to be, Harry had put the posters up in the club advertising us and there was already quite a buzz about our forthcoming appearance. There was no backing out now.

While Vera was in hospital I stayed at his brother's house, looking after the dogs and spending the evenings altering costumes to fit him. As always we were doing 'You Gotta Have A Gimmick' from *Gypsy* and I was attaching Christmas tree lights to my old blue-sequinned bra and G-string, once part of a strip costume for Vera to wear as Electra. The lights were connected to an extension cord that plugged into the

LEFT: Publicity photo for *The Lion Roars Back* at the Donmar Warehouse. I didn't half fancy myself in this.

BELOW: As Roxanne, the copper's nark, in *The Bill* with Tony Scannell as DS Roach.

ABOVE: Vera in Chrissie's kitchen, obviously not amused, after the chip-pan fire.

BELOW: Pat looking on as Vera takes to the floor. Christmas night '87, the Vauxhall Tavern.

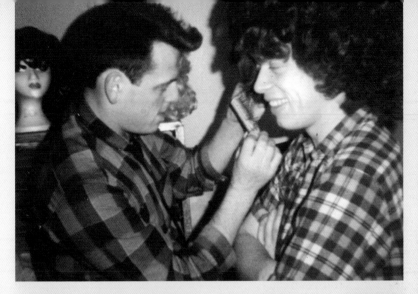

TOP: The two Davids, Hush and Doris, in the dressing room of the Vauxhall.

CENTRE: Chrissie and me. Like Vera, we could never resist a hat.

RIGHT: The irrepressible Regina Fong (Reg Bundy) enjoying a beverage with Skippy on his head.

LEFT: Victoria Mansions. My flat, middle row.

CENTRE: The 'womb-like' bathroom before a clean-up.

BOTTOM: The wartime fireplace.

LEFT: Vera after a few sherries, Vicky Mansions.

CENTRE LEFT: Dolly.

CENTRE RIGHT: Lucy.

BOTTOM: Scott.

ABOVE: Murphy.

RIGHT: Murphy on the Isle of Skye.

BELOW: Chrissie and Murphy in the parlour, Vicky Mansions.

BELOW LEFT: With Vera in the back of a car. Vera could never resist transforming a plastic bag into a headscarf.

BELOW RIGHT: The Citroën, my substitute for a Lotus Europa, parked in Witney with Chrissie.

ABOVE: Age is a shocking thing ... Murphy and me, Vicky Mansions.

RIGHT: The view from my room over Madame Arthur's in Copenhagen that was pure fairy tale.

BELOW: With the glorious Lisa in Denmark, enjoying a few Jagermeisters. She's obviously just said something highly amusing.

ABOVE: Three great ladies – Vera Lalley, Aunty Anne and Alice Strong.

LEFT: My mother. I don't know what she's going to do with a funnel, a pair of binoculars and the *Liverpool Echo*.

BELOW: Me at Woodside Ferry, the week my mum died.

mains and had a drunken punter thrown a pint of lager over Vera he'd have no doubt fused the national grid.

I had to really work hard to convince Vera to go out on stage in such a skimpy outfit. Mine wasn't much better for Mazeppa, just a few strips of black plastic hung with chains topped off with a gladiator helmet, but I didn't care. Vera on the other hand wasn't too happy at the prospect of standing in front of a packed club full of people, most of whom he knew, wearing not much more than a string of potentially lethal fairy lights.

As Vera slowly recovered, we rehearsed; the doctor had told him to rest and here he was bumping and grinding like a maniac and turning his lights on and off in time to the drumrolls by means of a little switch in his hand. He was wearing an eye patch now as his eye was still slightly swollen and bruised, but nothing, I reassured him, that couldn't be fixed with a bit of make-up.

On the night of Vera's debut as the new Playgirl we got ready in Diane's flat, putting Vera's make-up on and then my own. The facilities in the Masquerade weren't that good, even though Harry had gone to the trouble of erecting a curtain at the back of the dance floor for us to do our quick changes behind. We'd had a dress run that afternoon with Sharon as our audience. Diane was sulking as she'd wanted to watch too but couldn't as she was acting as our dresser and was stuck in the bedroom. We performed in the front room for Sharon, who sat cross-legged and open-mouthed on the floor, enraptured by all she was witnessing. It didn't bother her in the least that her father was dressed in the teeniest of gladiator outfits and blowing a bugle between his legs. She took it all in her stride.

When I asked her what she'd liked best, she replied, 'Vera dressed as Snow White.' We did a little routine as Snow White and the Wicked Queen. Vera thought he made a beautiful Snow White when he put on the little black bobbed wig and the perfect replica of her costume that Hush had made for me last year, holding the frock out like she did in the animation and skipping around the room to 'Whistle While You Work'.

'I look just like her, don't I?' Vera kept saying. Sharon obviously thought so too. She was bedazzled by him, staring saucer-eyed in wonder at the vision before her.

I thought Vera would be petrified before the show, but he seemed unperturbed. His only concern was whether or not people would notice his eye. I'd done my very best to disguise the bruising and swelling with the aid of lots of make-up and thick false eyelashes, but even so I couldn't help thinking that one half of his face had a look of Bette Davis while the other bore more than a hint of Anna May Wong.

The show went off without a hitch. Vera raised the roof when he switched his light bulbs on and by the time we got to the finale, a Phil Spector medley of Christmas songs, the crowd went wild.

I wanted to collapse with relief after the show as I'd privately had strong reservations about Vera's ability to pull this off. My fears had been unfounded as Vera was a hit, we both were, and to celebrate we all got very merry on the drinks that punters kept buying us.

'You're mad if you don't give this a go again,' Diane said. 'Look how you went down tonight. I'd give that agent a ring if I were you and get some bookings in.'

On cue, a guy in the audience stuck his head around the curtain and asked if we'd come and work his pub in Bolton in the New Year.

'What do you think, Vera?' I asked my new partner. 'D'ya want to give it a go then? Shall I ring Paul up at the Stone Chair and get some work in?'

Vera was so giddy on success and booze that at that moment he'd have agreed to join the SS if I'd suggested it.

'Why not?' he said, bursting with confidence. 'Say yes to the booking in Bolton and then first thing tomorrow get on that phone to Paul, tell him the Playgirls are back in business.'

The coach pulled into Leeds Bus Station. In the last eight months I must've made this trip from Liverpool over a hundred times. Vera was asleep in his seat with his mouth wide open and his face pressed up against the window. I gave him a shove to wake him.

'What?' he muttered, half asleep.

'We're here,' I said, collecting the bin-liner containing the wigs from the luggage rack. Since Hush's departure I'd had to learn how to dress the wigs and found after a series of trial and error that the most successful method was plenty of back-combing. Early attempts had resulted in a look that bore more resemblance to an electrified Persian cat than a finely teased coiffure. After a while I got better, although it had to be said that the wigs were far from the masterpieces that Hush created.

'Did you get eyelash glue?' Vera yawned.

'And where the hell am I going to find eyelash glue in Birkenhead?' I snapped back. 'I'll get some in Leeds, we'll have to make do with the Copydex till then.'

Copydex was more suited to DIY than sticking false eyelashes on, but it did the job even if it did tend to take the skin off your eyelids when you removed the lashes. Vera couldn't do his own make-up, he couldn't see to do it even if he wanted to, so the task fell to me. For a drag queen I hated putting make-up on, it was like painting the same section of kitchen wall over and over again, so having to do Vera's make-up as well as my own was a double chore. On nights when we were running late or if I had the hump, I'd pound the powder into poor Vera's face with the gusto of a debt collector hammering on a front door.

Since Vera and I had hit the road we'd travelled the length and breadth of northern England. For the first time in my life I got to see Blackpool. I'd always wanted to go there when I was a kid but my mother thought it was 'common' so we went to the Isle of Man to stay in a boarding house in Douglas instead. That she considered to be a lot more upmarket.

We'd been working at Heroes, a club in Manchester, and Basil Newby, the owner of the newly opened Flamingo club in Blackpool, asked us if we'd like to work there. The contract was for a Sunday lunchtime and two nights and it was like a holiday with pay. We stayed in a B and B called Trades, and Vera and I were like kids at Disneyland caught up in the carnival feel of the town. I've always thought Blackpool has a unique atmosphere, you either love it or loathe it, but either way you have to admit there's nowhere else quite like it.

That summer Blackpool was buzzing, all the pubs were packed, most of them belting out Captain Sensible's 'Happy Talk' (which drove me insane) and Madness's 'Welcome To The House Of Fun' (which I loved but that had me doing 'the walk' every time I heard it). Yates's Wine Lodge sold champagne on tap, around the corner you could see Burden and Moran in Olde Tyme Music Hall and for 50 pence you could get a three-course meal (tinned soup followed by meat and two veg and sponge pudding with custard).

One of my favourite haunts was the Tower Ballroom, a magical place that Lucinda Lambton penned the best description of when she compared it to a giantess's boudoir. We loved to sit and watch the couples dancing to the strains of Phil Kelsall on his mighty Wurlitzer, surely the true sound of Blackpool.

We'd invent life stories for the people. That elderly couple gliding effortlessly as one across the dance floor had met during the war when he'd been stationed in Blackpool and she'd worked in a fish-gutting shed in Fleetwood. Now they came back once a year on the anniversary of the night when they'd first met to dance again. Those two middle-aged women dancing together, an incongruous couple with the smaller of the two leading her much taller and wider partner in a tango? Well, they never married and have been coming here looking for love, albeit unsuccessfully, for the last twenty years. We could spend all day playing this game and even though we knew that the characters were only figments of our imagination they became, for that moment, reality.

I'm glad I got to see the museum piece that was the Fun House at the Pleasure Beach before it regrettably burned down in 1991. It had been featured in the film *Sing As We Go* with Gracie Fields and I'd always wanted to have a go in the large barrel that perpetually spun slowly around. The aim of the game was to walk through it without falling over, a trick that was very hard to pull off. I got stuck in it once after a horde of schoolchildren piled in, pinning me underneath them, until eventually after what seemed like hours I managed to escape, emerging with a black eye and no skin on my hands, knees and elbows.

We were the first act to work at the Flamingo club. It's changed beyond recognition since its early incarnation, but it was a club that I always enjoyed working at – just as well as I ended up working there regularly for over a decade.

Accommodation was always a major problem. Fortunately for us, we'd become friendly with the Sisters Slim and Bridie O'Brian, two drag acts based in Leeds who came to our rescue, kindly offering to put us up when we had a block of work in that city.

The Sisters Slim (Ten Tons of Fun!) lived in the notorious Leek Street Flats in Hunslet, South Leeds. The Slims, alias Alan and Danny, were big boys who had capitalized on their mammoth girth. Alan, the bigger of the two, would strip out of a nun's outfit to reveal a Wonder Woman costume underneath. After a bout of spinning around to the Wonder Woman theme he would then remove this to reveal rolls of fat and layer upon layer of a belly that hung down to his knees. The act was certainly unpretentious and could be described without malice as pretty gross – the London drag queens were appalled by it – yet the Slims were hugely (no pun intended) popular with audiences and never stopped working. They refused to take any money off us for allowing us to stay there so we'd contribute bags of groceries to the household instead – although considering the amount they consumed on a daily basis it would've probably been cheaper to pay rent.

Alan and Danny were a very good-natured pair and they let us share their driver, a happily married man with children who just happened to have a penchant for ladies' clothes of the British Home Stores variety. His beige pleated skirts and chiffon blouses in delicate pastel shades seemed at odds with the many tattoos covering his arms, hands and neck that he'd acquired during his stint in the merchant navy.

I liked the Leek Street Flats and never felt threatened walking around there, despite their reputation, as the place had a strong neighbourly feel to it. They were a sociable lot, characters were always popping into the Slims' for a cup of tea and a session of gossip and slander, and some of the conversations I heard would have me falling about laughing. I'd sit on the sofa absorbing the atmosphere and the chatter, thriving on it and subconsciously storing it all up for future use.

The other act who provided shelter from the storm was Bridie O'Brian. He mainly worked solo as a patter act but occasionally teamed up with Leeds' most infamous drag queen – Vicki Graham. The two of them worked under a name some would say was very apt: the Sisters Grimm. Silver-haired Bridie spoke with a hint of a soft Irish burr. He was very hospitable and every night at six o'clock we sat down around the table for our tea. If we weren't working, once we'd washed up and watched *Corrie* we'd repair to the New Penny for another night of revelry.

I liked Leeds, so much so that I seemed to spend more time there than I did in Birkenhead. I was also very keen on Bradford and in particular a pub called the Fleece where we frequently worked. The Fleece was owned by a tough little Australian lesbian of the old-school variety called Maureen who loved the bones of us and we felt exactly the same about her. We spent a lot of time in the Fleece, sitting up till all hours of the night drinking in the bar. In fact it was here that I hung up my wig and retired from drag for a second time.

The act was popular enough and we were earning a decent living, not enough to start digging the back yard up and building a swimming pool but enough to pay my mother her housekeeping and then not have to borrow it back again in the middle of the week. But the travelling around on coaches and relying on the good nature of friends to put us up could be dispiriting at times.

We started noticing that the pubs were cutting down

on cabaret as they couldn't afford a midweek act any more. A lot of the factories and collieries had shut down and times were hard, a fact made evident by the number of pubs boarded up and the lack of work. We couldn't afford to be picky, which was just as well as some of the venues we were finding ourselves booked into left a lot to be desired. Tickles in Wakefield was one such venue that for some inexplicable reason had drag acts on every Sunday afternoon. All the acts hated working there and none more than me. I felt that bear-baiting or a public execution would've been more appropriate entertainment for this establishment.

Walking through the pub to the room at the back to get ready, I took one look at the audience of pre-dominantly young males, most of them steaming drunk and aggressive with it, and didn't need to be Doris Stokes to know that two grown men dressed as Snow White and her stepmother skipping around the stage was akin to suicide.

Our opening number was a nod to *Hi-de-Hi!* with me as Gladys Pugh and Vera looking remarkably like the real thing as Peggy.

'Hello, campers! Hi-de-Hi!' went the familiar cry.

'Fuck off, you queers,' came the response, followed by a shower of beer bottles.

After I'd done my bit poor Vera had to stay on, strip out of the chalet maid's overall and stand alone in nothing but a Marks and Spencer's vest and knickers.

I'd had enough. Wild horses wouldn't get me back out there so I sat on the stairs and started to take my make-up off. As I smeared on the Crowe's Cremine (the best make-up remover in the world) I could hear the mob in the bar going wild – God knows what Vera was doing out there but whatever it was, it was going down a treat. I opened the door a fraction and was treated to the sight of Vera being spun round by his arm and leg by a couple of Neanderthals in rugby shirts. I stood watching in horror as Vera flew through the air as limp as a rag doll before hitting the dance floor and sliding across it towards the wall with the speed of a sliotar during a violent game of hurling.

I roared at the DJ to stop the tape as Vera staggered past me. 'They've just spun me round, the bastards, and flung me into the wall,' he said indignantly. 'I'm not going back out there.'

'Too right you're not,' I said, handing him the tub of Cremine. 'Here, get your slap off.'

One of the staff came swaggering in dressed in a shiny powder-blue shell suit that was a little on the small side. He looked like ten pounds of shit in a two-pound bag.

'What the hell d'ya think you're doing?' he shouted. 'You should be out there.'

'What's it look like?' I snapped back through a mouthful of Crowe's Cremine. 'We're getting changed. You don't want cabaret in this dump, you want fairground rides. I think they mistook me for an Aunt Sally and Vera a fuckin' Chair-o-Plane. Just give us our fee and we'll be off.' I was losing it now. All self-control, like Elvis, had left the building.

'You want paying?' he said. 'For that?'

I wanted to kill this gormless moron in front of me

and then run amok among the crowd with a chainsaw, indiscriminately hacking off limbs.

'Look, mate, if I were you I'd get back out there cos if you don't you might not get out of this place in one piece,' Shell Suit said menacingly.

'Are you threatening me, gobshite?' I asked.

'Just a bit of advice. We don't put up with any messin' in here from the acts,' he warned. 'Now are you going back on?'

'Listen,' I hissed, 'have you ever heard of the O'Grady Brothers from Birkenhead?'

'No,' he said. 'Should I?'

'Well, if you don't know them now you soon will. I'm one of them, my eldest brother is doing life for murder, two others are serving eight for armed robbery and the remaining four, who aren't in nick, would think nothing of torching this dump with you inside it. Now are you going to pay up?'

He paid up. In full.

'Well at least you got the money out of him,' Vera said on the way home.

'To the O'Grady Brothers,' I said, raising a can of Coke by way of a salute. 'And long may they come in handy.'

We'd really plumbed new depths though when we ended up in the Queen's, a pub on the notorious Lumb Lane. The landlady was a very pleasant woman who gave us drinks on the house and took us into the snooker room, which she explained she'd closed off for the night so we could use it to get changed in. She'd even provided a large mirror for us.

'It might be OK here,' I said optimistically to Vera, busy punching a dent out of his Salvation Army bonnet. 'I'll just go and have a look at the stage, shall I?'

The stage was a crude plywood affair, about four foot high, that had been built right outside the ladies' toilet and closely facing a wall with a row of chairs along it. Ninety-eight per cent of this stage was occupied by a behemoth of a DJ console, leaving a tiny wedge at the corner that didn't look as if it could accommodate one person, let alone two.

The crowd were rowdy but good-humoured, a fair percentage of them obviously working girls and their 'protectors', which meant if all else failed our hookers routine would go down well.

The DJ spoke over an excruciating bout of feedback from the mike which we took to be an introduction. Turning our tape on, we trooped out through the crowd, who groped us, squeezed us and touched us up in places that were thankfully well protected under three pairs of supermarket tights and a panty girdle.

Despite the enormity of the DJ console the sound was appalling. It was as if the tape was being played from an ice cream van three streets away – not that it mattered that the sound was so distorted, you couldn't have heard it anyway over the screams of the crowd. We climbed up on to a chair and on to the wedge, barely able to move in case we fell off, not helped by a group of women on their way to the toilet stopping to have a good feel of our ankles and legs. Their hands were all over us. I tapped one of them on the head with my trumpet in a vain attempt to get her to let go of my ankle but she was so stoned she didn't feel it.

I was glad to get off and leave Vera to it.

'It's going well,' the landlady shouted cheerily across the bar as I ran semi-demented into the snooker room to get changed. 'They love you.' I just wished they weren't so physical in showing it.

During Vera's big number with the blue-sequinned bra and G-string decked in fairy lights, one of the women sitting opposite the stage lifted her skirt and, opening her legs wide, she calmly pulled back the crotch of her knickers and gave Vera a bird's-eye view of her vagina. Now Vera had never seen one of these before, especially at such close quarters and in the flesh so to speak, and this unexpected revelation of the female anatomy caused him to fall off the wedge in shocked horror, the extension cord attached to the fairy lights pulling the plugs out with him and all the sound with it.

Somehow we got through the rest of the show intact. The cherry on the cake was finding that somebody had nicked my shoes from the snooker room, which meant I had to go home in a pair of glittery kitten-heel mules I'd bought in Leeds Market for £2.99.

For New Year's Eve we were booked into one of our favourite pubs, the Fleece in Bradford. We hadn't worked there for a while and were looking forward to spending the night with Maureen and her cronies. There was a strange atmosphere that night as instead of the usual regulars the place was packed to the rafters with very young students who seemed unsure what to do with themselves.

You couldn't move in there. Getting through the crowd to the stage was impossible and we both missed most of our changes – not that it mattered much as it was obvious they couldn't have cared less if a member of the royal family was up there giving birth to Siamese twins, let alone us two trying to kick in unison to 'If You Don't See What You Want Up Here'. Apparently they didn't.

This was the straw that broke the camel's back. I told Maureen that it wasn't worth going on for the second spot and went upstairs to get changed. As the bells chimed in 1983 we sat in the bathroom, me on the toilet with the lid down flicking ash into the palm of my hand as my aunty Chrissie had done and Vera perched on the end of the bath.

'I've had enough, Vera,' I said bitterly, painfully aware that at this moment we should have been celebrating the dawn of a new year, not stuck in a bathroom over a pub. 'It has to stop. We've had a good run for our money but it's just not worth all the effort any more. It's time for a change.'

'This is the second time we've had this conversation in the toilet of a pub,' he said. 'But I know what you mean, it's no fun any more. It wouldn't bother me if we quit.'

'Let's call it a day then,' I said, glad we'd come to an amicable decision and relieved that tonight was the last of it. Just what I was going to do instead I really didn't know.

CHAPTER 6

'*DIRTY BITCH!*' ERIC SHOUTED AS WE SAT ON THE TOP deck of a bus on our way to the Tower of London. '*Arseholes and wankers.*'

The man sat in front of us turned round and glared. 'If this foul-mouthed yob doesn't stop swearing in front of these women and children I'll throw him off the bus myself,' he said angrily.

'I'm really sorry,' I said apologetically, leaning forward in my seat so I could keep my voice down, 'but he can't help it, he has Tourette's.'

'He'll have a fat lip in a minute if he doesn't stop swearing,' the man said, not in the least appeased by my explanation.

'*Fuck face, smelly arsehole.*'

'I'm so sorry but he really can't stop himself from swearing. It's called coprolalia.'

'*Bollocks.*'

'Are you a doctor then?' the man asked sceptically.

'No,' I said in my best professional voice, 'I work for Camden social services. I'm looking after him.'

'*Cunt!*'

159

'Well, you're not doing a very good job of it, are you? Now if you don't shut him up, I will.'

'*PissFlaps!*'

A woman down the end of the bus piped up about how disgraceful she thought it all was and if the conductor had any sense he'd stop the bus and call the police to throw us off, pair of hooligans that we were ... blah, blah, blah. I'd had enough. Grabbing my young charge, I dragged him down the aisle.

'About time as well,' the woman sniffed. 'Such language! And you allowing it, you ought to be behind bars, the pair of you.'

'*Old fucking cow!*'

'What did he call me?' the woman screeched.

'An old fucking cow, would you like it in writing?' I said, getting Eric down the stairs, off the bus and on to Tower Bridge Road. We'd got off the bus way before our stop but in view of such hostility I thought it was probably best. Back in the early eighties Tourette's didn't have the profile that it has now and people were less understanding about the disorder.

I was back working for Camden Council as a peripatetic and Eric was my first assignment. He was a big lad for fourteen, taller than me, twice as wide and blessed with a very loud voice and an extensive vocabulary of obscenities that would make a docker blush. People were intimidated by him, averting their eyes or crossing the road to get out of his way when they saw and heard him coming. We were thrown out of a café on Tottenham Court Road and asked to leave the British Museum, and once on a tube a woman kicked me as she got up to leave, denouncing me as 'evil' for allowing my 'younger brother' to swear the way he did. What saddened me the most was that if people had bothered to look beyond the disorder they would have found an intelligent and very endearing young man.

It was Beryl Chyat, my old friend the social worker, who eventually got me motivated again, encouraging me to reapply for my old job with Camden and even sorting out an interview for me. Since I'd given up the act I'd been working behind the bar at the Plaza Bingo, slowly vegetating as I pulled pints for the bingo fanatics, and Beryl was the one who bullied me out of my self-induced coma and back into life.

I went down to London for the interview, staying with Chrissie in his Victoria Mansions flat for a week. It was good to be back again after such a long time away and I realized just how much I'd missed it. Chrissie and I were on speaking terms again after our fight in the Camden squat and we went out every night, mainly to the Royal Vauxhall Tavern, which was just down the road, to watch the acts.

After a week in London, Birkenhead seemed very quiet. I went back behind the bar at the Plaza Bingo and waited to hear from Camden Council. The interview had gone quite well, I'd thought, but as I still hadn't heard from them after nearly a month I began to believe that I'd been unsuccessful and resigned myself to the bitter fact that I might be working at the Plaza ad infinitum.

* * *

'Remind me when it's three o'clock,' my mother said piously. 'That's the time that poor Jesus died and I like to say a little prayer. And you can turn that bloody telly off when the time comes, show a bit of respect yourself.'

As far as I was concerned, there was nothing good about Good Friday. I felt like writing to the Vatican to ask them to rename it something a little more appropriate like Bleak, Miserable, Meat-free, Sombre, Funereal Friday. My mother had already been to church that morning and was nagging me, as she always did, to 'get down to church, you heathen, and say a prayer'.

'I'm watching *The Ten Commandments*, aren't I?' I shouted after her as she made her way into our tiny hall to answer the phone. 'That's religious.'

You could always tell it was Easter as, apart from everything closing down, you could guarantee that Charlton Heston would be in some biblical epic on the telly.

'It's for you,' my mother said, coming back into the room highly excited. 'It's Camden Council.'

They said that they were sorry they hadn't been in touch and apologized for ringing me at such short notice, but could I possibly start work on Tuesday? A job had come up providing respite for the foster parents of a particularly difficult boy.

At that moment I'd have willingly agreed to give Magda Goebbels a break from the kids, I was so relieved to be offered the chance to get back to a decent job. I promised I'd be in the office on Tuesday at nine prompt.

* * *

Despite my longing to get back to London, when the time came to actually go, leaving home was tough as I knew deep down that this would be the last time. Although there would be frequent visits I felt I'd never return to live at Holly Grove again.

My daughter Sharon didn't seem the least bit bothered at my leaving. I'd been in and out of her life so many times that one more vanishing act wasn't going to matter and I was spared any tearful farewells. In fact I remember her being far more concerned with going out to play than hanging around me.

Vera and I had gone our separate ways as well. His brother had returned home and Vera had gone to live in Keighley, working as a barman at the Fleece.

On the train down to London I told myself that at twenty-eight it was time to get my act together and do something with my life. This time I was determined not to end up, as I'd done in the past, crawling home to Mother with my tail between my legs, down on my luck and skint.

Chrissie's flat in Victoria Mansions was what estate agents would call a studio and in typical Chrissie fashion the place was furnished courtesy of the skips of south London. He was forever bringing decrepit pieces of furniture home with him which he would patch up and repair, giving them new life. Even the fridge came from a skip in Dorset Road. It tilted violently to the side each time you opened the door but apart from that little tic it worked as well as any brand new model.

Chrissie knew everyone in Victoria Mansions. It was a lively block to say the least and there were frequent barbecues and parties on the roof, which had been transformed by the residents into an inner city garden filled with old kitchen sinks full of flowers, pots of honeysuckle and clematis climbing up the walls and among the chimney pots. The council eventually made the residents remove all trace of this lovely garden, claiming that it was damaging the roof. Bloody miseries.

Even so, Victoria Mansions was a great place to live. It was a friendly neighbourhood with a good bus service and handy for the tube and overground. The corner of the mansions was occupied by the surgery of an old German doctor who always, regardless of your ailment, gave you a powerful shot of vitamins that would have you buzzing for hours. Sadly he was hit by a bus and killed as he was crossing South Lambeth Road one evening.

The neighbours were a diverse lot to say the least. Among them were a rock singer and an opera singer, a theatre lighting designer, a writer and an actress, living side by side with married couples and single mums and an assortment of gay men, one of whom sold dope. I hadn't had any experience of drug dealers and had no idea what to expect when Chrissie took me up there one night to buy himself a 'little deal'. Apart from the time when I'd eaten some (described in my first book), I'd never smoked a joint, as the idea of sucking on a soggy old roll-up that had been passed around a group of people revolted me. Now here I was in a drug dealer's den with Chrissie drinking tea while trying to hold a polite conversation over the top of Mahler blaring out of a sound system so vast and complicated it could've accommodated the Stones at Wembley.

Mine host was called Blake, an ex-public schoolboy who was more than a little eccentric, sitting cross-legged on a mound of Indian cushions surrounded by a flock of chattering budgies that he allowed to fly free around the flat.

'Now, what can I get for you?' he asked Chrissie once the formalities of the tea ceremony were over. 'Got a nice bit of black in,' he said, as affable as a Kensington butcher recommending a choice piece of bacon he had round the back of the shop.

'Give us a quarter of that then,' Chrissie said, all smiles, in his genteel voice.

Blake leaned over and turned a dial on a little black box that sat on the floor. It was the controls to a train set, the track of which I noticed ran all around the room and out of the door.

'Toot, toot,' he smiled, 'stand back please, one quarter of finest Lebanese coming up on the eight forty-five.'

From around the door frame a model train appeared with a budgie sitting as proud as punch on the back of the locomotive, pulling a line of trucks that carried a slab of what looked like dark chocolate.

Blake cut a tiny piece of the slab and, after weighing it carefully on a little pair of scales, wrapped it in a piece of clingfilm and handed it over, putting the money Chrissie had given him in a little cash box. Apart from our bizarre surroundings and the nature of the goods purchased, we really could have been at our friendly neighbourhood shop.

Once the deal was done, the little train, complete with budgie, backed out of the door and vanished out of sight.

'If you fancy some acid, I'm getting some on Thursday,' Blake said as he undid the many locks on his front door to let us out.

'No thanks,' Chrissie replied. 'I'm teetering on the brink of insanity as it is without acid tipping me over the edge, thank you very much.'

I experimented with LSD once or twice and despite what Aldous Huxley has to say about it I wouldn't recommend it to anyone. I was seeing a guy called Luke, not his real name I found out later on but a name given to him after Luke Skywalker, who, just like my Luke, was frequently on another planet. One night in a club called the Cellar Bar, a haunt of leather queens that used to be at the back of Heaven nightclub, Luke and I were having a drink with Derek Jarman when Luke suggested that we 'drop a tab of acid'. Mr Jarman sensibly declined, having more important fish to fry, while I, anxious not to look like a killjoy in the eyes of Luke (with whom I was besotted, bloody fool that I was), took one.

I don't recall much about the rest of the evening except for when we got back to Luke's flat. He turned on the stairs in front of me to ask if I was all right and there before my very eyes he'd turned into the spectre of the man who had haunted my childhood dreams – Sweeney Todd, the Demon Barber of Fleet Street. The front door key in Luke's hand had transformed itself into a cut-throat razor and Luke himself into the image of the man I'd feared most.

I took off down the stairs like a whippet and ran down the road, screaming that Sweeney Todd was trying to kill me. Luke was in hot pursuit, trying to calm me down, which he managed to do eventually but not without a lot of fuss. Luke and I didn't last long. He got a job with a fancy PR company, ditched the leather jacket for a more preppy look and ditched me for a more powerful squeeze who he hoped would further his career in the dizzy world of public relations.

The second time I took acid I did so unknowingly. I'd stayed overnight at a friend's flat and was walking around the kitchen barefoot the next morning. Unbeknown to me he'd had a tab of acid in a saucer on a side table, put there for safe keeping, and somehow it transferred itself to the sole of my bare foot. It wasn't until a few hours later on the bus going home through Brixton that it hit me. Again I can't remember much apart from trying not to panic as my ears were assaulted by distorted waves of sound and the world around me melted into a blurred mess of colours and shapes. Somehow I got back to the flat where luckily Chrissie was at home and, recognizing my condition, forced gallons of orange juice down me to help bring me back to earth. After a few hours the violence of the trip subsided, leaving me in a dreamlike state during which I stared intently at a framed picture of Disney's Wicked Queen and watched her come alive and hold a conversation.

Never again, I vowed, and I never have.

*   *   *

One night in a pub called the Two Brewers in Clapham I bumped into Hush. I hadn't seen him since he'd left me in the lurch in Slaithwaite but as I was glad to see him again I didn't see the point of throwing up old grievances. Instead we simply picked up where we'd left off as if nothing had happened.

Hush was working at Allders in Clapham as a window dresser by day and doing the rounds by night in a double act with his old partner, John. As much as I'd vowed never to set foot on a stage again, he asked me to join him in a 50s/60s act that he'd got together for a May bank holiday at the Two Brewers as they were a drag queen short. I flatly refused at first but after constant badgering from Chrissie, Luke and Hush I eventually gave in, taking myself down to Fox's in Covent Garden to purchase the necessary slap for the occasion. Hush knocked up a few costumes for me and supplied the wigs. Not feeling the least bit nervous about getting up in front of a packed pub again, I sailed on stage and thoroughly enjoyed myself, safe in the knowledge that this wasn't a career move but just a bit of fun on a bank holiday for beer money. Well, that's what I thought at the time. Hush and John split up and three weeks later I was back with Hush doing the rounds again in the Playgirls, juggling drag with social services, telling myself that maybe one day I'd make a decision and stick to it. I'm still waiting for this great day of enlightenment to arrive. I won't hold my bloody breath.

*   *   *

The landlord of the Two Brewers was the incomparable Phil Starr. We all loved Phil. He was one of the old school who'd been a drag entertainer since the early fifties. A superb comedian and teller of bawdy jokes, he was blessed with the sort of razor-sharp timing that simply can't be taught. Doing his act one night at the Vauxhall Tavern he said of me with his usual deadpan delivery, 'I saw Lily Savage at a bus stop the other night, blind drunk and eating a bag of chips with her drawers around her ankles. Well, I was ever so concerned so I went up to her and asked if she was all right, to which she answered, "Has he finished?"'

Hush would set his wig for him and occasionally if he was too busy on the sewing machine to deliver it himself I'd drop this freshly teased sheitel off at the pub. Phil liked his wigs blond, high and flat at the back.

'Very nice, very nice,' he'd say in his unmistakable London drawl, running his hand gently over the surface of the wig. 'But I do wish you'd bring it in something a bit more glamorous than a fucking bin-liner, dear.'

In later years Phil moved to Brighton and formed a double act with another legendary stalwart of the gay scene, Maisie Trollette. They called themselves Arsenic and Old Lace. Phil never stopped working up to the day he died aged seventy-two in 2005, a quality act right up to the end and an impossibly hard one to follow.

Despite the irregular hours that played havoc with bookings for the act and the sometimes extremely difficult assignments, I was still enjoying working as a peripatetic.

At the time I was providing respite care for a notoriously cantankerous old woman called Miss Lacey, enabling her foster carer to have a much-needed break. They lived in a very comfortable flat in Cranley Gardens, Muswell Hill, a few doors down from the flat where Dennis Nilsen was carving up the bodies of his victims and disposing of their grisly remains down the drains. Nilsen had once asked Vera if he wanted a lift home from the Black Cap. Thankfully Vera refused and went off to Bangs Disco instead, or God knows what fate might have awaited him.

Miss Lacey had her own cosy bedsitting room in the front of the house which she very rarely left except to complain about something. She was able to get around the flat quite smartly with the help of a stick if she chose to, but usually if she wanted me I was summoned by an electric bell. It went off in the kitchen each time she pushed the button in her room, which she did at least twenty times an hour in order to criticize everything I did for her, from the meals I prepared to the way I made her bed. After a week of dancing attendance on this old bitch's every whim, running around after her as if I were a maid of all works, I finally cracked.

Awoken from a deep sleep at 5 a.m. one morning by the ringing of her bell, I jumped out of bed thinking something was wrong and in my confusion walked straight into the wardrobe, nearly breaking my nose in the process. I danced around the bedroom in pain, dripping blood on the beautiful cream carpet, the bell ringing incessantly as a soundtrack to my agony.

Grabbing some kitchen roll to try to stop the flow of

blood from my nose, I marched into Miss Lacey's room. Instead of being sprawled on the bedroom floor with a broken hip and hypothermia as I'd imagined, she was sat up in bed knitting and listening to the World Service on her little transistor radio.

'You took your time,' she sniped, ignoring my bloodied nose and the wad of kitchen roll pressed against it, 'and in future can you remember to knock before entering my room.'

At that moment if someone had rung the front door with a petition to make euthanasia compulsory I would have cheerfully signed it. Instead I put all such thoughts temporarily out of my mind and asked with as much civility as I could muster, given the hour, what she wanted.

'I'd like a cup of tea if it's not too much trouble,' she said, maddeningly calm, 'and before you go would you please pick up my ball of wool. It's fallen off the bed.'

'Is that all?' I asked, furious. 'You dragged me out of bed to pick up your bloody knitting and make tea? Have you any idea what time it is?'

'It's coming up to ten past five,' she said, addressing me as if she were talking to an imbecile, 'and I'm still waiting for a cup of tea.'

I read her the riot act, during which she remained unmoved and tight-lipped.

'You are employed to care for me twenty-four hours a day, are you not?' she asked.

'Within reason,' I faltered.

'Are you or are you not employed to care for me twenty-four hours a day? Simply answer the question,' she went on, in tones more suited to a crown prosecutor.

'I suppose I am,' I replied feebly.

'Then in that case it's not unreasonable to ask you, my carer, to pick up my ball of wool and make me a cup of tea, is it? So off you go and do what you are paid to do,' she said, dismissing me imperiously with a wave of her hand.

I picked up the wool and then stomped into the kitchen in search of the tea caddy and some strychnine, annoyed with myself that I'd let her get the better of me yet again.

Earlier in the week I'd asked her if I might pop out and leave her for a few hours on Friday night while I visited a sick friend, a pitiful excuse but I really needed to get out. In reality I had a booking at the Black Cap and if I cancelled Hush wouldn't be very pleased and neither would Babs the landlady of the Cap, who quite rightly might not book us again if we cancelled at such short notice.

Miss Lacey had replied that she'd consider it and would give me her decision before Friday approached.

'I've given your request to visit your friend this coming Friday evening some thought,' she said as I gave her a cup of tea, 'and in view of this morning's behaviour I have come to the decision that the answer will not be in the affirmative.'

I wanted to pick up her knitting needles and shove them up her nose, but somehow I managed to resist this urge and try another approach.

'Listen, Miss Lacey,' I said, sitting on the end of her

bed, ignoring her protests to get off it. 'I don't have a sick friend, I made that up.'

'I knew it,' she declared triumphantly, like the cat who'd got the cream. 'I knew it was pure fabrication.'

'Yes, well, I'm sorry for that,' I said, picking at the candlewick. 'But the truth is this. I don't earn very much doing this job, so to supplement my income I do an act with a friend.'

'What sort of an act?' she interrupted.

It was far too early to start inventing a convoluted tissue of lies so I told her the truth, that I was part of a drag act.

She sat in bed staring at me. Then she slowly lowered her cup and saucer on to the bedside table and spoke.

'I thought there was more to you than met the eye,' she said, smiling for the first time since we'd met. 'Do your employers know about this drag act?'

'No, and I'd rather they didn't.'

'Understandably,' she said, smiling again. 'It would be disastrous for the council's reputation to have an employee who looked after children and the elderly exposed as a drag act. The press would have a field day.'

I could hear her in my head, straight on the phone to the *News of the World* to tell them she was an elderly lady who'd been left on her own by her care officer because he was prancing around a pub in a dress. She'd probably add that she was making the call from the hall phone, having fallen down the stairs and broken both legs.

'Well, I'll tell you what I'm going to do,' she said after what felt like a lifetime. 'You can stay out for as long as you like on Friday, and I'll never breathe a word to anyone of your extracurricular activities, providing, that is . . .'

Here it comes, I thought.

'Providing, that is,' she said again, prolonging the agony by reaching out for her cup and taking a long thoughtful sip before she pronounced sentence. 'Providing you take me with you. I've never seen a drag act before and it's been so long since I was in a pub and it's about time I had a night out.'

It was not what I was expecting and no matter how much I protested, Miss Lacey was adamant that she was accompanying me to the Cap on Friday night come hell or high water and that was that.

Her attitude towards me changed after my early morning confessional and she was far less demanding, hardly ever ringing her bell to summon me. Instead she made the effort to leave her room and come into the kitchen and talk. Over a coffee she revealed that in her day she'd been a highly respected cook, working in some of the grandest homes in England, preparing banquets and meals for royalty and for what she reverently referred to as 'the gentry'. She had photos and references to back up her claim, and insisted that I unearth from under her bed a large suitcase that contained the evidence of her life and career.

I studied a menu she'd prepared for a gala dinner at Henley in 1955, the year I was born. After reading the bill of fare, written out in her own hand in perfect French, I could understand why she'd turned her nose up at the burnt offerings I'd been serving up. This woman was a culinary artisan and here was I turning out lukewarm fish fingers and lumpy mashed spuds.

Come the day of the booking at the Cap, Miss Lacey spent a lot of time in her room, emerging around 6.45 looking smart in a well-cut coat and a blue felt hat. I wanted to get to the Cap extra early so I could find a space down the front for her to park her wheelchair, and I'd ordered a cab for 7 p.m.

'Shall we have a gin and tonic while we're waiting for the taxi?' she asked graciously. 'It seems appropriate. Or do you not like to drink alcohol before a performance?'

'I never drink before I go on stage,' I lied. 'But as this is a special occasion I'll join you in a very small one.' This wasn't hard to do as I wasn't keen on gin, unlike Miss Lacey, who demolished a large one as we waited for the cab.

'There he is,' she said at the sound of the doorbell, getting out of her chair a lot faster than she had got in it. 'Let me take your arm and you can walk me to the car, the driver can fold up my wheelchair and put it in the boot.' All those years of working for the upper classes had obviously rubbed off on Miss Lacey and she glided down the path and into the back of the car as to the manor born.

I parked her near to the stage, next to a couple of women who promised they'd keep an eye on her.

'And if you wanna go to the toilet, love,' one of them said kindly, 'just give me the nod and I'll take you.'

Miss Lacey inclined her head graciously by way of

175

thanks, and relieved that she was in good hands I escaped to the dressing room to get ready. Hush was already there sipping a pint of the freshly mixed 'baby'.

'I see you've brought your mother' was his only comment.

It was gone one o'clock in the morning when we got home and Miss Lacey was slightly pissed. Apart from the obvious signs, she asked me, as she prepared for bed, for a glass of water and her Steradent tablets, a request that would've grated on a sober Miss Lacey's gentility.

When I knocked with her mug of Milo she was sitting up in bed, the teeth still in. She wasn't so sloshed that she'd allow me to see her sans dentures.

'I've had a very enjoyable time,' she said, beckoning me to sit on her bed. 'Although I do have a confession to make.'

Now, what could an old lady in a wheelchair surrounded by lesbians in a gay bar have got up to?

'I used the gents' lavatory,' she said gleefully, her face lighting up like a young girl's. 'The ladies' was right at the back of the pub and I'd never have got through the crowd in my chair, so Pat suggested I use the gents' as it was closer and far more convenient.'

'Pat?'

'One of those women you left me with. They're lesbians, by the way, but then I expect you already know that. Pat was the big one in the sweater, a very nice woman, as was her girlfriend.' She paused to take a sip of her Milo. 'Pat's the man in the relationship,' she said knowingly.

I'd asked her if she'd enjoyed the act in the taxi home but she hadn't answered so I asked her again.

'Yes I did, very much,' she enthused. 'And I fully understand why you mime.'

'Why?'

'Well, you can't inflict a voice like yours on the public, can you? I've heard you singing in the kitchen, don't forget. No, very inventive of you to hide behind those who have a real vocal talent and stay mute. Don't wake me in the morning, dear, I'll have a lie-in, I think. Good night.'

Living at Vicky Mansions suited me fine. Chrissie liked to describe life there as 'Bohemian' but I just wished he had not been so bloody laissez-faire about getting his name officially on the rent book, which although he'd lived there for a few years he'd never got round to doing. Consequently Lambeth Council refused to accept him as a legitimate tenant and served him with an eviction notice.

Chrissie simply packed his belongings and moved in with a neighbour downstairs while I vacated to an enormous flat over a cobblers on Streatham High Street with Hush and a guy he worked with in Allders. We only stayed two nights, realizing that this flat was hideously expensive and unaffordable even with the rent split three ways. Before the landlord came round with the contract for us to sign we did a moonlight flit, hampered slightly by Hush's long, low, extremely heavy sideboard. He'd bought it in Allders' sale using his staff discount and christened it 'the good piece', though it looked for all the world like an Ikea coffin.

We strapped the sideboard to the roof of a friend's car and set off for our new lodgings on Somerleyton Road in Brixton. Coming down Brixton Hill the good piece started to break free of its moorings and as we braked at the lights outside the town hall it slid off the roof, across the bonnet and launched itself on its maiden voyage into the middle of the road. There was a bit of a tailback with the traffic and a chorus of car horns rent the air until we managed to carry it on to the pavement. As we struggled with this bloody thing a couple of coppers turned up to smugly inform us that it was illegal to transport something the size of Hush's good piece on the roof of a Ford Cortina. We ended up having to carry it to the flat in Somerleyton Road, receiving some strange looks en route and a group of gentlemen outside a pub in Coldharbour Lane asked us in all sincerity where the funeral was. Carrying that thing nearly killed us and I had hoped that when it fell off the roof of the car it would've smashed to pieces; however, it proved indestructible and apart from a few scratches survived unscathed.

The flat in Somerleyton Road belonged to a friend of Hush's called David, better known as Blanche. He was extremely good company and had earned his drag name because he was crazy for the film *Mommie Dearest* starring Faye Dunaway in the part of Joan Crawford. Our Blanche would stay in the character of Joan for most of the time we lived there. As it was only a one-bedroom flat we all shared a room and it wasn't uncommon to wake up and find Blanche standing at the foot of the bed clutching a wire coat hanger and scream-ing, 'No *wire hangers!*' This would be followed by a rant about how hard he worked at the studios to pro-vide me with the decent things in life and for what thanks? I'm surprised he didn't have Hush strapped to the bed à la Christopher.

We had a good time in that flat, lots of laughs but not a lot of room for three people, especially when one of them is Joan Crawford. So when we got the offer of an empty flat in a high-rise on the Winstanley Estate in Battersea we loaded up the good piece – in a van this time – and waving bye-bye to Mommie Dearest we set off for life 'up the junction'.

Our new abode had no cooking facilities so until we got round to buying a cooker I bought a tiny Baby Belling stove that had an oven, grill and hotplate that you could make a roast dinner on. It was money well spent as in later years when I was on tours around the country the Baby Belling proved indispensable, allowing me to knock up a decent meal in my dressing room when I didn't want to take my make-up off between shows on matinee days.

Between us we scrubbed this flat out. Hush decorated the bedroom and living room and did any necessary repairs and once the three-piece suite that Hush's mate Larn had given us was in place, together with the hated good piece with Hush's prized Lladró collection taste-fully arranged on top of it, the new place looked quite homey. I went up to Clapham Junction and rented a telly and an item I'd coveted since they'd first come out but could never afford: a video recorder. *The Avengers* was being shown again on Channel 4 and crazed fan that I was I was determined to own it all on videotape and watch it repeatedly at my leisure.

We worked a lot at a pub on Battersea Park Road called the Cricketers, which had been a famous drag pub for years. Once upon a time in the very early sixties when the house band at the Cricketers had consisted of two elderly ladies on piano and drums, an act called Alvis and O'Dell were arrested here, charged with aiding and abetting the running of a disorderly house and fined fifteen pounds each. Their crime? Miming to a recording of 'Speedy Gonzales', the exact same act they performed at Butlin's for the kids. Attitudes had certainly changed since those unenlightened times, for if you wandered into the Cricketers in '83 for a drink you'd have found a heavily pregnant nun doing 'The Vatican Rag' and not a truncheon was raised nor a whistle blown.

The Cricketers was only a twenty-minute walk from the new flat and to save on the expense of a taxi we'd load everything into the wheelchair and push it there. I should explain the wheelchair. We did a take on the movie *Whatever Happened to Baby Jane?*, a cult classic particularly among gays but one that I've always found slightly disturbing. Chrissie had found the wheelchair for us in a skip (where else?) and after a bit of patching up it was nearly as good as new. When 'the wheelie' wasn't on active service in the pubs and clubs, it substituted as a very convenient armchair back at the flat.

'I could get used to this,' I remarked to Hush one day as I spun across our sizeable living room to turn the telly over. 'It saves you walking.' Be careful what you wish for . . .

It was in the Union Tavern in Camberwell that I was 'struck down'. During the Baby Jane routine with Hush in the wheelchair as Blanche and me poncing around as Jane complete with clown-white make-up and a scarlet slash for a mouth, Hush spun the chair around rather energetically, trapping my knee awkwardly between one of the speakers and a wheel and dislocating it.

I lay on the stage in agony, unable to move. The bar staff called an ambulance and I was whisked off to King's College Hospital in full Baby Jane Hudson drag. Friday night in the A and E department of King's College Hospital was how I imagine Bedlam must have been on the night of a full moon.

As there were obviously not enough staff to attend to all the casualties I was parked on my trolley next to a radiator to await my turn to see the doctor. A combination of intense pain, the heat from the radiator and the sheer volume of noise soon had me giving out louder than any of the drunks waiting to be seen, causing a fiery Irish nurse to threaten me with a 'bar of soap in that mouth if you don't stop using that kind of language in here'.

Eventually a harassed young doctor arrived and peering over the trolley at the apparition that lay before him asked me what my name was.

'I'm Baby Jane Hudson,' I simpered in my best Bette Davis voice. 'Perhaps you remember me?'

The doctor wrote something down and then asked me if I'd had anything to eat or drink, which I had: I'd drunk two pints of cider and eaten one of Hush's mammoth teas.

'I'm afraid in that case you'll have to wait a few hours before we can take you down to theatre and give you an anaesthetic,' he said. 'In the meantime I'll give you a little something for the pain.'

A little something? For this amount of pain? I wanted a massive something, preferably in the form of a hypodermic full of morphine. Anything, as long as it stopped the agony.

Hours later, when I was being prepared for theatre, I kicked off again. They wanted to cut my tights off, but as they were new on that day I begged them to peel them off instead. It was bad enough being in this condition without having to fork out another £1.50 for a pack of four from the supermarket.

'You'll never guess what?' Chrissie said gleefully, strolling into the ward all smiles. 'You're in the loony ward.'

They'd obviously taken me at my word when I'd given my name as Baby Jane Hudson. I'd thought it was odd when I woke up to find the man in the bed opposite throwing oranges at me, while the only other occupant of our ward was sat on the floor by his bed tearing paper.

The nurse who brought me a cup of tea was quick to placate me, having obviously heard about my carry-on in A and E. Giving me a smile that she probably reserved for the seriously bewildered, she reassured me that my dress, tights and wig were perfectly happy in my locker and that she'd put my eyelashes in a little sputum cup on the side for safe keeping.

Despite Chrissie's attempts at persuading the nursing staff that I really did have severe mental health problems and they weren't to listen to my protestations of sanity, I was eventually moved on to the huge ward that was Men's Surgical, my left leg encased in plaster from hip to ankle. They kept me in over the weekend and I sat in my bed on the Saturday night feeling very sorry for myself, my bottom lip wobbling like a four-year-old's. Not only was I in hospital but I was missing the television event of the year – the return of *The Avengers*. Here I was, stuck in bed with no telly and Hush at home not having the faintest idea of how to operate the video recorder. Life really did stink at times.

To add to my misery, it looked like I wouldn't be able to do the panto that year. Together with some of the other acts, Hush and I had met up at Adrella's Soho flat to discuss ideas for an epic *Cinderella* panto that we'd planned to take around the pubs and clubs over Christmas. After a few lengthy living-in assignments since my return to the peripatetic team I was owed a lot of time off in lieu, part of which I had intended to take over the Christmas and New Year period. Now that I was going to be in a hip-to-ankle plaster cast for some time, it no longer mattered. I would be stuck in the flat on my own, unable to go to work of a day and, even worse, forced to watch everyone else go off and have fun in the panto.

I spent the first few days in my wheelchair watching everyone rehearse in the big front room. The sewing machine was set up in the corner and when Hush wasn't going through the routines he was bent over it furiously running up batches of costumes that I'd designed. During these rehearsals, egos clashed and tempers flared, particularly between the old queen of the jungle, Regina Fong, and reigning monarch Doris Dale.

David Dale, known in ladies' sewing circles as Doris, was one of the most popular acts on the circuit. He'd recently had a big success with an autobiographical documentary on C4 called *If They'd Asked for a Lion Tamer*. As well as working solo, David Dale and Adrella worked together in a very clever act called High Society. They worked brilliantly as a team on stage but offstage it was a different matter. They had recently returned from a month in Copenhagen, working and living in such close proximity that a break from each other was wise for all concerned, before one of them committed murder. Adrella, who had enough work of his own over Christmas, tactfully and quietly withdrew from the panto and was replaced as the Prince by a pretty young lad with a ripped body (as they say) called Ian.

Reg, alias Regina Fong, was going through a tough time. The popularity of his brainchild, the once hugely successful trio the Disapointer Sisters, had waned long ago, and his costumes, stored at the Black Cap in bin-liners, had been mistaken for rubbish and inadvertently thrown out. Prior to becoming the little darling of the drag scene, Reg had been a 'West-End Wendy', dancing in many West End shows and even a couple of movies, as he never tired of telling us. Because of his experience he felt superior to the rest of us and as a result he could be, on occasions, terribly grand and overbearing.

Reg rarely appeared on any stage now, pub or West End. He spent most of his time in his Kentish Town flat, skint and worrying how he was going to feed his two cats. Once in a while Hush, Reg and I would get a little thirty-minute spot together and do a few shows around the pubs. It wasn't very good. Reg never knew a word of what he was supposed to be miming to and even if he had it wouldn't have made any difference as he'd forgotten how to lip-sync. Nevertheless I loved working with him, for as far as I was concerned he was a legend. I also loved his surreal sense of humour and my suggestion that we tackle Peggy Lee's 'Don't Smoke In Bed' was met with whoops of glee.

The idea was that Reg would sit on a stool dressed in a diaphanous negligee while I lay behind him in a sleeping bag, wearing a wig full of rollers and lighting endless fags. Finally, at the number's conclusion, I'd let off a smoke bomb in the sleeping bag and engulf the stage in thick green smoke. It all sounded very good on paper but at the Black Cap one night I let off one of these smoke bombs without anticipating the effect the acrid fumes would create in such an enclosed space. They opened the fire doors to try to clear the air, to no avail. The smoke belching continuously out of the sleeping bag seemed to be growing stronger instead of diminishing, forcing the choking customers out of the bar and into the street. All that was left behind were a few diehards who were so pissed and such heavy smokers anyway that they never noticed any change in the atmosphere.

Apart from *Sons and Daughters* on daytime TV, an Aussie soap which I'd become addicted to since being laid up, there wasn't much for me to look forward to.

'Look, de-ah,' Reg drawled one day during a break in the panto rehearsals in our front room, 'I'll get straight to the point. We cannot find a replacement for you anywhere and as you seem to be quite agile, getting about, de-ah, without the crutches, why don't you come and do the show with us? We'll simplify the dance routines and we'll all help you.'

So for the Christmas and New Year period I hobbled around nearly every pub and club in London in a full-length plaster cast as an Ugly Sister. It amazes me to this day how six people, seven counting the dresser, with over thirty costumes and an assortment of elaborate wigs and headdresses managed to get changed in dressing rooms no bigger than a cupboard. Determination, I suppose, and the firm belief that obstacles are there to be overcome and anything is possible if you put your mind to it. If we'd been offered Cinderella's coach and a couple of Shetland ponies I dare say we'd have found somewhere to put them.

This panto went down so well that we had to do it again later in the year. As Ian, our Prince, was unavailable he was replaced by an actor called Scotland, who surprisingly enough happened to be Scottish. We

all know that in the panto Prince Charming goes off
with Cinderella in the end but off stage it was one of the
Ugly Sisters he was sharing his bed with. Scotland, or
Scott as I preferred to call him, was to become a big part
of my life. As well as lovers we became great friends –
important, I think, if a relationship is to have any legs,
don't you?

CHAPTER 7

March 1983

BECOMING A MEMBER OF EQUITY, THE ACTORS' UNION, was virtually impossible in 1983. You were unemployable in the theatre unless you were a member and, for drama students and a certain drag queen, getting hold of an Equity card was akin to the quest for the Holy Grail. You needed proof that you had been employed professionally for forty weeks and yet without a card you couldn't work, so it was a catch-22 situation. Young actors would take on the strangest jobs to meet the quota of weeks required: I heard of one who became a magician's assistant on a North Sea ferry and another who became a star stripper at Raymond's Revue Bar.

I'd been collecting contracts since I'd started the act and eventually, when I had the required forty weeks' worth, I took myself off to the Equity offices in Harley Street to apply for the precious card. As there was already a Paul O'Grady on the books I had to change my name and so I chose my mother's maiden name, Savage.

To go with my new name I had a new address as well. The tenant who had supposedly moved out of the Battersea flat suddenly decided she wanted to move back in and could we please vacate the premises by, say, yesterday? Hush went back to Upper Norwood and me to Vicky Mansions. Chrissie, who had taken over the tenancy of a flat there, knew of a neighbour, Andy, who was keen to sublet his flat. This was very convenient for me and I moved in, delighted that for the first time since I'd set foot in London I had a flat and, unbelievably, a bedroom all to myself.

Following the success of David Dale's *If They'd Asked for a Lion Tamer* on TV, a stage version was planned to open in March for three weeks at the Donmar Warehouse. The plot involved David's relationship with the two hard-bitten drag queens he worked with, his mother and his boyfriend. It was written by Bernard Padden with some very clever music and lyrics by Kit and the Widow and produced by Paul Oremland.

Reg teamed up again with Peter Durkin, his old pal from his days as a dancer in West End musicals, to play the drag queens. Sheila Collings, an actor who has been treading the boards since 1949 and is now recognized as one of the Knitting Nanas on the Shredded Wheat commercial, had a lot of fun bringing Bernard Padden's surreal script alive as a wonderfully eccentric mother, while I grew a beard, lowered my voice considerably and gave my best Scouse Bill Sykes impression as David's violent and abusive boyfriend.

During one tense scene I had to punch him in the

face, knocking him to the floor, and one night after I'd delivered the stage whack he hit the deck with a little more force than usual, groaning on impact with an 'Oomph' straight out of the *Beano*. That little oomph was enough to set me off laughing uncontrollably. I'd heard about corpsing on stage and now here I was, experiencing it for the first time in a packed Donmar Warehouse during what was supposed to be a serious moment. Corpsing is a bit like laughing in church or during a funeral, you are fully aware that you shouldn't be doing it yet you can't stop yourself. That night I had to run off the stage unable to finish the scene, hoping that the audience mistook my hysterics for the maniacal laugh of the triumphant bully.

I was still having regular physiotherapy sessions on my leg during the run of the play. After six weeks of wearing a plaster cast, the muscles had atrophied to the proportions of a POW's in a Japanese prison camp. The constant trips to the physio department of King's College Hospital were transforming my skinny pins into something resembling muscle and I couldn't believe it when I received a letter from a gentleman admirer claiming that I had 'nice thighs' – music to the ears of someone who had always been told that he had legs like 'two Woodbines hanging out of the packet' and for a brief moment I even considered buying a pair of shorts.

Strolling menacingly on and off the stage of the Donmar each night wasn't taxing but it was certainly exciting and I enjoyed every moment of the three-week run.

'You're making your West End acting debut, dahling,'

Reg drawled from his perch in the corner of the dressing room he shared with Durkin. 'So I'll be keeping an eye on your performance and giving you notes when and where I think they're needed.'

Reg had adopted an attitude grander than Sarah Bernhardt and Dame Nellie Melba put together from the moment he'd first set foot in the building and Nica Burns, who was running the Donmar at the time (she now runs the best part of the West End), would watch from her office, both amused and bemused by some of the carry-on during rehearsals.

'Now about your first entrance, de-ar,' Reg said to me one day in the dressing room, unaware that David was on the other side of the partition. 'You're supposed to be a "geezer", dahling, your character is basically a rent boy and only after poor Miss Dale for the money. Your entrance is far too low-key and I don't feel you're conveying the true menace of the character. Why don't you try something a little different?'

He laid his *Guardian* crossword aside on the make-up shelf and stood up to demonstrate how a real geezer would walk.

'Like this, dahling,' he said, swaying exaggeratedly from side to side, legs apart with his arms bent, swaggering across the dressing room like John Wayne carrying two imaginary pigs under each arm. To further enhance this illusion of masculinity he bit his lower lip and scowled, which together with the swagger gave the impression that here was a queen who was heavily and painfully constipated and badly in need of a lav.

'Who the hell are you to go around giving notes,

Regina?' David said angrily, coming out sharply from around the partition. They'd been winding each other up all morning during rehearsals and now here it was, the showdown.

'I'm merely offering advice based on twenty-five years in the theatre, Miss Dale,' Regina sniffed, looking down his nose at him.

'Oh, here we go,' David moaned. '"When I was in *Fiddler on the Roof*, dahling . . ."'

'All I'm saying is I've had more experience in the theatre than you, de-ar, so listen and learn,' Reg said icily, returning to his seat and waving his hand dismissively in David's direction, the equivalent of lighting the blue touchpaper to a highly explosive firecracker but failing to retire.

'Oh, dear,' Sheila Collings groaned from her seat next to me as the fireworks began. 'Here we go again.'

They might have torn into each other verbally on occasions, borne grudges and got on each other's nerves but deep down there was a mutual love and respect between these two. However, as David's star ascended Reg's was declining and he avoided what he saw as a loss of face by adopting the persona of the *grande théâtricale*, a mask that rarely slipped even in front of trusted friends.

Reg was a true eccentric and endless fun, sober or drunk, although when seriously intoxicated he could become a bit loud and rowdy, alienating people around him and sometimes getting into trouble. Working with David in Copenhagen at Madame Arthur's club he got arrested and nearly deported for writing 'Regina woz 'ere' on a shop window with a candle that he'd stolen from the Cosy Bar, and one weekend in Amsterdam, blind drunk after a night on the genever and a couple of 'mother's little helpers' (small blue pills that were a form of amphetamine), he nicked a bike.

'Help!' we heard him shout as he went careering down a fairly steep incline at speed. 'I can't ride a bike, de-ah.'

He hit a barrier at the end of a bridge and would've tipped into the canal had it not been for the swift action of two passing leather queens, one of whom after rescuing Reg took him back to his houseboat, lustfully muttering that he wanted to dress him in rubber. After much tugging and heaving and half a bottle of brandy, Reg apparently ended up wearing what he later described as a frogman's suit.

'There I was, de-ar, all dressed up like Buster Crabbe only with a gas mask on instead of a snorkel, trying to keep my balance on the boat. It was hard to stay standing as the boat was still rocking violently from the exertions of getting into the suit. It didn't help that I was pissed as a fart and had a bottle of poppers in the end of me gas mask either.'

'What did he do?' we all asked, eager to know every gory detail of this evening with a rubber fetishist.

'Nothing, dahl-ling,' he replied. 'He just sat there and stared at me. I couldn't tell if he was playing with himself as the gas mask had steamed up and I couldn't see. However, it was a fucking wonderful evening, verrry erotic.'

We went over to Amsterdam for a weekend of drink

and debauchery quite frequently. There was an offer on the back of soap powder packets that enabled the lucky shopper who collected enough of these vouchers to travel by boat and train to Amsterdam for relatively nothing. Consequently we bought boxes of soap powder by the dozen, collecting vouchers like mad until we had enough for a trip.

We'd get pissed on the boat on duty-free booze and after docking at the Hook of Holland would catch the boat train into Amsterdam and check in at the Hotel Orfeo. You got what you paid for at the Orfeo: the rooms were extremely basic but clean and as it was central and ridiculously cheap it became our base in Amsterdam each time we took a trip on the Soap Powder Trail. Today I'd sooner stay at the Orfeo than some of the so-called superior hotels in Amsterdam.

When Reg had been a member of the Disapointer Sisters he'd worked in Amsterdam many times.

'We performed at the comedy theatre in front of the Queen, de-ar,' Reg would boast, 'and it was Juliana then.'

One night in the Amstel Tavern as Reg, Hush and I gave an impromptu performance on the bar to the Andrews Sisters' 'Boogie Woogie Bugle Boy', a club owner recognized Reg from the old days and offered us a booking at his club. We returned a few weeks later courtesy of Daz and gave the Dutch gays, at Reg's insistence, the Hollywood show.

The real Queen may not have turned up but we got one hell of a reception. Hush had literally thrown a few costumes and headdresses together for this one-off show yet the crowd in the club reacted as if they were witnessing the splendour of the *Ziegfeld Follies*. We did the show the next night to an even bigger response from the crowd and the manager asked if we would consider doing a residency at the club. We made all sorts of grand plans about moving to Amsterdam and how we would rent a flat overlooking a canal, none of which came to fruition as the club closed down a few weeks later and we never heard any more.

'Oh well, de-ah,' Reg said philosophically when I told him the news. '"Que Sera, Sera", probably just as well we didn't go. We'd have been dead within the month.'

At the end of its three-week run the play, much to my regret, came to a close and I went off to Denmark with Hush for a month to work at Madame Arthur's. The agent got a shock when we arrived as I still had my beard.

'You haven't been working?' he asked, suddenly anxious in case we'd gone down the pan and he'd booked a dud. 'Has the act not been doing very well?'

'I've been in a play,' I replied airily, adding in tones that I hoped implied I was no stranger to the London stage, 'in the West End', to which he responded contemptuously, as if I'd let the side down.

'Acting? The theatre? Bah, all a waste of time. There's no money in the arts, cabaret is where the big bucks are and where all the excitement is.'

Hush wholeheartedly agreed with this sentiment. He was glad that the play was over and I'd returned to the fold and to the world he felt comfortable in, that of drag.

'C'mon,' he said cheerfully after we'd unpacked, 'get that beard shaved off, wench, and let's have Miss Savage back.'

Copenhagen in May was a lot livelier than when we'd last been here. The city had shed its winter coat and put its party frock on. We'd arrived just in time for the carnival and Hush and I took to the streets dressed as Snow White and the Queen. While the kids might have enjoyed the sight of a six-foot-three Snow White and her equally lofty stepmother, I was beginning to regret my choice of costume as the weather was balmy and it wasn't much fun dragging a heavy black velvet cloak around the streets, sweating like a whore in confession under a cowl and tin crown. I went back to the club to get changed, bumping into Lisa on the stairs.

'Where are you going? Get back out on the streets,' she roared, sounding like a madam ordering one of her girls about. Even though it was only two in the afternoon it was easy to see that she was already more than half cut as one eye was looking at me while the other was looking vacantly at the wall. I tried to explain I was getting changed as it was too hot, but she was having none of it and insisted that I put something else on.

'It's carnival,' she shouted, breaking into a frenzied dance and losing her shoe in the process. 'The Danes are stodgy,' she slurred, leaning against the wall for support as she tapped around the floor with her foot to find her shoe and missing it by miles. 'This is only the second carnival to be held here and we need to show them how it's done! Let's liberate the people!'

Well in that case, I thought, it would be priggish to

ignore this call to arms so I dumped the Wicked Queen and got into my hooker's outfit, which was comfortable and, as there was hardly anything of it, would undoubtedly be a lot cooler than a velvet cloak. Our first port of call was the Why Not bar across the street where she ordered two Jägermeisters. As Lisa was about to down her glass in one, a drunk backed into her, knocking the glass out of her hand and setting off an angry argument between them. The drunk suddenly lunged at Lisa, grabbing her by the hair, and as there was an enormous ashtray sitting on the bar doing nothing I let him have it – unfortunately just as two Politi happened to be coming down the stairs.

The drunk made a terrible racket and as he had no idea where the blow had come from started lashing out indiscriminately at everyone around him. Within seconds the Why Not, normally a fairly reserved little bar, had transformed into a Wild West saloon. In the midst of the melee we managed to evade one of the coppers, who was fighting his way through the crowd and making a beeline for me. We escaped into the street and vanished among the mass of people outside, not easy when you're wearing a wig bigger than the Hindenburg.

'That was fun,' Lisa cackled above the racket of the drums, a monotonous rhythm beaten in unison by the crowd. 'What next? How about we hit the Tivoli Gardens?'

I turned her down and instead headed back to our digs above the club to change into mufti and avoid a possible arrest.

*   *   *

'Be adventurous in life, but not in restaurants' is my maxim and I always order dishes that I know, unable to see the point in spending good money experimenting on a previously unfamiliar dish only to find it's inedible. So having lunch with Hush one day in a restaurant in the Tivoli Gardens I ordered sole, considering it a safe option.

To my horror, when this dish was served up, the fish still had its head, tail and every bone in its body. Revolted, I picked at it half-heartedly with my fork, rooting among the exceedingly bony framework of this monster for some flesh, even though I had no intention of eating any. To make matters worse, this fish bore an expression of abject misery, as if it had died of fright and in excruciating pain. It was like looking at an aquatic autopsy.

'Something wrong with the fish?' the dominatrix masquerading as a waitress asked, hovering menacingly over me. 'It's fresh. Very nice. Now eat it.'

It was a threat, not a request, and instead of telling her that I'd like it served sans head and tail and off the bone I sheepishly assured her that there was nothing wrong and I was just about to eat it.

'I hope you do,' she said, making her way back to the kitchen, probably to get a meat cleaver to decapitate me with.

'What am I going to do?' I hissed. Hush sat opposite me, tucking into his steak with no problem at all.

'Leave it on the plate if you don't want it,' he replied, not understanding my panic.

I hate complaining in restaurants, always have and

always will, and I'm absolutely hopeless when it comes to sending anything back. I've gone to extraordinary lengths over the years to hide the evidence of an uneaten meal and escape the inevitable 'Is there anything wrong with your meal, sir?' from the waiter. I've surreptitiously swiped many an undercooked steak off the plate and into a tissue, smuggling it out in my pocket and dumping it once I'm a safe distance from the restaurant.

The Tivoli Gardens fish was going to be a bit of a problem to smuggle out. It was an enormous beast that only just fitted on the plate, so there was no shoving this distant relative of Moby Dick in my jeans pocket. Weighing up the options, I took the only one available to me and when I thought no one was looking I slung the fish into the hedge next to the table.

'You enjoyed the fish then?' Irma Grese's aunty asked suspiciously when she returned to clear our table and saw my empty plate. 'You must have been hungry, very hungry indeed.'

'I was indeed very hungry,' I answered cheerily, rubbing my stomach like a kids' presenter doing Little Tommy Tucker to demonstrate how full up I was.

'Very hungry indeed,' she mocked, looking into the hedge, 'to have eaten all the bones and the head and tail as well. Do you want dessert? Coffee?' she enquired.

'No thanks,' I mumbled before an outraged Hush could ask to see the dessert menu. 'Just the bill.'

'Do you know what to do?' she asked slyly when she brought it.

'How do you mean?' I muttered.

'You just leave the money on the plate, you don't have to hide it in the hedge.' As she walked away she added, 'Is that an English custom?'

Needless to say she didn't get a tip. Apart from the breakfasts, which I loved, I didn't have much luck with food in Denmark.

When we got back to England I found I was homeless again. Andy had reclaimed his flat but thankfully Chrissie offered to put me up. This musical flats game was becoming very wearing but at least Chrissie's flat was pleasant. He'd inherited it from a very nice dental nurse who'd decorated it in shades of beige and magnolia with an oatmeal fitted carpet throughout.

'Beige,' Chrissie snorted in disgust, 'the hallmark of the bourgeoisie,' and set about redecorating in his own inimitable style courtesy of the skips of London. His first acquisition was a faux medieval wrought-iron chandelier that was far too big for the front room, and once all twenty-eight candles were lit it became a positive death trap. Still, it looked nice and as Chrissie said it saved on the electricity, not that our bills were high as he'd drilled a hole in the side of the meter and stuck a needle in to stop the wheel going round. Suspended from this needle on a length of cotton was a miniature Eiffel Tower acting as a weight, effective but a dead giveaway as to Chrissie's game, and I was threatened on pain of death never to open the door to strangers in case it was the leccy man.

It was time to go back to my proper job at Camden. Instead of returning to the peripatetic team, I was reassigned to the offices of Area One on Theobalds Road as the powers that be were worried that my dislocated knee was not up to the heavy work required of a peri. This suited me down to the ground as working nine to five in a very pleasant office would leave me free to perform in the pubs of an evening.

Hush and I occasionally teamed up with David Dale as an act called LSD: nothing to do with hallucinogenic drugs or pre-decimalization coinage, it stood for Lily, Sandra and Doris. We resurrected and improved some of the old Disapointer Sisters routines and I spent weeks editing a *Watch With Mother* sketch with Doris as Andy Pandy, Hush as Looby Loo and me as Teddy. I had an extremely primitive editing suite involving a video player and a tape recorder set up in the front room and would sit on the floor with one eye on the television and the other on the pause button of the tape machine, cobbling together lines from various episodes of *Andy Pandy*. It was worth it in the end but the effort nearly drove me and Chrissie insane.

'I'm going out,' he'd snap, slapping Oil of Ulay on his face in the mirror over the gas fire. 'That woman's voice saying the same thing over and over again, day in, day friggin' out, is going to put me in the mental ward.'

The BBC and the lovely Vera McKechnie, the lady who narrated the *Andy Pandy* series and a childhood heroine of mine, would undoubtedly have sued if they had known what I was making of their much treasured and fondly remembered kiddies' series.

'Look at Teddy, boys and girls, what can he be looking for?' Vera would say as Teddy on screen ponced about the garden in search of something he'd misplaced. Cut to the stage of the Vauxhall Tavern and me dressed as Teddy, rooting in an oversized handbag for a bottle of amyl nitrite.

'What has he got there?' Vera would enquire as I triumphantly produced the amyl and rammed it up my nose.

'Why look! See how he's sniffing it,' Vera would giggle, referring to Teddy's encounter with a flower in the garden from a different episode.

On cue I'd totter about the stage and bounce off the walls, supposedly out of my mind.

'See how high he's gone!' Vera would chuckle from yet another episode when Teddy had a go on a swing. 'What will Andy say when he gets back, boys and girls? I should imagine he'll have a go and try to get higher than Teddy.'

As for our reinterpretation of 'The Jumping Song' involving me, Andy and Looby . . . well, it would've given the head of BBC children's broadcasting a seizure. Even though the sketch was extremely rude it was done with great affection and never failed to go down a storm with the audience.

We also did a big burlesque opening routine years before the genre had a revival and became fashionable, with the three of us traipsing around as worn-out, hardbitten Minsky chorus girls, culminating with me on a violin bumping and grinding to 'Hungarian Rhapsody'. At my insistence we even did a spot of Irish dancing long before the *Riverdance* phenomenon, flying around the stage in wild red wigs and lurid emerald-green Irish dancing dresses run up by Hush, to a rousing version of 'Lanigan's Ball' until we were fit to drop dead. As a drag act I suppose you could say we were a bit before our time.

We loved working in Edinburgh. There was a gay club on Princes Street called Fire Island with a very appreciative audience. They loved our 'Blood Women' routine, much to Hush's dismay as it involved getting messy, smearing Kensington Gore – fake blood bought from Fox's in Covent Garden – all over our faces and wigs and donning cheap blood-soaked nighties. Hush didn't like getting messy and was appalled at the idea of appearing on any stage, no matter how humble, looking anything less than one hundred per cent glamorous perfection.

Doris had been doing Jennifer Holliday's 'And I Am Telling You' in his solo act, giving the number a macabre twist by appearing as a woman scorned, more than a little deranged and brandishing a carving knife, the bloody evidence of the violent demise of her lover splattered all over her. Doris would encourage us to cover ourselves in the fake blood but the furthest the reluctant Hush ever went was to delicately apply a couple of tiny smears across his cheek and a few cursory dabs on his hands. I'd sling it liberally all over myself as I enjoyed getting messy but I never went as far as Doris, who would literally pour an entire bottle over his head and even take a good mouthful, spewing it out all down his already saturated nightie.

Getting it all off after the show was usually a nightmare. Dressing rooms were primitive and we were very lucky if there was a sink on hand. Even so, there was never any hot water and getting the sticky sweet-smelling Kensington Gore off with cold water and no soap was virtually impossible so we invariably went home with our skin stained a bright pink. This Kensington Gore wasn't cheap either and we were going through gallons of the stuff. Even though we were supposed to take it in turns to buy it, just lately the task seemed to have been left to me. I'd noticed one morning as I was sorting out the drag case that there was only half a bottle left and as we were working in Bournemouth that night once again I took myself of to Fox's, complaining to Fred behind the counter about the expense.

'What are you doing with the stuff? Decorating the front room with it?' he asked. 'I'm not surprised it's costing you a fortune, you're buying the champagne of Kensington Gore,' he explained. 'There's a much cheaper one available, twice the size, almost a quarter of the price and just as good. Thicker and much more glutinous, if you catch my drift, not that I'm an expert on gaping wounds gushing oceans of viscous blood, thank heavens. So come on then, which one do you want?'

Needless to say it was the cheaper brand I took home on the 88 bus.

That night in Bournemouth Hush and I used up what was left of the old bottle, leaving the cheaper but untested new stuff for Doris. He drenched himself in it as usual but after the show found it impossible to remove. It clung to his skin like gloss paint and even though the management had supplied us with a comfortable room with a shower to get changed in (the club was below a gay hotel), no matter how long he scrubbed himself under a scalding shower the fake blood refused to budge. To add to his mounting fury and frustration he was on a promise and was anxious to get back down to the club in case his beau lost interest and went home.

Eventually, an hour and a half and two cans of Vim applied vigorously with a scrubbing brush later, Doris made his entrance into the club. The Vim might have removed the fake blood but it had left his skin with a deathly vampiric pallor tinged with blue. He glowed under the club lighting but it didn't seem to put the totty off. Maybe he was into vampires who smelt like well-scrubbed kitchen sinks.

It was the summer of 1984 when Lily Savage first reared her head properly for the first time and, typically, it all happened by accident rather than design. Andy, a friend of mine, worked in the bingo hall in Kennington, and on his nights off, being an industrious soul, he pulled pints behind the bar of the Elephant and Castle in Vauxhall.

I mentioned this establishment in my last book and to call it rough would be a gross understatement. It was here that the detritus of south London society gathered to drink. The majority of acts refused to work at the Elly as, apart from the notoriously lousy fee, it was seen as the last chance saloon, the place you ended up in when you couldn't get work anywhere else. This was damaging for the reputation of an act who fancied themselves as 'quality', as pub managements might just question why they were paying you decent money when the Elly was getting the same thing for a quarter of the price.

Hush didn't subscribe to this attitude. Work was work as far as he was concerned, and when John, the current manager, asked if he'd like to compère the Ladies' Night, an amateur drag competition that had been held every Tuesday night since the place had first opened its doors, he jumped at it. I couldn't believe it at first. Hush on a microphone? Talking? The same Hush who used to flee if anyone so much as went near him with a mike? I was full of admiration for his daring to go live, if not secretly a little envious. After all, if Hush could do it then why couldn't I?

The evening of his debut as presentatrice of the Elly's Ladies' Night, Doris, Chrissie and I went down to support him. The pub was busier than usual, with familiar faces we normally only saw in the audience of the more 'respectable' pubs dotted among the usual crowd of crazies, dossers, drunks, dog-rough trannies and tough little rent boys. Dickens would've loved the Elly. Hush sat at the back of the stage on a high stool like a hot-house flower in a broken-down greenhouse full of weeds, resplendent in a magnificent red wig (freshly teased to within an inch of its life that afternoon) and a shimmering sapphire-blue evening gown. He took delicate little puffs on a menthol cigarette and introduced the acts in clipped, 'refined' tones as each one lumbered out on to the tiny stage, in the manner of a directrice of a smart Bond Street fashion house revealing this year's spring collection.

The acts had to be seen to be believed. Some of them made the exhibits in a Victorian freak show look like the models in an Abercrombie & Fitch catalogue, a fact Hush was fully aware of yet chose to ignore, sending them up kindly yet remaining consistently supportive. A continuous stream of large vodka and tonics was sent up to the stage from behind the bar, and the more Hush drank the more he relaxed and the funnier he became, and consequently he was a riot.

Tuesday nights at the Elly were picking up, thanks to Hush. Throwing himself wholeheartedly into his new role as compère and mother hen, he would patiently try to smarten up his ladies, running up costumes for them out of remnants of fabric he had lying about the flat and bringing new life into their desperate old wigs.

'You can't polish turds, wench,' he'd say, 'but you can disguise them by rolling 'em in glitter and sequins.'

'We need extra bar staff,' Andy told me as he stood at the pump pouring me a pint of cider. 'Tuesdays in particular. It's getting busy.'

'I wouldn't mind a job behind the bar,' I replied in a moment of insanity. I certainly didn't need another job, having two already, but a couple of nights behind the bar would be fun. It would be a laugh working with Andy, John and his partner Colin and I fancied the idea of working at the notorious Elephant and Castle. Had I been a deb I'd have said it was deliciously low but as I'm not now and wasn't then I just saw it as a rough pub, and as I've always been drawn to the more seamy side of life the more I thought about it the more the idea appealed to me. Besides, I had a safety net, it wasn't a career move, I was free to leave at any time.

'D'ya hear this, John,' Andy shouted down the bar in his broad Glaswegian accent. 'Savage here is interested in applying for the job.'

John looked up momentarily and muttered something unintelligible, then returned to rooting around the till in search of something.

'Well, I'm the best offer you'll get. I'm a highly experienced barman,' I said indignantly to his back, suddenly aware that I wanted this job.

'I've worked behind bars for years,' I went on, adding for effect, 'I was trained at the Royal Air Force Club.'

To be turned down for a job at the Elephant and Castle public house was unthinkable. I had to get this job now. It was a matter of principle.

'If you're serious,' John spluttered, 'I'll think about it. I'm not taking you on only for you to leave after one session.'

It took me all night to persuade him I meant what I said and that I was prepared to live and die in the service of the Elephant and Castle. Eventually, worn down by my nagging, he gave in, telling me, still a little reservedly, that I could start on Sunday night.

The moment I set foot behind the bar of the Elly I regretted ever opening my big mouth. Some of the customers left a lot to be desired and there was certainly no time for any of the 'fun' I'd imagined I'd be having. I didn't stop all night. This crowd could really drink, particularly the lot in the back bar, the haunt of the gentlemen who resided in the men's hostel next door and who were mostly pissed, argumentative and troublesome to serve. If they got really out of hand then we'd throw them out, only for them to run round to the door of the front bar to try to get back in. Their attempts would then be thwarted by Campella, the incredibly camp but ferociously tough bouncer.

As John had predicted, after one session I wanted to quit – but rather than prove him right I kept my own counsel, gritted my teeth and got on with it.

Hush suddenly decided that he'd had enough of hosting Ladies' Night and left, but his succession of replacements weren't very good. In fact, on the whole they were appalling.

'Jesus, I could do better than that,' I moaned to Andy as we emptied out the dishwasher. 'These dogs that they've got in since Hush left are shocking.'

'Why don't you then, hen,' he said, avoiding the steam from the machine. 'Get yourself up there. Go on, I dare you.'

The matter was brought up again after the pub had closed and we were gathered around the bar having 'late gates'. After a lot of persuasion and a quantity of whisky and Coke I agreed to give it a go, unwittingly changing my life in an instant.

I didn't give it much thought until a few nights later when, coming out of Vauxhall tube station on my way home from work, I saw a crudely drawn poster in the window of the Elly proclaiming 'Tuesday Night Ladies' Night. Compère Lily Savage'. My stomach turned over. Why the hell do I keep opening my mouth without first considering what I'm about to say? It always leads me into situations that I later regret. And this was one of them. How was I going to get out of this one?

'Oh, shurrup giving out,' Chrissie said when I got home and told him my predicament. He was sitting in front of the gas fire in his vest and boxers eating toast and smoking simultaneously in an armchair that I'd never seen before. 'D'ye like me chair?' he simpered, flicking his ash in the direction of the gas fire. 'It was in a skip at the top of Fentiman Road. It's shocking what people throw out, there's nothing wrong with it.' He stood up to reveal his latest acquisition in all its glory. 'Look at it,' he said proudly, brushing toast crumbs off the cushion. 'Why would you throw this out?'

'Maybe it was something to do with the shitty green colour and the wobbly wooden arm,' I said. 'Or maybe it's haunted, somebody could've died a terrible death in that chair.'

'Haunted, me arse,' Chrissie said dismissively, giving the cushion one last brush down. 'Don't start that game.'

Chrissie was terrified of ghosts and all things supernatural. He couldn't even watch the tamest of horror films and would have hysterics if he heard the violin chords that accompanied the stabbing in the shower scene in Hitchcock's *Psycho*. I once arranged all the furniture in the middle of the front room and piled the kitchen chairs on the table after he'd gone to work. When I got home I found him standing in the hall still in his overcoat, afraid to move in case the poltergeist threw something at him, and when I eventually confessed that I was the poltergeist he never spoke to me for a week, which was nothing new as we were always falling out.

'Anyway, forget the chair, what are you going to do about the Elly?' he asked, closing the subject of haunted furniture. 'You'll have to go on, you've said you would.'

I had to agree there was no backing out now and I'd have to get on with it.

'Who knows?' Chrissie said, firing his Parthian shot as he swanned off in the direction of the bathroom. 'You might even be good . . . although I don't hold out much hope.'

On the big night, which came round far too quickly for my liking, I got ready in a room over the pub. As I painted the slap on I tried to think of things to say but my mind was too preoccupied with the task ahead to start coming up with gags. Andy and John kept appearing with words of encouragement and a supply of cider, and certainly not calming my nerves with the news that the pub was filling up nicely.

'Look at you!' Chrissie screeched as he came into the room with a large whisky in one hand and a carrier bag in the other. 'You look like a right old slag.'

I was meant to. I'd eschewed any attempts at glamour and opted instead for the uniform of the full-blown whore: a short black plastic mac with an even shorter leopard-print miniskirt underneath, each arm covered in a multitude of jangling bangles with garish ropes of multicoloured beads around my neck, topped off with an enormous confection of peroxide ringlets and artfully placed curls.

'Here, I got you this from work,' Chrissie said, producing some sort of dead animal out of the carrier bag. 'They were going to chuck it out but I saved it as I knew you'd love it.' He was working in C. & W. May, theatrical costumiers in Covent Garden, now long gone and replaced with a Waterstones bookshop. May's expansive basements were a veritable Aladdin's cave and when Chrissie and I were on good terms we'd spend hours trying on the costumes. I was in my element parading around as a White Russian officer one minute and Queen Elizabeth I the next. Chrissie, even though he claimed to be an atheist, preferred the clerical look, admiring himself in the mirror in the robes of the Archbishop of Canterbury.

The dead animal turned out to be a mangy fox fur.

'Throw it over your arm,' Chrissie said, shaking it violently to remove any dust. 'It'll look really whorey, not that you need much help in that department.'

When John came upstairs to tell me it was time to go on I felt like Ruth Ellis with Pierrepoint, only she probably didn't laugh nervously and make inane remarks to cover her terror as she was led to the scaffold, which in my case was the stage. I stood by the toilets trying to look cheerful and confident as the DJ introduced me, silently chanting the mantra I'd used since childhood and always reverted to in times of stress: 'Please God, let me get through this and I'll never be bad again . . .'

God was obviously manning the hotline that night because for the two hours I was on I did more than get through it, I had one of the best times of my life.

Something happened the moment I stepped on that stage, my personality as I knew it became warped and amplified a thousand times and I transformed into a knowing, louche and satisfyingly empowering character, coming out with the kind of talk I'd never thought I'd dare say in public in front of a packed pub. I'd reckoned attack was my best form of defence and so, suspecting every member of the audience of being a potential heckler, I tore into them one by one, hopefully establishing the ground rules.

With my conscience tucked safely away in bed, I was free to make no concessions and went for the jugular, tearing anyone foolish enough to try their hand into little pieces. I had no option to be anything less than evil-tongued. To show weakness in the face of the enemy would be disastrous and the stage of the Elephant and Castle was certainly no place for cissies. They ate their young alive in there.

What astonished me was the speed with which I delivered these put-downs. Where was I getting them from? Satisfyingly pithy ripostes seemed to be effortlessly spewing out of me with the rapidity of a tommy gun and to the audience's increasing delight. It was all very edifying.

A drunken woman who had been shouting inane remarks all night made her way to the front of the stage with a little man in tow. At first I wondered if she was bad drag as she was over six foot tall while her partner, who just about came up to her waist and looked for all the world as if he'd been cast as a comedy Asian in an unenlightened Dick Emery sketch, seemed incongruous standing beside this hulking creature who was as wide as she was tall. For a moment I found myself wondering what they looked like together naked in bed, an obscene image that I quickly banished from my mind.

'I've got something every queen in here wants,' the woman shouted proudly.

'What's that, love? Penicillin?' I asked.

'No, a fuckin' 'usband!' Oh, she was rough. I felt like a character from Jane Austen compared to her. 'We only got married yesterday and he goes like a rabbit. Bin on me back all day,' she bragged in a voice like a foghorn. 'D'ya want to see my ring?'

I didn't need to reply to that one. Pulling a wry face was sufficient to bring the house down.

This woman was a comedy gift but as I looked at her seemingly placid and inoffensive Borrower-sized groom, gazing up adoringly at his blushing bride, her flush brought on by alcohol rather than innocence, I wondered where the attraction lay. What chemical reaction had gone on here to bring such an unlikely couple together? What pheromones were they squirting at each other to induce such sexual attraction? To quote my mother again, 'Every pan has a lid . . .'

'Isn't anyone in 'ere going to buy us a bloody drink then?' she bellowed. 'Help us celebrate me marriage?' The groom looked up at me, probably dislocating his neck in the process, and grinned drunkenly.

'Tell me,' I asked him as I watched his bride drain the last of her pint in one, 'was it the prospect of British citizenship that got you down the aisle?'

Even Chrissie became the butt of a hoary old joke

I'd heard one of the comics in the Stone Chair use.

'See that frizzy-haired old queen over there, the miserable one with a face like a peanut?' I shouted. 'I had to take her back up to the hospital today. She's had a crippling case of piles. The doctor recommended that she smother them in tea leaves for a week, which she dutifully did. We sat up all night opening teabags with nail scissors to meet the demand.

'Anyway, when we went back today the quack told her to drop her drawers and bend over the sofa, a request she's no stranger to, believe me. Well, the doctor stared for what seemed like hours at Chrissie's tea-leaf-encrusted hoop, not saying a word.

'Eventually Chrissie piped up, "What do you see, doctor?"

'"Well, your piles are no better,' the doctor said, '"but I see an encounter with a tall dark stranger and a possible trip abroad . . ."'

Whereas Hush had introduced each act as if they were debs being presented at the Court of St James, I adopted the attitude of a Midwest carnival barker and introduced the girls as if they were the epitome of pulchritude.

'Roll up, ladies and gents, our first little lady to skip down the illuminated runway of joy sings, dances and crawls on her belly like the very serpent that St Patrick ground underneath his sandal. Please welcome the Fair Maid of Fife herself, the lovely Stella!'

Stella was one of my favourites, a skinny Scottish queen blissfully unaware of just how bad he was as he 'sang' 'New York, New York' in a key that hadn't been invented yet, four beats behind his backing track in a voice that could shatter marble. When eventually the catcalls and booing started drowning out Stella's remarkable vocal talents he'd abandon the song and go into a striptease instead, slowly removing everything, right down to his false teeth. These he'd place in a pint glass and hand to me for safe keeping. I in turn would pop them on the moving turntable of the DJ's console, setting them spinning around and grinning maniacally in a residue of warm cider at the bottom of the glass. Quite a spectacular finale to anyone's act, I'm sure you'll agree.

The undisputed star of the amateurs was Rose-Marie. His real name was John and he worked in the kitchens of one of the big hotels and lived for his Tuesday nights when he could get into his little crimplene charity-shop frock and take to the stage.

I find it hard to describe Rose-Marie without sounding cruel, though I felt very protective towards him. He had many physical deformities and while he didn't have serious learning difficulties he was what my mother, in an attempt to be kind, would term 'not the full shilling'. He was a happy soul, perfectly affable and good-natured until someone crossed him. Then his mood would switch in a flash, transforming him into a filthy-mouthed Mr Hyde with a violent temper. The first time I ever saw Rose-Marie shuffling back and forth on the stage I was horrified. His unlovely face smeared with make-up was set fast in a faintly obscene leer as he hobbled on his club feet, encased in Doc Marten boots, to Susan Maughan's 'Bobby's Girl', touching his

216

makeshift breasts and lifting the hem of his dress to reveal misshapen legs.

He was a dancing bear, an Elephant Man for the eighties, a monster in drag performing for an audience who at first cruelly laughed at him instead of with him. Thankfully the audience's attitude quickly changed towards Rose and he became a cult figure on the gay scene. Even though he was still looked upon as an oddity, he was our oddity and was greeted with great warmth and genuine affection each time he appeared.

He was murdered one night by a lad he'd picked up in a pub and taken back to his flat. The gay community were appalled by the senseless killing of such an innocent, but at least Rose had had his moment in the sun. That was when the agent Paul Wilde booked him in at the Hippodrome, formerly the Talk of the Town, fulfilling a dream Rose would never have thought possible.

That night at the Elly was a revelation to me, a real eye-opener as to what I was capable of, but even though I was high as a kite on adrenalin and flushed with success, I was not so giddy as to get carried away by the requests from other pub landlords in the audience to book me for their own venues. I realized that compèring a crappy talent show was one thing but actually launching myself on the circuit as a live patter act was another. I wasn't ready yet by any means and I knew it and besides, I told myself, one swallow doesn't make a summer and next Tuesday I might die on my arse.

No, I told myself, far wiser to stay in the Elly for the

time being. If I was to seriously make a go of this 'going live' lark then I'd have to work at it first and try to hone whatever skills I was developing, and the Elly seemed as good a place as any for me to practise in.

'A star is born, dear,' Campella said, kissing me on both cheeks and giving me a hug. 'Pure fuckin' anarchy, love.'

The star that had just been born staggered down South Lambeth Road with Chrissie in tow. He was drunkenly waving at cars and swinging a bin-liner containing the head of the disassembled Lily Savage around in the air while I, equally pissed, lugged the rest of her in a holdall and wondered how the hell we were going to get up for work in four hours' time.

'I'll gerrus up,' Chrissie slurred confidently, pausing momentarily as we crossed the road to moon at a lorry driver who'd stopped for the lights.

'Call that an arse?' the lorry driver shouted out of the cab window.

'What are yer talking about?' Chrissie shouted back, breaking into peals of flirtatious laughter and slapping a bare cheek. 'It's like a full moon, that is.'

'Shame you didn't see it last night,' I chimed in. 'There was a man in it.'

Oh dear. Rapier wit on the South Lambeth Road at 3 a.m. I really did need to hone those skills.

After a couple of Tuesday nights, word went round like a bush fire that the Elly was the place to be.

'There's this new drag queen on, Lily Savage – one half of the Playgirls, common as muck, mouth like a

218

viper, hosting a talent show with the worst acts you've ever seen.' Soon, as well as the usual melting pot of perfectly nice people, rent boys, drunks and the mentally unstable, Ladies' Night began to draw an eclectic crowd with the likes of fashion designer Katharine Hamnett and her team, the artist Patrick Proktor and the film-maker Derek Jarman rubbing shoulders with the hoi polloi of the Elly.

The BBC made a programme called *Patrick Proktor's Britain* with Patrick trailing all over the country visiting people and places that he liked. Lily was one of these people and he interviewed me in the dressing room of the Vauxhall Tavern, making this one of my very first television appearances.

Patrick wrote me a letter in which he compared Tuesday nights at the Elly to the cabaret of the Weimar Republic. 'There's nothing else quite like it in London, or indeed the British Isles,' he wrote, 'than spending an evening in the company of the most mordant of hostesses, blessed with the tongue of Medusa and the unnerving ability to turn any foolhardy heckler into stone and of whom I am her most ardent of fans. There is a maternal side to this tough, funny conferencier that I find most endearing in the way that she protects the "girls" of her troupe against the cruel jeers and drunken catcalls from the raucous crowd.' He went on to say of the 'girls' that 'despite their obvious lack of talent and peculiar physicalities' he found their naivety and self-effacement refreshing and that 'if one ever imagined what a working class gay cabaret on the Karlstrasse in pre-war Berlin was like then it could be found in a corner of Vauxhall'.

I don't know about that but it was certainly lively. One night during the show a punter made his entrance via the unorthodox means of a window. This drunken homophobe had already been ejected by Campella but had hung around outside, turning his wrath on a couple taking some air who, despite their appearance, were not the sort of queens you'd mess with, and with little effort they threw him through the window. As I said, it was rough but good fun.

Among the ragbag of queens who made up the cast of Ladies' Night was a solitary woman called Linda. Along with a line-up of her gay mates dressed as zombies, she would drag up as Michael Jackson and bring the house down with their version of *Thriller*. Linda had what I considered to be a pure cockney accent and the wit to go with it and could make a simple remark such as 'Put the kettle on, will ya,' sound funny. As I sat in her front room with her one afternoon, smoking and drinking tea and listening to her in full flight, she suddenly shot out of her chair mid-conversation and starting hammering on the window.

'Get orf my wall, you cunt,' she roared at the unfortunate youth who'd had the temerity to sit on the wall outside her window. Once satisfied that her request had been obeyed, she returned to her chair and carried on where she'd left off, bemused as to why I was suffocating with laughter. We all went trailing off in a coach to Manchester to give the unsuspecting patrons of a club called Napoleon's a taste of Ladies' Night, organized for us by a shop called Clone Zone. After the audience got over the shock they quite enjoyed it, I think, anyway we all got roaring drunk and I had a fling with one of the zombies in the hotel Clone Zone had put us all up in.

The next day on the way back to London I pulled out the old fox fur that Chrissie had given me and started playing with it, discovering that if I slid my hand inside this decrepit old scavenger and manipulated the clip that served as a bottom jaw I could bring it to life. I christened it Skippy and would sit on the stage having imaginary conversations with the moth-eaten thing, unknowingly creating a cult figure in the process.

After six months working on and off at the Elly I defected to the other side, the other side of the road that is, to the Royal Vauxhall Tavern. I was already a regular at the Tavern, working there with Hush and Doris at least once a week, and on my nights off I could invariably be found perched on a stool at the end of the bar, chatting to Paul, the manager. It was Paul who, after plying me with copious amounts of cider at one of the regular lock-ins, persuaded me with the offer of fifty quid as opposed to the fifteen I was getting at the Elly to jump ship and bring the amateur night over to the Tavern.

'I'll do it for a few weeks' were my famous last words.

I was to sit in my chair at the end of the stage presenting 'Stars of the Future' on a Thursday night for over eight years.

CHAPTER 8

T HE ROYAL VAUXHALL TAVERN WAS TO PLAY AN extremely important role in my life.

For us locals the Vauxhall was our village hall, a place where we congregated most nights to chew the cud and get bevvied in the process. All the big occasions in our lives, like birthdays and Christmas, were celebrated at the Vauxhall, and after each New Year's Eve's shenanigans I rarely got home to my bed before ten the next morning.

And when the nightmare of Aids hit us, devastating our community, wiping out most of our friends, the reception following the funeral was frequently held in the Vauxhall.

The 'Stars of the Future' talent show on a Thursday night became even more popular than Ladies' Night at the Elly, and over the years it seemed that the whole world passed through those doors on a Thursday night at one time or another.

Years later, on the Eastern and Oriental Express travelling from Singapore to Thailand, one of the inscrutable staff dressed in full Thai costume knocked on my cabin door just as we were pulling into Bangkok station, and dropping the gentle Thai twang he'd spoken with for the entire trip asked me in an accent that owed more to the banks of the Thames than the Chao Phraya if I'd sign the visitors' book, as he never used to miss a Thursday night down the Vauxhall. Up a mountain on the Isle of Skye a climber stopped to tell me how much she enjoyed Thursday nights in the Vauxhall, and even in a tea room in Shanghai I was approached and asked for a photo 'for old times' sake', to remind them of the good old days down the Vauxhall.

Looking back now, I might be recalling the past through a slightly sentimental and rose-tinted pair of specs, but I can see that those pre-Aids times in that pub really were the Good Old Days, scratching around, earning a living, going about our daily business not expecting much and not getting it either but managing to have a good time nevertheless. Our social life revolved around the Vauxhall, the Elly, the Market Tavern in Nine Elms Lane and the Union Tavern in Camberwell and we very rarely strayed outside the vicinity to go drinking.

My first few Thursday nights at the Vauxhall were not so much a baptism by fire as a roasting in the white heat of the core of a volcano.

Paul had promoted his new show heavily in *Capital Gay*, a free weekly paper for the London gay and lesbian community, and there was a bit of a buzz of anticipation about it going around the gay pubs which did nothing to boost my confidence. Instead it had the opposite effect, making me question my ability to carry it off. I'd lie in bed anticipating the heckles that might come my way and thinking up suitable put-downs for them just in case.

'When embarking on a new venture,' I remember Aunty Chris saying when she was promoted to manageress of Ashe and Nephew's off-licence, 'be prepared for all eventualities.'

Just as well I was, for on the very first Thursday night I walked out on to the stage of the Vauxhall and straight into a veritable heckle hole. They came thick and fast for the three hours I was on stage, but just as in the Elly I somehow managed to shoot them all down in flames, wiping the floor with the most persistent of hecklers with a relentless flow of venom that never seemed to dry up.

I needn't have bothered with the nocturnal preparation as the put-downs came naturally and, more important, instantaneously. It's no good dithering with a heckler, you have to go for them with the speed of a cobra – and it never ceased to amaze me that I always managed to do it. I had always had a bit of a reputation for possessing a 'sharp tongue', a gift undoubtedly inherited from my mother and her sisters – but that's where any similarities to Lily end.

For the years I performed as Lily I was constantly being asked in interviews who was the inspiration behind her and I can honestly say that it certainly wasn't my mother. Lilian Maeve Veronica Savage was a divorcee single mother of two, not averse to a little light prostitution to supplement her income and prone to shoplifting and receiving stolen goods. She drank, smoked, openly took drugs, fiddled her gas and electricity meters, believed in plain speaking and possessed a mouth that would make the inbreds who appear on *Jeremy Kyle* blush.

Apart from the plain speaking my mother had none of these attributes. She neither drank nor smoked, and apart from nicking the odd cutting off a plant from the gardens of the stately homes she visited over the years she was incapable of dishonesty. Infidelity and divorce were things that occurred among couples 'down south' and the only drugs she ever took, overlooking the night we were snowbound and housebound and got accidentally stoned after eating some dope that I'd been given at a party, were thyroxin and Valium, the latter for 'the nerves'. My mum's world revolved around her grandkids, her knitting and her garden, the Birkenhead Central Library, solitary bus rides to visit places she'd 'always wanted to see' and the Catholic Church.

Lily's world was a lot darker. The only flora that she ever cultivated were 'marahawana' plants, and libraries were places to pop into for a pee if she was caught short or to dump some 'stash' if she were being pursued by the police. Yet despite her shortcomings or maybe because of them she was a leading light of the Union of Catholic Mothers, an organization with which as a child I went on many a coach trip to the various spots dotted around the country where the Virgin Mary had put in an appearance.

I've always thought that comedy is formed in your childhood years, and now experiences from my past were being resurrected, repainted and morphed into pieces of Lily's life. The edges between us frequently blurred and sometimes as I was painting the slap on in a mirror I'd become aware that I was unconsciously aping Aunty Chris as she applied her warpaint back in Lowther Street, and on many occasions I noticed that I was adopting both her and my mother's way of delivering a punchline. Both of them were mistresses of the impeccably timed throwaway line, and more than capable of stopping you in your tracks with a pithy put-down.

Lily was an amalgamation of characters I'd encountered both in real life and in the fantasy world of TV and film who had left a lasting impression on me. Lily's roots (origins not hair) and lifestyle were strictly working class but her dress sense owed a lot to the ladies of *The Avengers*, the gaudy dance hall hostesses from the film *Sweet Charity* and the ubiquitous saloon gals and hard-boiled gangsters' molls who brightened up all those old movies, frequently stealing them from under the stars' noses.

The white wig that became a sort of trademark came about because it was the only colour that I really suited. Three times a year I'd make the trip to Lisson Grove on the 2b bus for a couple of 96Ks from Hairaisers, stopping off for a mooch around Alfie's Antique Market beforehand and annoying myself in the process as I could never afford the many curiosities that I desperately coveted.

I loved what I called 'mooching', just strolling around taking my time, mulling over all that was going on in my life, both the good and the bad, as I explored unfamiliar districts and shops as well as favourite old haunts like the New Piccadilly Café in Denman Street, a shrine to the fifties now sadly demolished, where I'd sit at a window table with my usual meal of sausage, beans and chips selected from the horseshoe-shaped menu over the serving counter and worry about the future.

As one wig wasn't sufficient for the required height and volume that I was seeking I always bought two which Hush would pin together, stuffing a bin-liner and some bubble wrap between them before launching an attack armed with the familiar tailcomb and brush until they resembled a mass of gravity-defying snow-white candyfloss. The addition of the black roots didn't come until much later on when I was at a photo shoot for *Gay Times* one afternoon. Finding myself hanging around between shots I came across a can of black spray paint, and for want of something better to do I squirted a bit on the hairline of the wig and combed it in, creating black roots in the process. The look suited the type of character that Lily was developing into, and from that day on I never wore a wig without the roots.

The Thursday night audience soon tired of their relentless heckling. Unable to get the better of me, they eventually gave in and allowed me to sit back and let my imagination run riot. Fuelled by the endless stream of whisky and cider sent up to the stage by the punters, I began to mould and create what would become Lily Savage.

Lilian Maeve Veronica Savage was born on the steps

of the Legs of Man public house, Lime Street, Liverpool, on a policeman's overcoat. Her mother, the lady wrestler Hell Cat Savage, had no such luxuries as gas and air or an 'epidermis' to relieve the pain of labour; she just bit down on the policeman's torch, recovering afterwards with the aid of a large pale ale at the bar of the pub she'd just given birth outside. According to Lily she was a rare beauty as a child, a former Miss Pears and the holder of the title 'Little Miss Duraglit', winning this accolade for being the only child able to suck the wadding without flinching. Despite her libertine attitudes she was a convent-educated girl and even considered taking the veil herself as a girl, entering a Carmelite order for a brief period as a novice, a habit – no pun intended – that she would return to much later on in life when I decided to kill her off. The convent of the Flagellated Flesh of St Philomena of Wigan was a silent order and the nuns were only allowed to say two words each year.

After the first year the young Lily approached the Mother Superior and spoke her two words.

'What have you to say, Lily?' the Mother Superior enquired.

'Damp beds,' Lily replied.

The following year Lily once again stood in front of Mother Superior's desk and delivered her two words.

'Anything to say, Lily?' Mother Superior asked.

'Lousy food.'

In the third year Lily repeated the process.

'Speak your two words, Lily,' she was told.

'I quit,' she said.

'Thank fuck for that,' Mother Superior replied. 'You've done nothing but fuckin' moan since you got here.'

A lousy old gag that I can promise is funnier in the telling and the only one I can ever remember. I never told structured jokes of the old-school variety as I'd invariably stray from the plot and forget the punchline.

After abandoning the convent Lily took on a variety of occupations ranging from working on the line in Cadbury's packing fudge to whoring, earning herself the international soubriquet of the Deadly White Flower of the Wirral among her many naval admirers.

There was a spell in St Risley's Remand Home for Girls following a raid by the police on a council house on the Woodchurch Estate, the headquarters of a thriving porn industry. One of Lily's films was shown as evidence during the sensational trial that sent sales of the *Birkenhead News* soaring thanks to such lurid headlines as 'Tranmere Tramp in Three-in-a-bed Lesbian Romp'. This film, entitled *Nativity 2 – Just when you thought it was safe to go back in the stable*, had been released as that year's big Christmas blockbuster only to be withdrawn two hours after its premiere, deemed as obscene and blasphemous by Christian fundamentalists. Lily was packed off to St Risley's and her co-star, Neddy, retired to a donkey sanctuary outside Blackpool once they'd managed to get it out of the rubber suit.

Incidentally, *Nativity 2* is considered these days to be an art house film with a respectably sized cult following and the few prints that remain are highly prized among collectors. It's particularly popular in rural Sweden where it is shown regularly every year at the film festival of St Botvid of Kodhe.

On her release from the months of incarceration in St Risley's Lily embarked on a short-lived career as a beauty queen following her crowning as Miss New Brighton Baths, a title she defends to this day, refuting all malicious claims that her success owed nothing to her uncanny resemblance to the stunning Hollywood actress Kim Novak but everything to the fact she'd had it off with all the judges beforehand round the back of the baths.

The young Lily was much in demand after her success at New Brighton, landing her some dubious cheesecake work for *Reveille* and *Saturday Titbits*, posing in a see-through chiffon nightie on a fake fur rug in front of a two-bar electric fire claiming that 'she loved working with animals and that she knelt by the side of her bed each night and prayed for world peace'. There was also a memorable spread in the *Angler's Weekly* when she appeared suitably attired as the 'Queen of the Crustaceans', wearing nothing but two winkles and a scallop shell.

Life was good for a while until the morning she set out for an engagement in Bury to pose tastefully caressing a link of black pudding and was overcome by a violent bout of nausea. At first she put it down to a suspect kebab she had eaten the previous night, but as the vomiting continued she paid a visit to the doctor and was told that she was pregnant.

Her grandmother, Erica Von Savage, advised her to sit in a hot bath and drink a bottle of gin, a practice that she kept up long after the baby was born. Being a good Catholic girl at heart, Lily tracked down the father of her child and after a little persuasion (Lily was the one on her knees when he proposed) she sailed down the aisle in virginal white, six months pregnant.

Following the birth of her daughter Bunty, the man she had married – who thought it great sport to fart in bed and then hold her head under the blankets until her rollers melted into the pillowcase – abandoned her, forcing her to seek employment in the Blue Balloon, a notoriously low strip club, as one of the featured strippers. It was the young Lil's first taste of showbiz and prompted her exodus to London, with her daughter, her whippet Queenie and her sister Vera Cheeseman in tow.

It was great fun thinking up all this nonsense, and at the Vauxhall I had plenty of time between the acts to spin all manner of impromptu yarns, creating a highly improbable and bizarre world for Lily to live in. I was to learn later that in comedy circles this was known as improv, a skill that was much admired, but at the time I just thought of it as 'letting my soft out'. I wrote Lily's history down in a book called *An A to Z Sort of Thing* with some glorious photos of the old slapper and her kin taken by my favourite photographer (Nicky Johnston, if you're interested).

Paul eventually left the Vauxhall, and the landlord, Pat McConnon, and his wife Breda took up residence with their family in his place. Pat was the former landlord of the Coleherne, the famous Earl's Court pub beloved of the leather queens, who had turned me down years earlier when I'd applied for a job as barman – a fact of which I constantly reminded him. Pat was a good-natured sort, the type of landlord one rarely finds running a boozer any more. He and Breda became trusted friends and part of our 'London family'.

Pat loved the craic, enjoying nothing more than a session slinging good-natured abuse, and I was happy to oblige. Our relationship became a running gag over the years as I sniped at him from the stage. 'You know why there are no snakes in Ireland? Cos they're all running gay bars in London.' My jibes slid off Pat like water off a duck's back, his response being to dismiss me with a cheery 'Yer a feckin' bowsy, Savage, a feckin' bowsy'.

As well as the regular stable of 'talent' inherited from the Elly, 'Stars of the Future' began drawing other hopefuls out of the woodwork who craved the spotlight. Sometimes there would be over twenty acts waiting to go on, most of which were dire. However, occasionally some real gems came along. One night I announced a new act called Betty Legs Diamond who spun confidently on to the stage and proceeded to go into a dance routine that would have had the judging panel on *Strictly Come Dancing* wetting their knickers. Simon Green (Betty Legs) was a professional dancer who had appeared in many a West End show and entered 'Stars of the Future' just for the sheer hell of it. He used to tear the place apart and I've never seen anyone, then or since, male or female, to rival him. He went on to be the star of Blackpool's Funny Girls for years, choreographed lots of my early shows and is currently residing in the Boulevard Show Bar in Newcastle.

Another favourite with both me and the crowds was the diminutive Tilly, who in full Brunhilde drag would give the crowd a taste of grand opera to thunderous applause as enthusiastic as any Dame Kiri received at Covent Garden. His other great crowd pleaser was 'The Lonely Goatherd', to which he'd lead the audience in a rousing chorus while flinging himself around the stage, a performance that was all the more remarkable considering Tilly was disabled, not that he ever let such a trifling matter bother him. Tilly got on with his life in a way that left supposedly able-bodied people behind in the dust.

Tony, the Liverpudlian behind Tilly, was blessed with that dry wit peculiar to Scousers and he could cut an upstart down to size with a withering look and a line sharper than a bee's arse. Self-deprecating and very funny, he frequently gave me and Vera a lift up the South Lambeth Road in his specially adapted car when we'd had one too many and Vera had temporarily lost the use of his legs.

First time visitors to the Thursday nights could never quite believe their eyes when they saw the talent that trod the Vauxhall's 'illuminated runway of joy'. There was the Princess Melina, a tall gangly queen who mimed in Greek, and Judy Luft, a young man who was rumoured to be the son of a famous film director and whose speciality was his unique interpretation of Judy Garland singing one of her most famous hits.

The recording he used of Judy was not one of the lady at her best, as when she wasn't slurring her words she was forgetting them, and to add insult to injury he included some of Judy's incomprehensible rambles in the cacophony. This was no tribute to the star once the idol of a generation of gay men and object of much reverential impersonation by the drag queens. Judy Luft's version was something entirely different. 'Avant-garde' I called it at the time, for want of a better explanation, as I attempted to pacify an angry audience following Judy's show-stopping performance.

Judy Luft was a big lad, well over six foot tall. He would paint his face clown white and stick on a little black dress that didn't fit and a black wig that could pass for roadkill. Finally, he would dunk his entire head in a sinkful of water to represent heavy perspiration just before he went on. I'd watch with a mixture of fascination and apprehension as he lurched into the spotlight, shaking his head as violently as a wet dog and soaking everyone who had the misfortune to be standing near the front as he careered up and down in an impossibly high pair of patent leather shoes that had a sense of direction all their own. Judy could hardly stand up in these death-trap shoes, let alone move, and he frequently lost all control, involuntarily launching himself upon the crowd who in turn would beat him off and throw him back up on to the stage, hurling pints of beer at him, furious that he'd soaked their neatly pressed jeans and shirts and smeared them in clown-white make-up. After a while Judy vanished as quickly as he'd appeared, never to be seen again, and even though I'd miss his insane contribution to the evening it was nice to be able to walk across the stage without needing waders.

On the whole the crowd, despite being extremely rowdy, were a good-natured lot, tolerant of even the most abysmal of acts and rarely hurling anything worse than friendly abuse and catcalls – until, that is, the night a post-op transsexual got up and proceeded to strip.

This person was highly unpopular, a pushy exhibitionist with an unpredictable temper who despite female hormones and extensive cosmetic surgery still looked about as feminine as Desperate Dan. She'd been missing for a while, reappearing to brag that her absence was due to a spell in Charing Cross Hospital undergoing gender reassignment surgery (although that's not quite how she put it) to become a fully fledged woman, the primary reason for this transition being so she could go on the game.

'I've got a licence to print money between my legs,' she announced proudly within earshot of anyone who might be interested, which apparently they weren't as everyone turned their backs on her and suddenly became engrossed in conversation.

Even though I was wary of her I was civil towards her, believing it easier to be pleasant than confrontational especially when dealing with a person who wouldn't hesitate to shove a glass in your face. She looked down on the others in the dressing room, boasting about how she was 'a real woman' whom men couldn't resist. She was that most dishonourable of prostitutes, a 'clipper', luring unsuspecting customers with the promise of a good time by giving them the key to a non-existent flat nearby in exchange for cash upfront. She told these suckers that she'd be along in a minute, which of course she never was, vanishing instead into the streets of Soho to reel in another fish. Any mug gullible enough to fall for this flimsy ruse deserved to be ripped off, but even so I disliked her for it.

From the moment she minced out on to the stage she managed to antagonize the audience. The chants for her to get off became deafening yet she completely ignored them, instead setting about writhing suggestively on a stool. In my experience, the audiences in the gay bars loved drag performers and female singers and comics but were intolerant of women pretending to be drag queens, and in particular post-op transsexuals still posing as drag queens. The attitude was: why? Why go through all that time, effort and pain to become female and then still hang around the gay bars acting like a screaming – and extremely annoying – tranny?

Letting her halter neck top drop she revealed a pair of breasts so tight and firm that it looked as if the surgeon had stitched a couple of bowling balls under her flesh. The groan from the crowd rivalled the one that went up when England lost to Portugal in the World Cup, and encouraged by this she proceeded to fondle these un-natural mammaries, flicking her tongue in and out obscenely as she pulled on her extraordinarily long nipples.

'You can milk them all night, love, but I doubt if you'll get anything out of them,' a wag in the crowd shouted to much merriment from the rest. The smiles were soon wiped from their faces, though, when she pulled the poppers on the denim miniskirt she was wearing and let it drop to the floor, revealing an absence of underwear and a lot more besides. The spectators gasped as one as she sat on the stool and slowly spread her legs, exposing the recent handiwork of the surgeon. Every chin in the pub, including mine, hit the deck with a thud as she stuck her fingers in and opened it up, leering at the crowd and shouting 'God bless the National Health Service'.

The reaction from the audience was terrifying. They stormed the stage, hurling bottles, glasses, ashtrays, stools and even a table. Someone threw me a golfing umbrella which I opened and hid behind, trying to quell the riot by screaming down the mike for them to pack it in, but to no avail. Eventually I gave up and crawled off the side of the stage and down to comparative safety behind the bar.

It was on the front page of *Capital Gay* the following week with me quoted as saying that I'd 'never seen anything like it – and I've been in the Toxteth riots'. I took a few weeks off from 'Stars of the Future' after that, giving the crowd down the Vauxhall some time to cool off and remember that it was a pub and not a war zone.

Most weekends there was a party to be had somewhere in the area. One house in particular, a squat in Vauxhall Grove, seemed to have a party going on seven days a week, and Judy London – one of the Stars of the Future who sang 'Secret Love' in such a way that had Doris Day been passing and just popped in for half a lager she would have failed to recognize one of her signature hits – who lived in a nice little house round the corner with his partner Reg, was frequently throwing his doors open for a 'do'.

Chrissie had been invited to a party in a high-rise. 'It's a fancy dress party. Come down to the shop and find a costume,' he said. Normally a good root around among the thousands of costumes on offer in the cellars of C. & W. May was like a holiday but I was working day and night that week and didn't have the time.

Chrissie, who despite loathing the clergy and anything to do with organized religion had a penchant for ecclesiastical garments, was standing in the tiny kitchen when I got home from work dressed as the Pope complete with mitre and sceptre, eating Kentucky Fried Chicken out of the box.

'What d'ya think, then?' he asked, licking his fingers. 'It's not too much, is it? Give us a ciggy, will you? I'm gaspin'.'

By the time the rest of our band of revellers had turned up at the flat to get ready for the party I was sulking because I didn't have anything to wear, telling anyone who would listen that I wasn't going. Robbie, who worked behind the bar and had been christened 'Maggie Muggins' by me, was going as Tarzan in a costume that consisted of nothing more than a couple of chamois leathers and a few leather shoelaces tied around his wrists which, considering that he could hardly be described as the Johnny Weissmuller type, I thought took a lot of bottle. George, one of our drinking cronies from the pub, was in the bathroom wearing a tie-dyed body stocking trimmed with a dubious-looking fur doing something elaborate to his face with a box of paints.

'I'm Grizabella the glamour cat,' he said proudly, painting whiskers on with a shaky hand. 'Y'know, from *Cats* . . . "Memory" . . .' Someone else was in the front room dressed in bad drag asking Chrissie if he had a spare pair of tights handy as there was a ladder creeping up the leg of his (Chrissie didn't), and on the sofa casually skinning up on the back of an LP was Noddy.

Looking at this lot preening and posing and having a good time made me all the more desperate to go to the party, but even though I didn't want to go without a costume I was adamant that I was not going to dig Lily out and go in drag.

'Oh, for Christ's sake,' Chrissie said, picking up a pair of dungarees off the bedroom floor, 'put these on and go as Huckleberry Finn. I'll lend you me straw hat as well if you'll shut up giving out.'

I quite fancied myself as Huckleberry Finn, in a gingham shirt under the dungarees that I'd rolled up at the hem, the rim of the straw hat frayed with a pair of nail scissors to give it that authentic whiff of hillbilly chic and, as the finishing touch, a red hanky hanging out of my back pocket.

'It's not bad, considering it's been flung together,' I said, pushing the hat further back on my head to create what I thought was a halo effect. 'I quite suit a hat, don't I?' I added, admiring myself in the mirror. 'What d'ya think, Chrissie?'

'Oh yeah,' he said, taking a pull on a joint before handing it to me. 'You should wear a hat more often – preferably one with a fuckin' big heavy veil.'

Nobody gave us a second glance as we made our way

down the South Lambeth Road, stopping to buy cheap booze in the newsagent's on the way. Dope always used to make me laugh uncontrollably and by the time we were going up in the lift of the high-rise I was in hysterics, setting off Maggie Muggins and Noddy, like a pair of sniggering kids.

'Behave yourselves,' Chrissie tut-tutted. 'These are very respectable people and I don't want to be shown up. Now pull yourselves together.'

'Nobody respectable lives in this block,' Grizabella muttered as we made our way down the landing, struggling to pull his body stocking up where the crutch had sagged almost down to his knees.

'Shurrup, George,' Chrissie said, ringing the bell. 'One of them's a teacher.'

The gentleman who answered the door to us was wearing a pair of leather chaps with nothing but a heavily studded leather jockstrap underneath, and apart from a coarse carpet of black hair that covered the best part of his Herculean body very little else.

'You sure you've got the right party?' he asked, his eyebrows vanishing into his hairline.

'This is Tommy's place, isn't it?' Chrissie enquired.

'Yes.'

'Then we're at the right party,' Chrissie announced, marching past King Kong and into the hall, the rest of us following suit. 'We're expected.'

'What made you think it was fancy dress?' Tommy, the host, asked when he caught up with us in the kitchen, hemmed in the corner by a gang of leather queens.

'Isn't it?' Chrissie asked.

'No,' Tommy replied, laughing. 'It's a heavy S and M party.'

I'd thought as much when I'd nearly tripped over a naked man crawling along the floor on all fours wearing a dog collar and muzzle, being pulled along on the end of a lead by an obese giant dressed from head to toe in leather.

'Come and see the show,' Tommy said, leading us out of the kitchen past disapproving Masters and Slaves who I assumed objected to the presence of the Pope, Huckleberry Finn, Noddy, Tarzan, Grizabella and a tranny as it probably broke the severity of the mood required for such a party. In the dimly lit bedroom, where the air was thick with the smell of sweat and stale amyl nitrate, and bin-liners adorned the window to prevent any light from creeping in, a naked man in a harness lay suspended from the ceiling.

'That's the teacher,' Chrissie hissed under his breath.

'What's he teach, gymnastics?' I asked, watching fascinated as he splayed his legs, wrapping them effortlessly around the chains that attached the harness to the ceiling, making himself comfortable for the big beefy chap who was advancing upon him with one of his hands covered in what looked like Trex.

'I hope they've screwed that into a reinforced beam,' Chrissie said, ignoring what was getting screwed in the harness below, 'otherwise they'll have that ceiling down on top of them.'

'Chrissie,' I gasped, grabbing his arm and making him jump. 'He's got his hand up his bum.'

241

'What did you expect? What type of show did you think they were putting on? *Sooty*?' Chrissie snapped, annoyed at my naivety and still preoccupied with the complexities of how you went about attaching a harness to the ceiling of a council flat.

The human puppet show that I was watching was not that dissimilar to Sooty's act, although I didn't think for one minute that it was in any way suitable entertainment for a children's party.

'Chrissie!' I squealed like a schoolgirl, breaking the heavy silence, unable to believe that the human body could actually tolerate what I was watching without incurring permanent damage. 'He's got his arm in now, right up to the elbow.'

'Dirty bastard,' Chrissie sniffed, wrinkling his nose up in disgust. 'Come on, let's go and see if there's any food knocking about. I could just fancy a pork pie.'

I couldn't, not after what I'd just witnessed, but I followed Chrissie out anyway, having seen enough.

'I can't believe that, Chrissie, I really can't,' I said, sounding like my mother. 'I honestly didn't think it was humanly possible.'

'Disgustin',' Chrissie said, heading for the kitchen. 'Like watching an episode of *All Creatures Great and Small*.'

As I stood in the queue for the bathroom a greasy little chap in a leather biker's jacket at least five sizes too big for him punched me hard in the arse. 'How far do you go?' he mocked. 'How much can you take?'

I looked at his thin weedy moustache growing above his nicotine-stained teeth like an unpleasantly hairy fungus and marvelled at the cheek of this rat in a leather jacket.

'About all I can take from you,' I snapped at him. 'So piss off. I'm not into stuff like that.'

'Then why have you got that hanging out your back pocket?' he demanded, pointing to the red handkerchief I'd stuffed into the pocket of my dungarees. 'You know what that means in the hanky code, don't you?'

The penny dropped. I'd completely forgotten that a red handkerchief in the back pocket meant that the wearer was into what's known in the business as 'that practice that got Julian Clary into trouble on the Comedy Awards' when he made a gag about doing it with Norman Lamont. There was a wide variation on this theme. White meant masturbation, light blue stood for oral sex, and as for yellow and brown, well, use your imagination.

'Oh,' I said, suddenly apologetic, quickly pulling the offending rag out of my back pocket. 'It's not what it means.'

'Then you shouldn't go round sending out signals if you're not prepared to follow them up.' The rat in the jacket turned round in contempt to reveal his own back pockets. 'Look at me.'

Hanging from the pockets of his 501s was an assortment of hankies in every conceivable colour, making his backside look like the rear end of a May Day float. By the look of things this queen wasn't leaving anything to chance. And it would take an open university course before the observer could attempt to decipher this array of multicoloured bunting. What in God's name was a tartan hanky meant to indicate? A predilection for having it off while listening to Jimmy Shand?

'C'mon,' Chrissie said, mooching out of the kitchen. 'Some old dog is being shagged over a sink full of plates in there, hard-faced bitch doing it right in front of me as I was eating a bowl of chilli, put me right off. Let's go home.'

As we were leaving I heard Chrissie saying to the yeti who'd let us in, 'Bless you, my child. Would you like to kiss my ring?'

Chrissie had been using this line as a way of introducing himself all night and like everyone else he'd tried it on the yeti was unimpressed.

'Suit yourself,' Chrissie said cheerfully, sailing off down the landing towards the lift. 'That's the trouble with leather queens – no sense of humour,' he said, smoothing down his cassock and straightening his mitre before our descent in the lift. 'And no sense of style either.'

On 1 February 1985 I finally got my wish and moved into my very own council flat in Vicky Mansions. Karen, a neighbour Chrissie was friendly with in the next block, was vacating her flat for pastures new and offered to sell me the keys for two hundred quid, a practice that was fairly common then. She took me down to the housing office to get my name on the rent book by telling the woman that I'd been living with her for the last five years and wasn't it about time I was recognized as a co-tenant?

I'd worried myself into the ground before this

interview in case the council failed to believe us and my chances of getting hold of that holiest of grails – a flat in the Mansions – were cruelly dashed. As it turned out the woman behind the desk couldn't have cared if Karen had been shacking up with the entire Court of St James, and instead of the grilling that I'd anticipated she simply waved a form in our direction and told us to sign it.

The morning I finally got the rent book and keys I stood in the empty front room beside myself with bliss in the knowledge that finally, at the ripe old age of twenty-nine, I had a place I could call my own.

The vacating tenant had obviously never bothered to decorate for years, and as she'd denied access to work-men when the Mansions were being modernized and given a major makeover in the early seventies the flat still had the original fireplaces, now boarded up and painted a hideous shade of bilious green, all the original light fittings, and Bakelite round-pin plug sockets – of which there were only three in the entire flat. My bath-room was painted a deep chocolate brown, which Karen explained made the room feel womb-like and comforting – even though I secretly thought that it looked more like a cell in the H block that had seen some heavy activity during a dirty protest – while the kitchen, which was a respectable size, was straight out of *A Taste of Honey*.

Russell, a friend of mine from the Vauxhall whom David Dale likened to my familiar, was small, cute and sexy. He came across as a little toughie but was as soft as a freshly dropped cowpat, and although he had the face of a cherub he was as mischievous as one of Satan's imps. It was Russell who offered to change my pre-war electrics. I had my doubts about his skill as an electrician, but he assured me in adenoidal tones that there was 'no need to worry, Liwl'. He removed the solitary socket in the front room and I stood in the tiny hall waiting for his instructions to turn the electricity off and on again when the time came for him to do whatever he was doing in there with two bare live wires in his hands.

'Off, Liwl,' came the cry, and I duly obliged.

'On, Liwl.'

'Off, Liwl.'

I stood in the hall flicking the switch on the fuse box up and down in time to this mantra.

'On, Liwl.'

Click.

'On, Liwl.'

Bored click. A bit slower this time. I was obviously losing concentration owing to the tedium of standing in the dark little hall flicking a bloody switch on and off.

'Off, Liwl.'

Bang!

Following the explosion there was a flash of light and a peculiar smell and through the crack in the half-open door I could see Russell being hurled across the room by an unknown force. I rushed in to find him slumped against the skirting board drooling, his eyes slightly crossed.

'I said off, Liwl,' he moaned in a tiny voice, one eye

looking at me, the other gazing over towards the fire-place. 'Off.'

Sitting on the sofa drinking tea after his impression of Lon Chaney in *Man-Made Monster*, Russell confided in me.

'I went for one of them HIV tests,' he said casually. 'I got the results back today.'

'And?' I asked.

'It came back positive,' he said, drinking his tea thoughtfully before asking, 'What happens now? Is it serious?'

'Didn't they tell you up the hospital?'

'Nah, they just said to come back if I felt ill. I'm not going to die, am I?'

'Don't talk rubbish. After all, it's not Aids, is it?' I said, trying to sound knowledgeable and convince myself in the process that this HIV business was nothing to panic about. 'It's only a virus, like a cold. I bet you it clears up in no time and even if it doesn't I dare say they'll have found a cure for it soon. You've got nowt to worry about.'

That's how naive we were in the early days. We were completely ignorant of the facts about the killer disease that was soon to be labelled the 'Gay Plague' by the tabloids.

'That's what I thought,' he said, obviously reassured by my pathetic prognosis. 'I won't worry about it then. I'll put that light fitting up for you.'

I watched him as he climbed the ladder, trying to put the news of his test results out of my mind together with the feeling of impending doom that, try as I might,

I couldn't get rid of. Listening to him chatting away up at the top of the ladder and enviously admiring his six-pack as he reached up to unscrew the old fitting, pulling his T-shirt out of his jeans, I couldn't imagine life without him. We shared the same evil sense of humour and Russell was a willing and inventive accomplice when it came to winding someone up, usually at my instigation. No, Russell wasn't going anywhere for a long time yet, I told myself. He was too young and healthy to die. Suddenly I wanted badly to rush up that ladder and hug him tight, promise him that everything was going to be all right and swear that no lousy American disease called Aids was going to finish off the likes of my lovely little mate.

Although ours was a platonic relationship we loved each other dearly, but we didn't go in for either private or public displays of emotion or affection. 'I'll put the kettle on,' I gabbled, making my way hastily to the kitchen, fighting to hold the tears back. Standing by the sink I tried to drink a cup of water but the hard lump in my throat wouldn't allow me to swallow.

'Please don't let Russell die, God,' I begged, calling upon this Lord of my childhood who seemed in those days to listen to my frequent petitions and was nearly always quick to lend a helping hand, a God surprisingly easily mollified simply by a reckless promise to 'never be bad again'.

He'd obviously got wise to my ruses since then, as despite repeated supplications in Westminster Cathedral, and the lighting of hundreds of offertory candles to show that I meant business, heavenly intervention was not forthcoming and, like so many, within a few years Russell was dead.

I went to see him just before he died and this time I did hug him tightly, openly weeping for the beautiful boy now degenerated into the wizened, incontinent, senile old man I held in my arms by this appalling disease, the threat of which hung over us all like the sword of Damocles.

First thing I did on moving in was throw a party. Bernard Padden, a brilliant writer and actor from Manchester who had written *The Lion Roars* back at the Donmar, had gathered a group of actors together and formed a company called Nervous Kitchens that was putting on a trilogy he'd written called *The Scythe of Reason* at the Ovalhouse theatre just up the road from the flat.

I was obsessed with these surreal yet very funny plays and to describe the trilogy as off the wall wouldn't do it justice. I went nearly every night that it was on, dragging various friends along with me, some of whom were totally unable to understand my enthusiasm. Chrissie, even though he didn't really enjoy it, was effusive in his praise after the show as he considered every production at the Ovalhouse, good, bad or incomprehensible, to be 'art', and to dismiss one would be seen as seriously uncool. I loved it, and found that enjoyment of this strange trilogy was enhanced if one sat through it heavily stoned.

The first act was set in a café and involved two men who were lovers having an argument while a waitress kept popping in and out to take their order. Reg played one of the lovers and an actor named Kate Ingram fresh from the success of the film *Scrubbers* was the demented waitress. This waitress morphed into a character called Madame in the second act and Kate had a ball with it playing the eccentric medium with a benign grin on a face that she'd partly covered with a face pack. On her head sat a hat similar to Nina la Roche's conch from the Canning Street days, and from under this she'd occasionally reach up and produce a Jaffa Cake and then nonchalantly eat it. Watching her was a master-class in comic timing.

Reg played a homophobic 'geezer', employing all the mannerisms Reg believed geezers had, such as sitting with his legs wide apart resting his arms on his thighs, nodding his head and sucking his lower lip. Bernard had given him an awful joke that he had to come out with during the séance scene that went 'What's the miracle of Aids? It turns a fruit into a vegetable', which made the audience angry and uncomfortable, exactly the effect that Bernard was seeking. Of course Reg loathed having to say it.

Bernard wrote some wonderful dialogue, such as: 'He falls in love at the drop of a hat.'

'Really? I had no idea that plummeting millinery was such a powerful aphrodisiac.'

The last act involved Madame in a nuclear plant, sitting on the floor with her legs wrapped around a bucket doing something with a potato on her head while the rest of the cast danced around her desperately trying not to corpse.

On their last night I threw a party for them in my empty flat, and since Chrissie had told me that the majority of actors who performed at the Oval were vegetarians I made a vegetable stew on the accident-waiting-to-happen gas stove that Karen had left behind. They weren't, so someone went and got a bucket of spare ribs from the Kentucky.

At the party Bernard told me that there was a chance that the play would be transferring to the Latchmere theatre in Battersea and asked if I would be interested in playing Madame, as Kate would be unavailable. Reg was very put out on hearing this news as he wanted to play Madame, and would no doubt have been wonderful. He was far more suited to the role than me, but as I was so desperate to say those crazy lines and be part of the company I jumped at the chance, although the proposed transfer took some time and I didn't get my chance to play Madame until 1988.

With the help of Chrissie, Hush, Russell and Scott I gave the flat a much needed scouring. Karen had not been one for domesticity and the walls ran yellow with nicotine as we washed them. Once they were clean Russell and Chrissie 'threw up' a few rolls of woodchip and lashed a pot of magnolia emulsion around while I painted the windowsills and skirting boards with white gloss: an unimaginative colour scheme, I know, but as Chrissie said at least it was 'clean-looking'.

What savings I had were evaporating fast as I went on a spending spree to furnish my new home. Invading Habitat I bought everything from plates and lamps (which I still have) and blinds (which I don't) for the kitchen and front room. The bedroom curtains Hush was going to run up for me, as despite being offered good money Chrissie had declined, claiming grandly that being a couturier he 'didn't do curtains'. I caught the bus up to Clapham and bought a Carnival gas cooker from the gas board to replace the wartime experience Karen had left behind, rented a telly and video recorder, ordered carpets for the front room and bedroom from a discount carpet shop and, pushing the boat out in Arding and Hobbs, a brand new double bed. Going home on the bus I chain-smoked in a frenzy on the upper deck from the shock of spending so much money and from the excitement of it all.

Chrissie laid the carpets for me, and from a shop at the back of the Mansions that sold ex-catalogue merchandise I managed to furnish the flat for next to nothing. In the midst of my gleaming magnolia front room one thing really jarred, and that was the fireplace. Even though I'd covered the hideous green paint with layers of white gloss it still stuck out like a sore thumb and was not, as interior designers would have you believe, aesthetically pleasing nor in harmony with the ambience of the room. I wondered what lay under all the layers of paint, bought a large tin of paint stripper, and set about scraping off the years. By about three o'clock in the morning a dappled light brown tiled hearth had been revealed.

Attempting to stand up to admire my handiwork was more difficult than I expected and I realized as I tried to focus that I was out of my mind from the fumes of the paint stripper. Sitting on the floor propped up against the sofa, a recent acquisition from Habitat that I was having a lot of trouble keeping clean as I'd stupidly bought it in cream, I closed one eye and took a long cyclopean look at the fireplace. Unfortunately, despite my hard work and consequent possible addiction to a certain brand of paint stripper, the bloody thing was still an eyesore. I sat there and contemplated this anachronistic grate, so out of place among my gleaming magnolia and Habitat acquisitions, and after a while it started to grow on me. There was something familiar about it that I found comforting. It was the kind of fireplace that someone had once sat down in front of to a nice boiled ham tea, or relaxed next to in an armchair listening to the Light Programme on the wireless, or stood in front of and rubbed their hands or quite possibly in Mum's case turned her back on and lifted her skirt, letting her freezing bum feel the benefit of a nice coal fire. As I allowed my fume-fugged mind to wander I felt a real sense of what the room must have looked like during the war years. What this fireplace needed was a mirror above it with a Bakelite clock in the middle of the mantelpiece with a pools coupon and a rent book wedged behind it. There should also be a packet of Players Weights, a couple of bits of something made from brass and maybe an ornament or two, one of which should be religious, and, perched on the far end, a separate shilling for the meter. Instead of fighting this fireplace I was going to make it the focal point of the room and decorate around it. Paint stripper doesn't half make your mind wander.

I found a chimney sweep who came round and proclaimed that I had a lovely clear flue and a strong draw, and after carting a bag of coke back from the garage on Nine Elms Lane I sat down with Chrissie in front of a roaring fire and had a nice boiled ham tea listening to the Light Programme on my newly acquired Bakelite wireless, which remarkably still worked even if it did take five minutes to warm up after being turned on.

Swept up in this wave of wartime nostalgia, Chrissie got me a beautiful shawl from somewhere in the bowels of C. & W. May to drape across the table and a gas mask that reeked of mould which he hung on the headboard of my bed, giving gentlemen callers the wrong idea. I gave it to the drug dealer upstairs who stuffed it with amyl nitrite-soaked wadding and had a ball sitting on his cushions blissfully happy listening to Mahler with a budgie on his head.

David Dale had started up a company called the Kopy Katz and under his direction they performed shows every night for a week at the Union Tavern. Welsh Chris, known to all as Maggie, and his partner John from New Zealand were now running it and living over the shop. The Union was a large pub that had the advantage of a big stage and the unheard of luxury of a custom-built dressing room with lots of mirrors and lights and a sink for us to wee in. It was a great pub to work in and Chris and John became good friends. I helped them move to their new pub, the Aquarium in Brighton, when the Union sadly closed down, carrying a fridge freezer on my own down three flights of stairs after taking one of Maggie's slimming tablets, which must've possessed the same strength-enhancing properties as Popeye's spinach. David's next big production was going to be *Annie* and he asked me if I fancied playing Lily St Regis.

'Go on,' Chrissie said. 'I'd love to make that outfit, all those flounces cut on the bias.' Chrissie and I were on speaking terms of late and he'd been making me a lot of outfits. He really was a skilled tailor but was growing tired 'wasting a five-year apprenticeship and all my fuckin' talents' on rubberized miniskirts and all things leopard print. He was longing to be let loose on a project that would get his creative juices flowing with the force of Niagara.

'Pink chiffon,' he said dreamily, running his fingers through an imaginary fabric. 'Tons of it, weighted and wired so it hangs beautifully and flows when you walk. Shame it's going to waste on your skinny back. Still, I dare say I'll pull the rabbit out of the 'at as always.'

Buying fabric for costumes was, and still is, a pastime that I very much enjoy. Thanks to Chrissie and the lads at Borovicks in Berwick Street Market I'd learned what worked and what didn't, how much fabric was needed and what sort of lining went with it, and how to appreciate the important factors like durability, practicality and value for money over highly expensive, poor quality fabrics that might look fabulous but wouldn't last the course.

Chrissie never got his yards and yards of chiffon as I went for a more practical floral cotton lined with pink satin, out of which Chrissie created a magnificent period costume complete with pill box hat and veil that was worthy of any West End stage.

As the dressing room was packed with twelve queens and a couple of dressers roped in to help I got made up in the bathroom upstairs, in the rooms David shared with two other people I vaguely knew to say hello to around the pubs. As I stood larding on the slap the next door along opened and a man wearing only a towel walked out. He didn't notice me at first and came straight into the bathroom.

'What the hell do you think you're doing?' he demanded angrily, startled by the sight of a shirtless drag queen leaning over the sink.

'What's it look like?' I replied. 'I'm from the department of sanitation. I've come to see if there's any vermin lurking around and from where I'm standing I can see there is.'

'Look, you,' he said, waving a toothbrush at me, 'when I walk into my bathroom—'

'Your bathroom?' I interrupted.

'That's right, my bathroom, I don't expect to find a gobby Scouser giving me lip, so shift your bony arse and piss off back downstairs before you get my boot up it.'

Who would've thought that with those eloquent words of endearment we would embark on a relationship that would last over twenty years.

'I've had a run-in with the most ignorant, arrogant 'ard-faced bastard that God ever put in shoe leather in your bathroom,' I said to David when I returned to the dressing room.

'Oh, that's Brendan Murphy,' David laughed, 'my

flatmate. I've got a feeling you two are going to get on well.'

'In your wildest dreams, Doris,' I snorted. 'From now on I'm getting made up down here.'

However, I continued to get made up in the bathroom over the following week as I was secretly interested in this argumentative, moody, sarcastic, devastatingly handsome man who, I was happy to see, would neglect his waiting boyfriend in his bedroom next door to sit on the end of the bath and talk to me. He was reluctant to reveal much about himself, but I managed to eventually winkle out of him that he was originally from Portsmouth but had recently returned from Spain where he had been teaching English, and was currently running a gay sauna in the Oval. He also reluctantly admitted to being a fan of the Playgirls and of me in particular, which instantly won him more Brownie points, but getting any further information out of him wasn't easy as he was a man of few words.

Our cosy little chats in that bathroom invariably ended up in a row. One such barney kicked off after he'd accused me of being schizophrenic and in need of medical help. He was serious, and when challenged claimed he could think of no other possible explanation for my strange behaviour when on some nights in the pubs I'd be affable and chatty and on others I'd glare at him as if he were shit and I were Ajax.

He had a twin brother, whom I remembered Chrissie saying he'd had a nasty run-in with one night in the Vauxhall.

'Narky little bugger,' he'd said at the time. 'Got a right mouth on him.'

'What's he look like?' I'd asked.

'Like his twin only without the glasses.'

Poor Murphy. No wonder he was confused, for when he wasn't wearing his glasses I'd mistaken him for his own twin, someone I was prepared to loathe on sight without having even met him, purely on the evidence supplied by Chrissie.

As it turned out Murphy's brother Kevin looked nothing like him, although he did have, as Chrissie had remarked, 'a right gob on him'. He dismissed me at first as a necessary evil, although he couldn't comprehend why his brother was having a relationship with some-one who most definitely did not conform to type, being quite unlike the usual brand of cuties Murphy was attracted to. These beat a steady path to his door while Maggie and I would sit in the kitchen below, me making sarcastic remarks on the passing traffic that crept down the stairs, Maggie humouring me, rightly suspecting that my snide comments were born out of jealousy.

Our romance was a very slow starter. I started visiting David Dale and Maggie a lot more often than I usually did, Maggie greeting me in his Welsh lilt with 'You here again, Lil? You'll be moving in next.' I'd also temporarily abandoned the Vauxhall as my regular haunt, instead drinking in the Union, engineering it so that Murphy and I would accidentally bump into each other, get chatting and end up spending the rest of the evening together, slowly getting to know each other until closing time.

Murphy's other flatmate, Joan, who had made the move from Portsmouth with him, was baffled by our behaviour, as any physical attraction that we felt for each other was expressed by bouts of boisterous play fighting. I'd walk in a pub and attempt to drag him to the ground; he'd get me in a headlock and rub my scalp with his knuckles, resulting in a violent struggle that ended up with us rolling around on the floor of the bar.

'What the hell is going on with those two?' a bemused Joan would ask.

'It's more what's not going on,' Chrissie would reply, bored with these constant brawls that had everyone talking. 'I wish they'd get it together.'

Eventually we did. I was on a date with a chap one night and we were sitting in the Vauxhall having a drink before heading off to Vicky Mansions and hitting the sack when at around closing time Murphy appeared.

'Who's this?' he asked, weighing up my date as if he were a freshly exhumed corpse. 'Get rid of him. You're with me tonight.'

I laughed, assuming it was just an attempt to embarrass me, but the date piped up, 'You what, mate?'

'Don't you "You what, mate" me,' Murphy said, hovering menacingly over him. 'You heard me, sunshine. Take a hike.'

'Now just hang on,' I started to protest.

'Shut it,' Murphy said, and turning once again to the date asked him when he was leaving. The date thought for a moment before deciding that I obviously wasn't worth the hassle and finished his drink in a hurry. He threw me a pitying look as he skulked out of the door.

'What did you do that for?' I asked Murphy, trying to sound annoyed with him.

'Cos he's an idiot, that's why. Now do you want a drink?'

We slept together for the first time that night. Up till then we hadn't even kissed and on the bus to work the next morning I realized that I was smitten, content to sit gazing contentedly out of the window at a world that suddenly seemed brighter instead of burying my head in the *Daily Mirror* and tucking into my usual breakfast of salt and vinegar crisps, Coke and a couple of Benson and Hedges.

It was exhausting juggling two jobs and two fellahs, as when I wasn't seeing Scott I was with Murphy. They were jealous of each other at first, giving me frequent ultimatums of the 'either he goes or I do' variety. I couldn't make my mind up as I liked them both and was happy with our status quo even if they weren't.

'You know what you are, don't you?' Chrissie said one night in the pub.

'Greedy?' I offered.

'No, a slag,' he said, mooching off in search of some-one to buy him half a lager.

In the end it was Scott who made the decision for me by moving to New York. He asked me to go with him and even though a new start in the USA sounded an exciting prospect I procrastinated as usual until Scott eventually gave up and went off to the States without me.

I felt the familiar hard lump in the back of the throat when the time came to say our goodbyes over a farewell drink in the Market Tavern. I stood outside the club at the top of the staircase watching him cross Nine Elms Lane until he was out of sight, wondering if I'd passed up a golden opportunity.

'Have I made the right choice?' I asked Russell, who was working temporarily at the Market as a doorman.

'I'll say,' he replied without hesitation. 'He's an actor, i'n't he? They're only interested in one fing.'

'What?' I asked.

'Themselves,' he sniffed. 'Murphy's the one for you, not Scott, and anyway, what you gonna do in New York?'

'I dunno. Get a job.'

'You need a green card before you can get a job.'

'I'll go on the game.'

'You!' Russell cackled. 'You're too old.'

'I'm only twenty-nine for chrissakes.'

'You'll be firty soon and that ain't no chicken so get back in there to Murphy and stop mooning over the other one. You and Murphy are made for each other.'

For a while nobody else existed and we'd spend days on end holed up in the flat watching videos in bed and talking endlessly. Our favourite films were *Darby O'Gill and the Little People*, *The Roaring Twenties* starring Jimmy Cagney and Gladys George, *Love Me or Leave Me*, *The Unsinkable Molly Brown*, Bergman's epic *Fanny and Alexander* and of course *Gypsy*.

That winter it snowed and one early morning after

yet another all-night session sitting up drinking and talking we took a cab to Westminster Cathedral and re-enacted the final scene of *The Roaring Twenties* in which Jimmy Cagney, riddled with bullets from a shoot-out with Humphrey Bogart, staggers towards a church, collapsing on the snow-covered steps before dying in the arms of Gladys George while a policeman looks on.

Chrissie executed the part of the copper while I gave it my all in the Gladys George role, rushing across the concourse outside Westminster Cathedral to catch Murphy as he staggered up the steps.

Chrissie: 'Who is this guy?'

Me: 'This is Eddie Bartlett.'

Chrissie: 'How are you hooked up with him?'

Me: 'I could never figure it out.'

Chrissie: 'What was his business?'

Me: 'He used to be a big shot.'

Chorus of the last few bars of 'My Melancholy Baby' and off to find a café for a bit of breakfast.

I think that it was the first time that Murphy had ever seen a musical as he was a man who preferred football and snooker to Rodgers and Hammerstein, and Kevin, now more perplexed than ever, could not believe that his tearaway twin was constantly declining every offer to roam the West End in favour of a night in front of the telly watching *South Pacific*. Without admitting it, Murphy and I were now officially courting and I found I had a genuine bona fide boyfriend, one that I'd never be able to rein in and tame even had I wanted to, although I'd certainly have an interesting time trying.

Bluebirds should've twittered around the window box, which sadly was full of dead herbs and not daisies, as I leaned over it and hung out the window to take a gulp of the early morning carbon monoxide emissions from the busy flow of traffic on the South Lambeth Road. Love, an overrated emotion as far as I'd been concerned, or at least as I'd always professed until now, was most definitely in the air in Victoria Mansions.

Today was my thirtieth birthday and I had a flat, a fellah and a following, and I couldn't believe my luck. I turned from the window to look at Murphy, lying on his back in bed, half covered by the duvet.

Murphy was one of these annoying people who not only always looked wonderful in repose but was positively stunning first thing in the morning, the swine, and lying in my bed asleep he resembled a fanciful artist's depiction of a romantic gypsy for the cover of a Barbara Cartland novel.

Murphy had been in a long-term relationship with a woman called Celia for years. He loved and adored her, but confused and at odds with his sexuality he took a job in Spain teaching English to give them both some breathing space while he tried to make sense of a painfully difficult situation, and hopefully arrive at a solution.

Celia, who by all accounts was a remarkable woman, had taught at Murphy's school. Their relationship, as you can imagine, caused a bit of a stink at the time with Celia being not only his teacher but an older woman having a fling with a teenager to boot.

Murphy was unfazed by the gossip, as even as a lad he was his own man with a will of iron and a resolve impossible to break, a kindly euphemism for one stubborn bastard. And as far as he was concerned Celia was the only woman for him and that was that. Case closed. His only concern was for Celia and the harm that the gossip might do to her, although she was more than capable of dealing with any detractors herself.

One ordinary morning, as Celia was cycling to school in Gosport, she fell under the wheels of a bus and was killed instantly.

On receiving this shattering news over the phone Murphy flew home from Spain immediately. At the funeral he refused to go in the church, as at the time he held strong opinions about the hypocrisy of organized religion. He considered the funeral service unsuitable and not what Celia would have approved of so he stayed outside, lurking in the doorway and smoking angrily, his heart broken. He moved back into the family home for a while, paying frequent visits to London to stay with his twin Kevin who conveniently also happened to be gay, and together they'd terrorize Soho, their favourite hang-outs being the Pink Panther club, a dive somewhere up one of Soho's seedier streets, and a pub called the Golden Lion in Dean Street, a popular hang-out for rent boys and their clients.

The rent boys loved Murphy, and although he wasn't interested in them sexually I believe he was offered loads of freebies, proposals he assured me that he always turned down, preferring to play a more avuncular role, offering advice and patiently listening to their pitiful stories of how they ended up working the streets. I once stood at the door of this pub shouting up the stairs to Murphy that 'if he didn't stop whoring with those filthy trollops and get himself down here I was going to punch his headlights in', a rant that didn't go down very well with Jack and his partner Ian who ran the Lion and were great friends of Murphy's. I have a feeling they barred me after that.

Kevin could be big trouble when the mood took him and was not one to sit on the fence when voicing his opinions, frequently getting himself into arguments that Murphy would inevitably end up having to sort out. These barroom squabbles would usually end in a fight, and Murphy, no slouch when it came to fisticuffs, would wade in regardless of whether he was out-numbered or not, a quality that I greatly admired.

Over the years the Murphy twins were chased by police, hotel managers, jealous boyfriends and, on one occasion, an angry mob through the streets of Barcelona, and if I was 'born to trouble as the sparks fly upward' as that Christian Brother at my old school had once declared to my mother then I'd met my match in Murphy.

He was now unemployed following a blazing row with the management of the gay sauna, and the evening before my birthday he'd blown the best part of his giro on a meal at Rebato's Wine and Tapas Bar on South Lambeth Road, a romantic gesture that I wouldn't have believed he was capable of. Loving him all the more for this surprising turn-up for the books I chose to ignore the fact, as I mopped up the juice from my garlic prawns, that as he'd blown his giro on the meal I'd probably have to support him for the rest of the week.

But that was last night, when I was still in my twenties. I was thirty now, which in gay years is Neolithic. Still, at least, in the words of the song, I still had my health, which is a damn sight more than a lot of my friends had.

I tiptoed quietly into the kitchen as I didn't want to wake him just yet. He'd had another restless night, his sleep disturbed by another bout of the horrors as he cried out in the dark for Celia. His entire body would shake as he sobbed, calling out her name and frantically twisting the Claddagh ring that had once been hers round and round on his finger until finally, his grief subsiding, he'd lie still. He lost that bloody Claddagh ring one night when, unusually for him, he was blind drunk. He was inconsolable when he found it was missing, as it was irreplaceable, and the next morning in desperation I rang Breda at the Vauxhall to see if she knew where I could buy one. The shop that she suggested in Lambeth Walk had long closed down when I got there, and after searching around the jewellers of the Walworth Road with no luck I eventually went home.

My mother always said that if you'd lost something precious you could petition your guardian angel to find it for you. Putting on the kettle I made a silent plea to mine, not expecting a positive response but employing the usual bargaining process of promising to go to church and so on. And then, as I sat on the sofa sipping my tea, something under the coffee table caught my eye. It was the Claddagh ring. We'd searched every inch of the carpet with a fine-tooth comb over and over again and it would've been impossible to miss, yet now here it was winking at me from under the coffee table.

I was so shocked and relieved to find it that I put my coat straight back on and caught the 88 bus to Victoria and the Cathedral to light the promised candle of thanks. I slipped a tenner in the box as I left only to realize that it was all I had on me, which meant a walk home in the rain.

A guardian angel with a warped sense of humour smirking down on me. Just what I needed.

I was working the evening of my birthday at the Goldsmiths Tavern, a pub where Vic Reeves was a regular with his Big Night Out. Murphy couldn't come for some reason so Vera accompanied me. It was nice to have someone to help with the baggage; when Murphy came with me on a booking he refused to carry anything as he didn't want to be seen as a drag queen's hanger-on and so I'd struggle through the pub while Murphy strolled twenty paces behind me pretending he didn't know me. I was slightly annoyed that he'd refused to come with me to the Goldsmiths but all was forgiven when on my return I found him bashfully standing next to a spray of thirty red roses.

'What grave did you nick those from?' was all I could say, shocked and suddenly shy at the sight of the beautiful floral display tastefully arranged in a plastic bucket on the front room table. To break the sudden tension of the lovey-dovey atmosphere I did what I normally did and leapt on him, dragging him on to the floor in an armlock only to be skilfully thwarted by a cunning move that resulted in me being flung under the table and sat on. As I said, love was in the air.

The Chief Constable of Greater Manchester, James Anderton, had described Aids as a 'self-inflicted scourge' and said that gay people were 'swirling around in a cesspit of their own making'. Mr Anderton claimed to have received these messages as a result of regular and direct communication with God himself. Inspired by Mr Anderton, the south London police raided the Vauxhall Tavern one evening just as I was about to go on. Over twenty police officers descended on the pub wearing rubber gloves as a 'preventative measure against catching Aids' to deal with alleged over-crowding. As a result eleven people were arrested, including Pat's wife Breda who was upstairs watching television with her children at the time. The charge of overcrowding was a poor excuse for a spot of police harassment and such was the outcry among reasonable civilized people following this phoney raid that the BBC's *Heart of the Matter* made a programme about it. The headline on *Capital Gay*'s front page that week quoted me as announcing 'We should riot' from the stage of the Vauxhall, which I did, as I believed that attitudes towards gay men and women were taking a nasty turn that was demonstrated by the frequent witch-hunts orchestrated by our police force.

The tabloids were quick to jump on the bandwagon of paranoia surrounding Aids, persecuting gay celebrities in an attempt to destroy careers and reputations. Kelvin MacKenzie, a fat ignorant oaf who was then editor of the *Sun*, knowingly printed a totally fabricated exposé of Elton John that cited him as paying for rent boys for the many drug-fuelled orgies that he held, even going as far as to state that Elton cut the vocal cords of his dogs as their barking annoyed them. All vicious lies of course, spun to sell a tabloid rag, and Elton, most upset by the claims that he'd silenced his beloved dogs in such a barbaric manner, quite rightly sued, winning a million pounds in damages with the *Sun* having to print a full page apology. The rent boy who had originally sold his sordid tale to the *Sun* later came clean to the *Daily Mirror*, admitting that he'd 'made it all up and only did it for the money and the *Sun* was easy to con'.

The *Daily Star*'s editor Ray Mills was expelled from the National Union of Journalists for his persistent racist and homophobic abuse, not that the expulsion bothered him as he still carried on referring to the gay employees of Camden Council as 'bent' and talking about the poofter persuasion, while up in south Staffordshire Bill Brownhill, the leader of the Tory council, announced that his cure for Aids would be to 'put ninety per cent of queers in the ruddy gas chambers'. A lesbian protester spat at a police officer during a small demonstration against 'the gas man's' comments, the police officer later demanding a blood test in case he'd contracted the Aids virus from her. To explain this hysterical behaviour away a spokesperson for the Police Association blamed the media, claiming that police officers picked up their information about Aids from the press and that it wasn't surprising that they were getting the wrong idea. Indeed.

The government finally stirred itself out of its lethargy and launched a massive ad campaign on television that was meant to be informative as to HIV/Aids and its transmission and prevention but only succeeded in confusing the public further with its histrionic images of icebergs and exploding volcanoes. Queer-bashings were on the increase and the general mood was anti-gay, the police frequently raiding house parties, clubs and pubs for no other reason than harassment.

At each and every venue I worked in up and down the country I named and shamed each and every one of these evil cretins via the medium of Lily Savage.

It was my way of fighting back.

Vera had come to stay for the weekend from Bradford and on the Sunday night the usual suspects gathered for a lock-in at the Elly as we'd been doing for the past few weeks. Gladys, one of the acts from the talent night, was a professional Irish dancing teacher who offered to give us lessons, resulting in a rousing shebeen where we charged around the floor to Irish music with Gladys standing in the middle of us in full drag shouting out instructions.

At around 4 a.m. the police raided. Scottish Andy was unfortunate enough to be holding a drink just as the law swanned in, and this was enough for the south London police, hell-bent at the time on harassing gays, to arrest him.

Vera, slightly the worse for drink, went to Andy's aid, challenging the police in a voice that was incomprehensible even to me. They nicked Vera as well, throwing him into the back of the van with Andy and holding them both in the cells of Horseferry Road police station. Vera was summonsed to appear in court the following week charged with being 'drunk and disorderly on the premises known as the Elephant and Castle Public House', but when he got back to the flat he had a quick cup of tea and a bacon butty, packed his bag and cleared off up to Yorkshire to vanish in the depths of Bradford, leaving me to deal with the coppers when they came looking for him. I was becoming adept at lying to policemen on the doorstep as only the week before they'd turned up looking for Murphy, whom they'd traced to the flat from the car hire company we'd recently hired a car from. A Mercedes had cut him up badly and while the offending vehicle sat at the traffic lights on Portman Street Murphy had taken the opportunity to get out and tell them what he thought of them, kicking the door of the car and denting it to show he meant business.

I gave the police some cock and bull story, hastily made up as I went along, which they seemed satisfied with, and happily they never came back.

The Goldsmiths was a mixed pub popular with the students from the college that rather snootily didn't book drag acts. Adrella and I had got together to form a double act called High Society that he'd once been in with David Dale. I didn't fancy jigging around in a leotard miming to *Cats* or prancing around with no wig on to 'Sweet Transvestite', so the ideas and numbers Peter (Adrella) and David had used that had made the act so popular were quickly abandoned for new ones.

We both wanted to do more live work. It was silly not to, as it was obvious by the reception we both got in the Vauxhall that that was what the audience wanted, but even so, as a safety precaution and to pad out the show, we'd throw a couple of mime numbers in.

Nigel, the pianist from the Piano Bar in Brewer Street, made some backing tracks for us to sing along to. I was reticent at first about singing in public but Peter talked me into it and we picked songs that were easy to fake. 'Oom-Pah-Pah' from *Oliver!* was popular as I could sing it in what I thought was a raucous cockney accent. 'Don't Tell Mama' from *Cabaret* was also a great opener as it was sung/spoken and the lyrics were so easy to parody:

> You can tell our Vera, suits me fine,
> Cos she's in the toilets chopping a line.
> But don't tell Mama what you know.

Peter desperately wanted to do the 'Mickey Mouse Club March', complete with mouse ears and banners, but his masterstroke was coming up with the idea of a song for Skippy.

Skippy, you may remember, was a fox fur that I'd turned into a vent doll. Inexplicably this mangy old fur became a celebrity with an enormous cult following, the cries for Skippy raising the roof of the old Vauxhall every time I appeared there. To keep the momentum going I arranged to have Skippy shot by an unknown assailant, resulting in a headline on the front page of *Capital Gay* demanding 'Who Shot Skippy?' and a subsequent queue down to the Oval to get into the Vauxhall on a Thursday night. There were all sorts of theories as to who actually did the dirty deed, which I kept going for a few weeks until the actual culprit was finally revealed as Lily's evil half-sister (me in a black wig) whose motive was hatred born out of jealousy for her sex-kitten sibling and who has strangely enough never been seen or heard of since.

High Society made their debut at the Union Tavern, the show running for over four hours. Coerced into doing my Cleo Laine impression I sang 'Who Can I Turn To?' while a bemused audience watched and wondered why I was doing Anthony Newley in a curly wig and purple kaftan. We also did our mind-reading act with Peter as the Svengali figure wandering around the audience holding items up for me to guess what they were, while I sat on stage wearing a paper bag over my head as Mrs Lilian Stokes, international psychic, guessing to the audience's surprise each item correctly, thanks to a clever code which if I tell you, I'll have to kill you.

Despite missing their last bus home the audience were very kind and the act went down well, particularly Skippy's performance of 'Manamana', which had the place going wild and provided me with a great way to close the act for many a year to come. Skippy the infallible crowd-pleaser was guaranteed to get them going even if I was dying on my arse. Skippy even gave birth to a stoat called Damien, a piece of vermin Chrissie had found in a drawer at May's and one that lived up to its namesake. I'd wheel this thing on in a baby buggy and have it spout the juicier lines, courtesy of a tape as it couldn't really speak, from the film *The Exorcist*.

Maggie offered us a residency at the Union every Sunday night and Pat, who knew when he was on to a good thing, offered us one at the Vauxhall on Mondays, which meant I was now working there three nights a week. It was little wonder that customers of the Vauxhall thought that I part owned it.

Despite the current atmosphere of anti-gay and Aids hysteria whipped up by the media, the politicians and the religious maniacs, and the increasing number of deaths from Aids-related illnesses of our friends and loved ones, morale was high. Gays and lesbians in general are a pretty tough breed, an indefatigable lot (we've had to be), able to deal with and adapt to any given situation.

I was optimistic. Life was good along south London's Barbary Coast on the rue de la South Lambeth, and I was earning good money, not surprising since I was at it from nine in the morning until midnight most days. Murphy had convinced me it was time to go professional and really make a go of it with Lily. My friend Beryl Chyat had also had a hand in my taking the plunge, pulling me quietly aside one day into one of the interview rooms at work.

'Is there something you've neglected to tell me?' she said, coming straight to the point as usual. 'Are you doing a drag act called Lily Savage?'

She handed me a copy of *Tomorrow*, a short-lived magazine that Katharine Hamnett had launched featuring me, Hush and David Dale in a photo strip entitled 'The Sex Kittens', which was, to coin a well-used phrase, big in Japan.

'What's this?' she asked, waving the offending article under my nose.

I came clean and confessed. Beryl was livid that I hadn't told her earlier and was straight down to the Vauxhall that Thursday to witness 'Stars of the Future' for herself.

The next day I asked her if she'd enjoyed it, not that I had to as she was clearly ecstatic, still riding high from the circus the night before.

'You know you're moonlighting,' she said solemnly after she'd calmed down.

'I know. That's why I kept it quiet. D'ya think they'd sack me if they found out?' I asked.

'No, you daft beggar,' she said, slapping me on the arm, 'this is the moonlighting job, working for Camden. It's Savage you should be concentrating all your time and effort on. Give this up.'

And so I eventually did, but not without a lot of soul-searching and angst at the thought of becoming self-employed. On the flip side, though, I told myself at three in the morning as I sat on the front-room floor writing material to reassure myself that I could do it, I would be my own boss, answerable to nobody, able to sleep all day and stay out of a night, hopefully earning good money in the process.

Splicing together all the gems that I'd come out with

at the Vauxhall – those that I could remember, that is – and the stuff I'd been scribbling down over the past few months, I managed to glean enough material for what I supposed was a fifteen-minute act, nowhere near enough I knew, but sufficient to try out at a birthday celebration at the George IV, an East End pub I'd been asked to appear at.

I'd been fortunate to have a deep well of material to draw from lately thanks to Vera's re-emergence, minus a tooth, from the wilds of Yorkshire and safe return to the Black Cap as a live-in barman, and a couple of Chrissie's friends who had recently arrived unexpectedly at the crack of dawn one morning from Birkenhead saying they were 'laying low for a while'. Chrissie was furious at first when Irene and Karen turned up on his doorstep unannounced but soon thawed out once Irene had rustled up a docker's breakfast followed by a strong pot of tea and a copious supply of fags and news from home.

They were a pair of lovable rogues, two tough ladies who had spent a fair amount of time enjoying Her Majesty's hospitality as a result of their habit of taking things from shops without paying. They were inveterate and highly skilled shoplifters and could spot a floor walker in a department store blindfolded, and both Murphy and I loved them. For me it felt like being with members of my tribe again, hearing that familiar accent rattle around the landings of the Mansions, enjoying sessions around Chrissie's kitchen table listening to conversations that were pure comedy joy. Each time Irene popped round to my flat she'd 'just throw the mop around while I'm here' as she was incapable of keeping still. It was like getting a visit from the 'how to turn a dump into a home' fairy, for she possessed the ability to sort order out of chaos and transform a room into somewhere that suddenly felt homely. It was comforting sitting on the sofa watching the condensation running down the windows from the steam emanating from the kitchen and listening to Irene 'just boiling this bit of cabbage and throwing a bit of dinner in the oven while I'm here'.

The stories about her life that she told me kept me in material for months. She was blissfully unaware of just how funny she was, and her tale of the day she had her coil removed, a form of contraception previously unfamiliar to me that she described as a device having the dimensions of an electricity pylon from which she swore she sometimes heard voices, was a godsend. I took this tragic-comic tale, warped it, and that night Lily was picking up Radio Luxembourg and taxi messages on her coil, much to her embarrassment, as she stood next to a microwave in the queue to pay her bill in the Electricity Board showroom.

Irene came banging frantically on my front door one night wearing just her bra and knickers and a headful of Carmen rollers, shouting that Chrissie's flat was on fire. I gave her a coat and together we ran over to Chrissie's flat to find thick black smoke belching out of the open front door and Chrissie emerging in a pair of baggy long johns and a blackened face covered in soot screaming, 'Evacuate the building!'

He'd put the chip pan on and forgotten about it, distracted by a film he was watching on the telly, and it wasn't till the flames came licking around the living room door that he remembered. Thankfully the fire brigade arrived extremely quickly and put the blazing pan out, but the resulting damage rendered the flat uninhabitable and forced Chrissie to vacate temporarily to a neighbour's. Some evil queen reported back to him that I'd been laughing about it in the Vauxhall, which I had, as the memory of a black-faced Chrissie in long johns still makes me laugh today when I think of it, but Chrissie was highly offended that I found the matter funny and didn't speak to me for months.

The birthday show at the George IV in the East End went extremely well, the fifteen minutes' worth of material I'd worked out lasting over forty-five when I got out there. Time just flew and when I came off I apologized to the compère, Lee Paris, for overrunning. He didn't mind in the least. A few acts hadn't turned up and there was plenty of time that needed filling.

Lee Paris had been working the south London pubs for years. He was one of the first acts I saw when I arrived in London and the sight of him flying down the bar of the Vauxhall on a pair of roller skates was not something you got to see every day. He offered me a bit of advice.

'You're very good, dear,' he said. 'Don't bury yourself in the Vauxhall. Get out and do the rounds. Take all the work you can get.'

And I did.

From a source around the back of the Mansions in Dorset Road, Irene 'just happened' to find herself in possession of a large collection of brand new bed sets – matching duvet cover, sheet and pillowcases – which sat stacked up to the ceiling in Chrissie's front room until Irene could think of a way to shift them.

'Can't you do something?' Chrissie moaned one morning from a gap in the multicoloured bedding that lined the room, completely surrounding him as he sat on what was left of the sofa drinking tea and sucking on a fag. 'Can't you flog them down the Vauxhall?'

'Ay, that's not a bad idea,' Irene said, running out of the kitchen waving a dishcloth. 'A tenner each, a bargain at the price and all good quality gear, one hundred per cent cotton with a bit of something else thrown in that washes beautifully and will last a lifetime.'

I remembered this spiel the following Monday night as I announced from the stage after our first act that I would be selling bed sets from the dressing room during the interval. A lengthy queue formed within seconds, prompting Pat to ask, 'What the feckin' hell is that bowsy selling up there?' I did a roaring trade for quite a few weeks until Pat, more than a little concerned about being busted for selling stolen goods, put a stop to it.

I had a great relationship with this genial Irishman who never seemed to let anything faze him. One Christmas Eve, after a particularly boozy lock-in, he mislaid the takings. As business had been more than brisk the money bag contained a substantial amount of cash. Pat was beside himself, but after searching the pub from top to bottom ten times over without uncovering the missing cash he could only conclude that someone had stolen it, which cast a bit of a shadow over the Christmas night party.

Since I worked the place so often I'd been elevated from the ground-floor dressing cupboard and given a bathroom for my own personal use upstairs. I kept a few costumes in here, piled up in the bath, and on the occasions when I ran out of Cremine I'd run along the hall and nick a bit of cooking oil from Breda's chip pan that did the job but left me smelling strongly of fried food. That night, the big holdall that I kept my drag in lay at the side of the bath where I'd left it, and reaching inside to see if I had any tights that were wearable I came across a large bag containing a wad of notes. It was the missing money, but what was it doing in my bag? I lit a fag and tried to recall what had happened after the pub had closed on Christmas Eve, and slowly the series of events that led to the case of the missing money began, as Mrs Christie would say, to unfold.

Pat was a man who could hold his liquor but on that Christmas Eve, like the rest of us, he had seriously partaken of the Christmas spirit. On his way to put the takings in the safe he'd dropped by the bathroom for a chat and dumped the bag of money on the edge of the bath. It must have slipped down into my bag while he indulged in a bit of play boxing, which he was wont to do when he'd had a few scoops. I had a bottle of whisky with me, and by the time we went downstairs to the bar we had forgotten all about the money. The look on his face when I returned it to him was a picture, and it made his Boxing Day.

* * *

I'd had a great year, one of the best of my life so far, but it was to be the lull before the storm. Like many others, I wasn't prepared for the horror and devastation that lay in wait just around the corner, and blissfully unaware of what loomed ahead I enjoyed every minute of every day.

I'd appeared at the Albert Hall for Fashion Aid, sharing a dressing room with Sandie Shaw and Ann Mitchell, Dolly from the TV series *Widows*, and had been down the Seine on a beautiful boat with Hush and David Dale, LSD booked as the cabaret for a party Katharine Hamnett was throwing to celebrate her new collection. We got ready in a section of the minuscule galley, putting our make-up on in the side of a highly polished fridge freezer as none of us had thought to bring a mirror.

I don't know what kicked it all off. Probably a few petty grudges reared their ugly heads and were transformed by alcohol into a snarling, sniping Hydra spouting extremely cross words that led to our physically laying into each other. I leapt on David, hauling his wig off and pushing him violently against the door which promptly fell in, sending us brawling like two hissing, spitting tomcats on the floor among Ms Hamnett's slightly startled guests.

Hush, resplendent as always in emerald-green sequin and flame-red wig, was chatting politely to the French minister of culture when we landed at their feet. 'Shall we go over there?' Hush said, pretending he didn't know us and steering the minister away from the scene of the crime. 'It's getting a little rowdy in here.'

It took four security guards to prise us off each other, and to prevent further reprisals David was removed from the boat at Notre Dame. We met up again later when Katharine took us to supper at La Coupole, where I threw oysters at David while he sat at the other end of the table weeping like the Mock Turtle.

We made it up the next day. Drunken spats like that aren't worth falling out over and anyway we were going to work in Israel together for a week, so it was best to clear the air.

I'd got the booking through Paul Wilde, an agent I worked for. Paul was a real wheeler-dealer. If you wanted to book an Inuit belly dancer who performed with singing parrots then Paul was your man. He had his fingers in many pies, all of them within the law of course, he'd claim with a twinkle in his eye, but he was straight down the line when it came to the acts. He was one of the good guys and he would never cheat you. I liked Paul a lot. He was bloody good fun and wasn't afraid of a challenge and when Tel Aviv's only gay bar, the Divine club, requested a drag act he booked the Playgirls in.

Hush wasn't having any of it.

'Under no circumstances am I going to bloody Tel Aviv to be blown to bits,' he declared through pursed lips. 'I've seen it on the telly, it's not safe and I'm not going.'

Nothing could persuade him to change his mind. I couldn't go alone as they wanted a mime double act so I went to work on David, who like Hush was also extremely doubtful about going to Israel and didn't want to know. David can be fearless in many respects but he is a natural born worrier, particularly when it comes to his health and safety, and if he has a headache he'll convince himself that it's actually a tumour.

I went back to work on Hush, but just as I was getting him to warm to the idea of Israel he fell off his high heels and broke his ankle, so it was back to David. This time I was more forceful, until in the end he agreed to go.

Parts of Tel Aviv looked as though they'd been thrown together that morning out of materials found in a skip but I loved the beaches, the weather and the food, and I thought the Israelis were some of the most beautiful men and women I'd ever seen.

It was great fun working at the Divine club, which I seem to remember had an Egyptian theme with mock columns and a frieze of hieroglyphics running round the walls.

We were asked if we would perform for the opening of a new clothes shop and had to get changed in the window as there was nowhere else for us to go. They'd sellotaped sheets of paper over the glass in an attempt at privacy but they soon came loose and fell off from the heat of the overhead lighting, and within minutes quite a crowd had gathered outside the shop to watch us getting changed like a couple of Amsterdam tarts until the police arrived wanting to know what was going on.

We also worked in Eilat at King Solomon's Palace, doing two shows a night, the first at five o'clock in front of a packed room full of nice Jewish families who sat open-mouthed and silent with shock all through the show. The late show was a lot better, while the reception we were given at the show we put on for the staff in their club made the entire trip worthwhile.

I picked up a right stunner that night – an Alsatian pup living rough on the streets who took a fancy to me. Eilat wasn't as built up then as it is now, although there were lots of hotels under construction, and the one that we stayed in hadn't even opened yet. Incredible as it might sound, when I opened my door the next morning the Alsatian puppy was curled up asleep outside. Somehow he'd worked out what room I was in and made his way up fifteen floors to stake it out. That was it. I was in love with this hound, and for the rest of my stay in Eilat we were inseparable. Even though on his side it probably had a lot to do with my feeding him regularly, when the time came to go home parting was agony. I'd enquired about bringing him back with me but he would've had to stay in quarantine for six months and I couldn't afford the expense.

I often wonder what became of him. He was smart as a whip and a real beauty. Of course I do realize that he will be dead by now, unless he was the canine version of Noah, who supposedly built the Ark at the grand old age of 480, but the sentimental side of me likes to think that he had a long, happy life. Sadly, the realist in me seriously doubts it.

CHAPTER 9

———

NOW THAT I WAS TRAVELLING THE LENGTH AND breadth of the country on such a regular basis, the train fares and hotel bills were taking a major slice out of the night's fee. I'd also just won *Capital Gay*'s Entertainer of the Year, the only thing I'd ever won since the Easter egg in Miss Bolger's raffle at St Joseph's Primary School. I pretended to be very nonchalant about this award but in secret I was overjoyed, and throwing caution to the wind I bought a car.

As I couldn't afford the Lotus Europa MK 2, the car Tara King had driven in *The Avengers* and the one I desperately wanted, I went for a bright red Citroën BX which I bought brand new on the HP. That car was my prized possession. I'd look out of the window each night to gaze down lovingly at it, parked proudly outside on the South Lambeth Road. It had electric windows, which we all thought were the height of sophistication, and as I couldn't drive Murphy took the wheel and together we covered miles, travelling to venues all over the country in luxury.

It wasn't unusual for me to work Cardiff, London,

Birmingham, Manchester, Sheffield and Bournemouth, all in one week. If we were eager to get home to our own bed then Murphy would drive through the night with an Elkie Brooks tape playing and me desperately trying to stay awake in case he fell asleep at the wheel, not that he ever did as in all the years I spent in a car with him we never had an accident. Murphy was an excellent if aggressive driver, who took no prisoners on the road. God help anyone who cut him up as he'd pursue them in a car chase worthy of *The Sweeney*. We had lots of arguments over this and many a journey was spent in silent anger.

The places we stayed in overnight ranged from decent to dumps. Grim little rooms with damp beds and grubby nylon sheets that sent sparks flying when you got into bed in the dark were a false economy, no matter how inexpensive they were. It was far better for the soul to shell out an extra fifteen quid and stay in a 'proper' hotel, if only for the luxury of a shower. In one such hotel in Cardiff after a night working in one of my favourite venues, the Tunnel Club, we lay in bed watching the telly and eating a box of Cadbury's Roses, pleasantly pissed. We fell asleep and the first thing that greeted me when I opened my eyes in the morning was the sight of Murphy's back smeared in what looked like shit.

I pulled the sheets back. The one we were lying on was slathered, as were my legs, and out of the corner of my eye I could see a lump hanging in my hair.

'Murphy, wake up! You've shit the bed,' I screamed.

'No I haven't,' he said matter-of-factly, patting his backside to check. 'It must have been you.'

I patted my nether regions as well, just in case, and found to my relief that I wasn't the guilty party either. Maybe the room was haunted by a ghost badly in need of an Imodium?

'It's chocolate, you lunatic,' Murphy said, bravely sniffing his fingers. 'You left those bloody chocolates in the bed, didn't you?'

'I did?'

Ding, ding, round one.

Concerned at what the chambermaid might think, I made Murphy get up so I could strip the bed and wash the sheets in the bath with a miniature bottle of shampoo.

'How are you going to dry them?' Murphy asked, amused by what he considered to be the actions of a madman. 'You can't put them back wet. They'll only think we've pissed the bed.'

As I'd been to Cardiff so many times, I knew the city centre pretty well and remembered seeing a launderette. Smuggling the sheets out in a carrier bag, I tracked it down and spun 'em and dried 'em and had them back on the bed by midday checkout, while Murphy sensibly read his paper over a leisurely breakfast.

If we weren't in a hurry to get to the next venue, we took the opportunity to visit the countryside on our way home. Each time I worked the Nightingale in Birmingham, another club that I worked regularly for years and always liked, we'd drive back to London via the Cotswolds. We'd stop off in Woodstock or Witney for something to eat and I'd be let loose around the antique shops. I never came away empty-handed from a trip to a market or an interesting junk shop piled high with what Murphy dismissively referred to as shite.

In York Market on our way back from Newcastle I bought a cheap ceramic statue of a cockatoo that I still have today as it reminded me of Kiki, the bird from Enid Blyton's 'Adventure' series, and in Witney there was a shop that sold all manner of bric-a-brac guaranteed to make me part with the previous night's fee. I once spent twenty-five quid on an art deco muffin dish that had Murphy asking repeatedly all the way home what in God's name did I want a muffin dish for, especially one that cost twenty-five quid, and did I actually know what a muffin was?

Soon the tiny front room of Vicky Mansions was crammed with the treasures that I'd picked up on my many travels up and down the country. Pictures covered my magnolia woodchip while every available surface was loaded with bibelots and curios, ranging from a wind-up gramophone that I had to stuff a towel down the horn of every time I played a 78 on it as it was so loud, to a set of Snow White and the Seven Dwarves garden ornaments that Vera had bought me for Christmas even though I only had a window box.

Murphy and I embarked on our first holiday together to the Greek island of Lefkas, courtesy of a raffle organized by my favourite agent, Paul Wilde, at the Hippodrome in Leicester Square. I'd been asked to draw this raffle and was genuinely amazed to see that the

ABOVE LEFT: Royal Vauxhall Tavern, about to go out and strip.

ABOVE RIGHT: 'But ya are, Blanche, ya are!' Baby Jane, Union Tavern.

LEFT: First appearance ever at the Black Cap.

BELOW: Compering 'Stars of the Future' at the Vauxhall Tavern.

ABOVE LEFT: Hush in full flight.

ABOVE RIGHT: Hush oozing glamour.

LEFT: Dressing room at the Donmar –
Peter Durkin, Hush and Reg.

BELOW LEFT: With Vera giving it our
all as Salvationists, The Fleece,
Bradford.

BELOW RIGHT: Vera.

NEWS

Who shot Skippy?

An assassination attempt took place in the Royal Vauxhall Tavern pub, SE11 on Thursday.

Skippy, the life-long fox fur friend of drag act Lily Savage was attacked and shot several times on stage during a performance of their act together.

The friendly glove puppet who has entertained pub-goers for a number of years was seriously injured in the attack and was immediately rushed away to a secret hideaway clinic, believed to be in the Paddington area.

The landlord of the pub, Paul Thompson, was an eye-witness to the shooting but isn't sure whether or not he could identify the attempted assassin.

"It was all over so quickly," said Paul. "Some maniac ra

Witness

A right 'Royal' riot

A riot broke out at the Royal Vauxhall Tavern on Thursday and some members of the audience stormed off stage.

Fury at bizarre gay showtime

Brighton and Hove Leader
Gazette & Herald and incorporating Brighton News

July 14 1988
Editorial ☎ 606799
Advertising ☎ 694433
10p WHERE SOLD

Hanningtons
SALE NOW ON

BRIGHTON has been slammed the cesspit of Europe over a gay sexy show due on stage on Sunday.

Brighton Council has been attacked by Tory councillor John Blackman for allowing the kinky Royal Burlesk show which features a drag artist and male strip-

'It's more than Brighton's ever seen before'

Exclusive by Anna Wood

Wisdens — whatever your Sports Interest

ALL YOU NEED FOR TENNIS...
Large selection including graphite rackets by Dunlop,

Benny Hill
See page 4...

ABOVE: The Blood Women – me and Hush.   **BELOW**: Doris, Hush, Savage.

RIGHT: Marlene and her nurse, Union Tavern.

BELOW: Old time music hall, the Union Tavern – Lee Paris on the end.

LEFT: Giving it my Vera Duckworth impression for Lynne Perry, the *Street*'s Ivy Tilsley, at the Union Tavern. Like Liz Dawn, Lynne served her time in the pubs and clubs. She gave us two hours of brilliant cabaret and the audience wouldn't let her go. The butch bit next to Lynne is Hush.

BELOW: Cinderella: Ian, Reg, Sheena Sean, Doris, me and Hush.

ABOVE: Barry Stevens having a good feel.

RIGHT: Yep, I'll come clean. That's me as Pinocchio. Don't ask.

ABOVE: Russell, me, Doris – Bournemouth.

ABOVE: Snow White and the Wicked Queen at the Cricketer's.

CLOCKWISE from top left:
The perfect outfit for
a court appearance;
with Beryl Reid at
John Addy's birthday
party; Lily; Regina,
Adrella, Breda, Pat
and me – the Royal
Vauxhall Tavern; early
publicity shot – I think
I'm trying to look sexy.
Either that or I've
been caught mid-shot
picking my nose.

holder of the winning ticket for 'an unforgettable, romantic holiday for two in a stunning resort on the beautiful tranquil island of Lefkas' just happened to be Murphy. It was only later that he told me that he and Paul had identical books of raffle tickets and simply tore the matching number out when I called it. It was Lefkas, and all its promised beauty, here we come.

We landed on Greek soil and stayed there trapped inside a boiling hot plane on the runway for over three hours as no landing docks were available. Of course Murphy and I kicked off, Murphy issuing an ultimatum to the cabin crew that he'd forcibly open the doors himself if they didn't let us off the plane immediately, a threat that fell on deaf ears and was met with the benign smile of a Stepford Wife, infuriating him even further.

Once we'd been released from this flying Black Hole of Calcutta and had cleared customs, we were piled on to an antique coach such as one would expect to find ferrying the campers around Maplin's Holiday Camp. We sat on this for a further hour while Jo, our airhead rep, sorted out the allocations. What struck me was just how placid all our fellow travellers were, taking this hanging about the airport in assorted forms of boiling hot transport as par for the course.

When I questioned the man behind me about this he simply said, 'Ah well, welcome to Lefkas.'

'That's if we ever bloody see any of it,' Murphy snarled, rising from his seat and going in search of Jo. She was hovering outside the coach looking anxious as she consulted her clipboard, wondering what she was going to do with the excess of holidaymakers. Our numbers didn't tally with her list. Eventually some sort of decision was made and the coach pulled out of the airport car park and off to somewhere called Nidri, which sounded to me like a Welsh brand of toilet cleaner.

Jo did her stuff on the mike, delivering the standard patter that she'd learned in her introductory course on how to be a travel rep, jollying us all along and getting us to stand up and introduce ourselves.

'She can fuck off, the daft cow,' Murphy muttered, a sentiment that I could only echo.

We were taken to a small hotel on the edge of an even smaller beach that seemed very pleasant at first glance, until I spotted the infestation – not of rats or cockroaches but of a group of jolly married couples and their progeny swapping suburbia for Greece for a fortnight. One of the men, fat and over forty and wearing a pair of swimming trunks that could only have belonged to a six-year-old they were so pornographically tight, greeted Jo like a long-lost daughter and she in return giggled gratefully. Here was a satisfied customer she could present to the Grinch, now sitting on his suitcase unsuitably attired for the sunny Greek weather in jumper and jeans, and sulking like a brat at the prospect of being stuck for a bloody week with the Waltons.

'Hi, I'm Mick,' the man said, bounding over. 'Welcome to our happy camp.'

'Tenko,' I muttered gloomily.

'It's a beautiful spot,' Mick went on, 'and there's absolutely loads to do. We normally have a group barbecue every evening on the beach – we're great believers in group activities here – and then the kids put on a show for us afterwards while us mummies and daddies sit back with a beer.'

He winked and mimed a nudge, nudge movement with his elbow in Murphy's direction. Murphy remained impassive and silent throughout this declaration of fast living, while I just moaned from my perch on my case behind him.

'Wait till you meet my lad,' the man crowed, turning his attention to me. 'He's nine going on fifty, a regular Paul Daniels he is, always trying out card tricks on you. He's got a miniature guillotine that he'll make you put your finger in, very clever trick it is, although there's no need to worry. I can promise you'll have all your fingers still intact when you go home.'

'Ohhh . . .' I moaned again, only this time from deep despair.

'And then there's lovely Jo over there,' he prattled on, drawing the life essence out of my body with his depressingly boundless enthusiasm. 'She organizes some great, and I mean Really Great [here he did the wink and the nudge, nudge action again] theme nights. You've just missed the Abba party.'

'What a shame,' I said, suicidal by now.

'There's a Roman Orgy on Thursday night,' he went on relentlessly. 'And me and the wife are . . . oh, hang on a minute, don't go away, there's my lad. I'll just go and fetch him—'

'Murphy,' I pleaded, seizing my chance as our tormentor took off in the direction of a boy waving an inflatable baseball bat, 'I'm not staying here and that's final. Not for a monkey up a stick. I am not spending a week with this bunch of naffs with their barbecues and community spirit and their rotten bloody kids with their card tricks and—'

'Everything all right?' Jo asked at what was probably the most inopportune moment in her career to date.

'No, it's bloody not,' I barked, all self-control now lost.

'We're just getting the room sorted out,' she stammered. 'I'm afraid it doesn't have a balcony or a sea view though, we're heavily overbooked you see . . .'

'Here he is, here's my lad,' the man in the obscene trunks said proudly, bounding back with a woman and kid in tow. 'And this is my wife June, better known as Loony June.'

'Why?' I asked.

'Cos I'm crazy, that's why!' June screeched, giving me a little push that nearly knocked me off my case. 'I can't help myself, can I, Terry?'

'Murphy . . .' I pleaded, adopting a voice actors use on *Casualty* just before they take their final breath.

'Sorry, mate,' Murphy said, thankfully springing into action at last. 'We're not stopping, we're moving on,' adding menacingly, 'aren't we, Jo?'

It was nightfall when we arrived at what Jo had described as a 'beautiful villa that has only just been completed'.

'Each of our villas has a housemother,' Jo told us gleefully. 'She organizes activities and bosses you about. You've got Freya, you'll adore her.'

We didn't. Freya wafted about in bare feet and a

voluminous kaftan, a garment that could've easily accommodated a wedding party of sixty. Her hair was unkempt and unwashed to show that she was Bohemian, and she rattled a selection of metal bangles ('a gift from an artist friend when I lived in Marrakech') that would've drowned out Big Ben.

Our room was empty apart from two very narrow single beds with a little pine bedside cabinet between them and a child's pine wardrobe. On the wall hung a cheap print of a Swiss mountain scene, a peculiar choice, I thought, for a Greek villa.

'Is this where Heidi and her grandad normally sleep?' I asked Freya. 'I'd hate to turf them out of their room.'

'It's got a lovely balcony,' Freya said, ignoring me. 'You share it with next door, a lovely girl called Shelley. She's a lot of fun and I'm sure you'll get on, she's extremely laid-back.'

Laid-back was an apt way to describe Shelley as she spent the entire holiday staring at her bedroom ceiling with the entire heterosexual male population of Lefkas banging away on top of her. Shelley was extremely vocal in her lovemaking and the paper-thin walls of the villa did little to drown out her pleas as she implored the latest hairy beast to go on doing whatever he was doing, only faster and harder. I'd lie in bed dreaming up fates worse than death for this slapper who, when she was actually vertical for a change, would clack noisily around on the marble floors of the villa in high heels, and when she was hit by a speedboat and temporarily concussed, rendering her blissfully silent for a day, I can't say I was sorry.

Our villa was unfinished, the plumbing still not really up to dealing with its residents' needs plus those of the endless stream of Shelley's gentlemen callers. Showers became a luxury, as did hot water, and the appalling Freya would shout, 'Remember to put your soiled toilet paper in the wastepaper bin and not down the lavatory after a shit,' each time one of us went into the communal bathroom.

The villa had been built on a thriving mosquito farm, or so it seemed from the number of the little swines that invaded our room each night, foiling Murphy's efforts to keep them at bay. He'd seal all the windows and the balcony door despite our room having no air condition- ing and turn all the lights off apart from the bedside light. It was OK, he said, to leave that one on as the two-watt bulb gave off a light so weak that a mozzy with binoculars wouldn't be able to find it. After spray- ing the room heavily with some toxic chemical guaranteed not only to kill mozzies but all fauna, flora and human life within a ten-mile radius, he'd light a number of coils around the room in an attempt to smoke them out. Curls of acrid smoke rose eerily in the dim yellow light, making the room look as if we were in the process of conducting a black mass. Adding to the fumes from the spray, the smoke made it near im- possible to breathe.

God help me if I left a window open and put the light on, for this was a hanging offence. Each night we had blazing rows over it with Murphy shouting, 'Get that light out!' like an ARP warden during the war.

Murphy could and would eat anything, unlike me. I

was and still am (although nowadays not quite as bad) a picky eater and after I discovered that my steak was actually goat meat I existed on a diet of fruit, ice cream, crisps and ouzo.

I hated every minute of my stay on Lefkas. Even though I've been interested in Greek mythology since I was a boy and in the burlesques of Aristophanes more recently, I've never set foot in Greece since, although I'm contemplating remedying that one day soon.

At the airport a different rep to Jo approached us.

'Oh, there you are,' she said, all smiles. 'We've been looking everywhere for you two, you naughty things, moving without telling us. Now which one of you is Brendan?'

'I am,' Murphy said. 'Why?'

'Well, you see, your brother has been ringing every day, desperate to get hold of you but as I've said we couldn't locate you . . .'

'That fool Jo knew where we were,' Murphy pointed out. 'Did my brother leave a message?'

'No he didn't, he just said it was very urgent that you called back. Jo is no longer with us, she's been transferred to the mainland . . .'

Her words died on her lips as Murphy rushed off in search of a phone box. After ringing his parents and getting no reply he had no choice but to board the plane and spend the next few hours agonizing over what might have happened at home.

'I bet something's happened to Homil,' he kept saying. Homil was his mother's name. 'I just know it's Hom, she's died, I just know it.'

It wasn't his mother, it was his father who had died. Tearful members of the family were there to meet us at the airport, to break the news to Murphy and take him back to Portsmouth.

On the train back to London I reviewed the week's events in my mind. I came to the conclusion that the reason we'd had such a lousy time, culminating in tragic news on our arrival home, was because we came about the damned holiday by dishonest means. I hadn't heard about karma yet but had I done so then it would've offered the perfect explanation for our disaster of a Greek holiday.

The death of Murphy's father prompted me to pay a long-overdue visit to my parent.

'You're looking well,' my mother said as I walked through the back door. 'A tan suits you, although you'll pay for it in later life. Look at my face, me cheeks look like an accordion, they're that bloody wrinkled.' She seemed smaller since the last time I'd seen her and her voice lacked its usual timbre.

'How are you, Mam?' I asked, giving her a kiss on the cheek, something I didn't normally do as we were not a particularly demonstrative lot.

'Well, apart from these rotten varicose veins throb, throb, throbbin' and the bunion on me toe crippling me and those new tablets that the doctor's put me on giving me dizzy spells and the blinding migraines that I'm getting, I'm all right thanks.'

It was nice to be home.

'What d'ya fancy for your tea?'

I fancied making the pilgrimage across Mersey Park to pay homage to 'the Duchess', as Mrs Cunningham, the proprietor of the finest fish and chip shop in the world, was fondly known. I still fantasize about Mrs Cunny's peppery fishcakes and her chips cooked to perfection in dripping as much as I did then, but unfortunately that good lady had long retired, taking her secret recipes with her.

'Is the Chinese takeaway still open in Downham Road?' I asked my mother.

'Yes, that is, but the wool shop's gone, the place is going to the dogs. Have you seen Borough Road? It's like a war zone, every shop boarded up and derelict, and as for Oxton Road, mother of God, it's got a porn shop.'

'There's pawn shops everywhere, Mam, it's a sign of the times. People are skint.'

'Not pawn, porn,' she corrected me, lowering her voice in case Dot-Next-Door heard her. 'Filthy books and dill-dolls and in Oxton Road as well. Who'd have thought it? The place will be crawling with whores next.'

Ten minutes later, after recovering from the fit of uncontrollable laughter brought on by my mother mispronouncing 'dildo', I managed to compose myself sufficiently to enquire how she was so knowledgeable about the stock available in the Oxton Road sex shop.

'Vera Lalley told me. She went in once for a nose – you know what Vera's like, she doesn't give a bugger. She was telling me about it in the casino the other night.'

'The what?'

'The casino at the top of Oxton Road, I was in there with Vera last week.'

'You were gambling?' What had been going on in my absence?

'Only a couple of bob on the roulette table,' she said casually in the manner of Omar Sharif. 'And I won twenty quid.'

'You didn't go and lose it again, did you?' I was fascinated by the notion of my mother at a roulette table.

'No,' she said, 'I split it with Vera and we had chicken and chips and then these two fellahs bought us a drink.'

'What two fellahs?' So, as well as booze and gambling, she was now cavorting with men? What would the Union of Catholic Mothers have to say about this? She'd more than likely have her badge torn from her cardigan and be forced to hand in her statue of Our Lady.

'I don't know, just two fellahs, nice they were, bought us a couple of drinks. They were just lonely, you know, being friendly, they were down from Glasgow on business. I got a taxi home, four quid he charged me. I gave him fifty pee for a tip. Half one in the morning I got in, God knows what Dot'll think next door.'

'What were you doing in a casino in the first place?' I asked, curious as to what had brought on this turn-around in my mother's behaviour. Was Vera Lalley leading her astray?

Vera had been a neighbour of Aunty Annie and Chrissie's in Lowther Street before those perfectly reasonable houses were demolished, victims of the development purge of the late sixties. She was a particular favourite of mine, famous for being able to play anything by ear on the piano as well if not better than Winifred Atwell. Vera was Aunty Chrissie's best friend and fellow member of the Lord Exmouth public house ladies' darts team. Her dark eyes sparkled with mischief and life was never dull when she was present, her corncrake laugh echoing around the room as she told us of her latest escapade with the skill and timing of a highly accomplished comedienne. Just writing about Vera and remembering her vivacity and optimistic outlook makes me smile.

'Well, I'd been down to the market, you see, to get a nice leg of lamb from that butcher's,' my mother said, settling down in her chair to explain. 'And I thought I'd walk up Grange Road to see if I could get myself a new leccy blanket from TJ's before they closed. Mine's had it, I'm just waiting for it to burst into flames, it's that old. Anyway,' she went on, picking absently at a run in her tights, 'I bumped into Vera coming out of the pub.'

'Who was coming out of the pub? You or her?'

'Vera, silly, she dragged me into McDonald's.'

'McDonald's?'

'Oh yes, we've gone all mod, there's a McDonald's on Charing Cross now. I had a cheeseburger and some chips. No plate or anything, you had to eat them with your fingers off a bit of paper on a plastic tray. Seemed clean enough though, the lavs were spotless.'

'Go on.'

'Then she says to me in the pub—'

'The pub?' I interrupted.

'That one on the corner of the Cross Uncle Al used to go in with Willy Fawcett. Vera dragged me in, I only had a port and lemon – so she says to me, do you fancy popping into the casino for a bit, Molly? And I said I'm hardly dressed for a casino, Vera, and what am I going to do with me two bags of shopping and me leg of lamb? And she said I could stick them in the cloakroom, which I did. It's a very smart casino, better than the last one I was in.'

'And when were you last in a casino?' I asked her, growing increasingly fascinated by my mother's apparent double life.

'In the Isle of Man with your dad. You couldn't see a thing, it was that dark, and there was a woman in the lav who expected a tip just for turning on the tap and handing you a paper towel. I gave her a couple of coppers though.'

'And what time did you go to this casino with Vera?'

'About half seven.'

'And you didn't get home till half one?'

'Says he who spends the night out tomcatting until the early hours. You're not the only one who can have a bit of fun, you know, so don't be condemning me to a life stuck in the house on me own. I'm a free agent and I can do what I like and if I fancy a bit of an adventure, not that I'll be doing it again, then it's no one's business but me own. Now, what are you having for your tea?'

At about two o'clock in the morning I was awoken by gunshots coming from my mother's bedroom. As I leapt out of bed the thought came into my mind as I looked around for a suitable weapon that perhaps she'd crossed a couple of gangsters in the casino and they'd turned up to avenge their honour.

'Jesus tonight,' I heard my mother shout. As I rushed into her bedroom clutching a wire coat hanger to fight the gangsters off with, I was hit in the face by a spray of water. Had the bullets gone through the ceiling and burst a pipe?

'What's going on?' I shouted.

'What d'ya think? Bloody ginger beer.'

Was my mother using cockney rhyming slang as a term of abuse? Surely not.

'The ginger beer,' she said irritably, pointing at some bottles lined up against the side of the wardrobe and pouring forth a mountain of frothy liquid. 'It's exploded. I must've used too much yeast again. I can never get it right. I put them in here out of the way of the kids. Now help me move the rest of these bottles into the lav in case they go off.'

Sleep was disturbed at regular intervals throughout the night by the sound of corks popping in the toilet, and in the morning Dot-Next-Door said she could hear someone messing around with fireworks all night, either that or someone was using explosives to break into the factory in Holt Road and should she call the police?

As I said, it was nice to be home.

Before I went back to London I made the trip to Landican Cemetery to visit my father's grave with my mother. We stopped by to see Aunty Anne on our way home and found her busy whitewashing the inside of the large cupboard that had once stored coal, before the advent of the gas fire.

'I just thought I'd throw a bit of distemper up those walls,' she said cheerfully. 'Wait till I rinse this brush out and I'll make a cup of tea.'

It was odd not to find Aunty Chris sat in her chair wearing the ubiquitous nylon housecoat, her head full of curlers and her sucking on a fag while studying the racing page. The flat felt empty without her and, like my mother, Aunty Anne seemed to have shrunk.

'What do you think of these Aids, Molly?' she asked my mother, drying her hands on a souvenir tea towel from Norfolk.

'Not much,' my mother said, taking her mac off. 'They taste foul and I never lost any weight on them.'

'No, not those Ayds, the other ones,' Aunty Anne said, flicking a fly with the tea towel. 'That new priest at mass said he'd heard that some members of the congregation were concerned that you could catch it from drinking out of the chalice at communion. What do you think?'

'I wouldn't know what to think,' my mother sighed. 'A woman on the bus told me you can catch it off toilet seats and from glasses in pubs, but that sounds a bit far-fetched to me. I wonder how poor Rock Hudson caught it?'

'Well, the priest told us that, as there was no evidence to prove the rumour and as he doubted that there were any homosexuals in the congregation, we were perfectly safe to take communion,' Aunty Annie said, heading off to make the tea.

'And how does he know there's no homosexuals at St Michael's then?' my mother shouted after her.

'Because I don't think homosexuals go to mass,' Aunty Anne replied from the kitchen.

'Don't talk daft, Annie,' my mother said, tut-tutting. 'The Catholic Church is littered with them. Why, in Ireland if a fellah doesn't fancy women he says he's had a vocation and becomes a priest. Not that I'm saying every priest is a homosexual but I'm bloody sure there's a few lurking about.'

'God forgive you, Molly,' Aunty Anne said piously, bringing the teapot in. 'Do you want a biscuit with your tea?'

I went over the road to Billy Lam's Chinese chippy to seek solace in a prawn curry with chips. All this talk of homosexuals coming from my mother and Aunty Anne was making me a little uncomfortable, especially any mention of Aids. I was trying to convince myself that it would soon be over and a cure found.

But it wasn't. The Spectre of Aids, as some of the press often dramatically called it, had now seriously ridden into town, bringing a vast army with it and wiping out thousands of our community – talented, brilliant men who had made enormous contributions to the theatre, ballet, the arts and music. All those incredible men bravely continued in their chosen profession until ill health finally forced them into retirement, hospital and inevitable death.

Regulars of the Vauxhall would suddenly vanish, re-emerging as shadows of their former selves, emaciated and frail, their faces bearing all the tell-tale signs that we had come to recognize: the sunken cheeks, the yellowing skin, teeth that appeared to be too big for the mouth, the unbearable sadness in the hollow eyes that burned brightly in skeletal sockets and called to mind the victims of the Nazi extermination camps.

Death became a way of life and when I wasn't visiting friends in hospitals I was at a funeral, often returning home to listen to my answerphone telling me that a friend I'd only just visited that morning had died. Reflecting on this in those dangerous wee small hours, I wondered if I myself was a grim reaper. Just lately everyone I came into contact with seemed to die and a visit from me to a hospital bedside would signal a fast-approaching demise.

The Westminster Hospital, now a block of fancy apartments, had an excellent Aids unit on the top floor, overseen by the remarkable Professor Brian Gazzard. Professor Gazzard, a pioneer in Aids research, was approachable and practical when it came to dealing with sensitive issues, for many of the parents of the patients in his care didn't even know that their son was gay, never mind dying of a terminal disease. Professor Gazzard spoke out against hypocrisy and fear generated by the media and deserves a medal for his continuing work in the fight against Aids.

The Salvation Army were regulars on the wards, practical and efficient as always, proving that they really were an army and a compassionate, non-judgemental one at that. I'd watch them in the day room, my respect growing each day as I saw them console the parents and lovers of the recently deceased. Through the long hours of the night they would tend to those who were alone in their final moments, then organize and pay for their funerals. The Quakers were another group of good people that I have the greatest respect for as they came frequently, volunteering to help when others wouldn't dare.

Lily took on a different role during those dark times, as did the majority of the acts. Our job was to boost morale, keep the spirits up and, most importantly, to make our audiences laugh, allowing them to forget for a brief while about this deadly killer that was sweeping through the gay community with a speed comparable to that of a bush fire.

I had frequent visits from anxious young men in the dressing room of the Vauxhall, all of them wondering if they 'could have a few words'. I always knew what was coming by the look on their faces and the oh so familiar opening line, 'I went for a test last week . . .'

A nineteen-year-old I'll call Tim broke down over the sink, dissolving into tears as he told me that he'd just learned he'd tested positive.

'But I've only slept with two men,' he sobbed. 'How is it possible?'

Aids wasn't selective, it didn't matter how many people you'd had unprotected sex with, it only took one who was carrying the virus to become infected.

When Tim went blind and lost the use of his legs I went to visit him in the Middlesex Hospital.

'You'd better put these on,' the nurse said, handing

me a mask and gown as she led me to a room with yellow tape across the door.

'I don't need them, thanks,' I'd say as I pushed back the curtains surrounding the bed, to which she'd reply, 'Your choice.'

The funny, pretty little design student who never missed a Thursday night at the Vauxhall and who had so much to live for now lay on the bed, blind, paralysed and disfigured by sarcoma, holding his mother's hand as she sat quietly by his bedside.

'He's just woken up,' she said gently. 'Are you a friend?'

I introduced myself to her and then bent down to kiss Tim.

'You came,' he said. 'Mum, this is the first person I told when I found out I was positive.'

We made polite conversation for a while, asking the usual banal questions one asks around hospital beds, 'How are you feeling?' and 'Are they looking after you OK?'

Tim's mother excused herself, leaving us alone for a while. 'Call me,' she said, the pain in her eyes belying the smile on her lips. 'If he needs anything, I'll be in the kitchen.'

We chatted quietly and just before I left Tim I asked him why he chose to tell me out of everyone when he was first diagnosed HIV positive.

'I didn't tell you,' he said, 'I told Lily.'

I went in search of his mother to tell her that I was leaving.

'Thank you for being his friend,' she said, struggling to keep her composure. 'He's a wonderful little boy, you know, I've never heard him complain once, not once. I don't know what I'm going to do without him.'

I took the stairs down instead of the lift in case anyone should get in and see me crying.

There were benefits and fundraisers held in every pub and club to raise money for hospices, the Terrence Higgins Trust and the London Lighthouse. Every act on the circuit turned out to support them. I did at least three charities a week, sometimes more, and between us we managed to raise thousands of pounds. Adrella and I did regular shows on the Aids ward at St Mary's in Paddington. I'd drag up as a nurse and dispense red and white wine from cardboard urine bottles to the nurses and patients. At Christmas it was particularly difficult to keep a smile on your face. Even though there was a celebratory air on the ward, it was tinged with sadness and a desperation to enjoy the moment as we all knew that the majority of men lying there and some of their friends would not live to see the New Year in.

I sat on the bed of an old friend from the Market Tavern, his youth, health and handsome good looks ravaged by Aids but his sense of humour still very much intact.

'Is there anything you'd like?' I asked

'I suppose a wank's out of the question, is it?' he replied wryly. 'Failing that I'd love a fag, but you'll have to hold it for me as I can't use my arms.'

I lit the fag and held it while he took a few drags.

'I needed that,' he said, coughing and spluttering, 'but no more, thanks.'

When I looked around for somewhere to put the fag out, he said, 'Don't waste it, smoke it.' The other people in the room, a couple from a charity, a young intern and some nurses, watched me intently to see what I'd do. Would I smoke a cigarette that had just left the lips of someone dying from Aids?

Dismissing any doubts of my own, to the amazement of the group I took a drag, not wishing to insult my friend and make him feel like a leper. It was still uncertain whether or not the virus could be transmitted by saliva but as this was a theory I didn't believe I was happy to sit and share a fag with an old pal.

Working the Vauxhall was akin to entertaining the troops at the front. You never knew who would be missing from the audience the next time you stood before them, which one would be the next to die, not from a sniper's bullet but from something equally deadly.

In the war against Aids, the Vauxhall, like so many other gay pubs and clubs, was in the forefront. It was no longer fashionable to be gay – homophobic attacks were now rising alarmingly. Gays carried disease and were solely responsible for the epidemic that was killing them off. Why should we be bothered, some people said. They have no one to blame but themselves, let it kill them all. Such talk made me boiling mad and I'd rant from the stage, expressing my feelings through Lily, trying to get the point across that we were all in this together, boosting morale and hopefully easing the burden in the process. I protected my gay audiences as fiercely as Lily guarded her two kids, Bunty and Jason, and wouldn't think twice about leaping off the stage and belting any disrespectful heterosexual who'd wandered in with his mates 'for a laugh' and stepped out of line.

The cabaret acts, drag or otherwise, fought like Trojans against ignorance and prejudice and have, apart from those of my generation, mostly gone unrecognized.

After Peter (Adrella) died in 2011 from cancer I was sent a copy of a blog that read: 'There was something about drag back then that forged the identity of many a gay man. The gratitude I feel to Adrella, Lily Savage, Regina Fong et al isn't confined to appreciating the bloody good entertainment they provided. They affirmed us all when few others did. They made the "gay scene" a less threatening place. They helped build a community during the darkest days of the epidemic which was killing so many of us.'

Other tributes poured in. 'The drag queens were and are the original freedom fighters for all lesbian, gay and transgendered persons. We owe them our lives.'

Thank you for that, Sebastian Sandys and Father Bernard Lynch, and when people ask me if I still mind being referred to as a 'drag queen' by the press, which I don't by the way, it's remarks like yours that make me extremely proud to belong to that extraordinary and much maligned group of entertainers.

Adrella had been offered two weeks' work in Finland if he could get a trio together. I signed up, as did Ebony (John), another act on the circuit. Both Adrella and

Ebony had been before and knew what to expect, whereas I was blissfully ignorant about the place and was looking forward to visiting and working in this Nordic country.

'They may appear icy, the Finns,' I informed Adrella and Ebony, 'but sexually they're very liberated and extremely friendly, or so I believe.'

'Really,' Adrella said flatly. 'You just keep believing that then.'

The first sight that greeted us as we piled off the train at Tampere station with mountains of luggage were posters stating 'AIDS TRAVELS ON TOURISTS!'

'Charming,' I said to Adrella. 'Talk about a warm welcome.'

There were further cheery welcomes awaiting us. The manager of the Black Emmanuel club we were working in was a surly bastard who insisted on searching our luggage for booze. Alcohol was illegal backstage in Finland, as were drugs, dogs, breathing and laughing.

The walls of the filthy cellar dressing room we found ourselves in were plastered with abusive graffiti: 'Abandon hope, all ye who enter here' some wag from a rock band called Stiff Lightning had written over the door, while acts who'd worked there previously had devoted an entire wall to describing the demerits of the club. It was hardly an encouraging sign, that and the hostile attitude from the staff in the kitchen adjoining our slum, and I wasn't relishing spending a fortnight here.

'Never mind,' Ebony said, forever the optimist, 'they might like us.'

They didn't. They hated us and sat glaring and silent throughout our half-hour spot. Ebony was black and when we walked through the city centre on our way to work with him people literally stopped in their tracks, blatantly staring open-mouthed, as if the African Queen was parading down the high street on the back of an elephant with a retinue of dancing girls in attendance.

'What are you bloody looking at?' I'd ask, somewhat childishly. 'You wanna photo?'

Ebony rose above it majestically, sailing up the high street to the club in Chanel sunglasses and trailing scarves.

We'd been told that Finland was a country of heavy drinkers. This was evident from the number of dead drunks sprawled across the pavement every Saturday night, far more than in the pedestrian zone of Copenhagen, which was like a Temperance Society meeting compared to this lot. Surprisingly, considering they drank alcohol like water, there were hardly any off-licences, and the few that there were only opened at certain times during the week.

I was delegated to go and buy some booze and when I finally managed to find an off-licence, located in a quiet street some distance from the flat, I had to join the end of a very long queue.

'A bottle of vodka, a bottle of gin and three bottles of whisky, please,' I asked the formidable matron in the chemist's white overall behind the counter.

'Three whisky?' she questioned, looking at me pityingly as if I were a raging alcoholic lying face down on the floor of the shop in my own vomit. 'Three?'

'That's right, three.' I battled on bravely, refusing to be intimidated by this dragon.

'Are you sure three's enough?' she sneered.

'Actually no,' I replied, seizing my chance to wipe the smug look off her gob. 'Make it four.'

It was a pyrrhic victory, for as well as having to carry six bottles of booze home in a paper bag I'd had to spend an outrageous amount for them.

We had the booze, now to root out the local gay scene. What did gay people do in this one-horse town apart from either move or drink themselves to death? To find out, Peter asked one of the kitchen staff who seemed less unfriendly than the rest if he knew where the gay bar was.

From the response he received, he might as well have asked the whereabouts of the nearest paedophile ring. In the end I rang Murphy, who, consulting his copy of *Spartacus*, the frequently out-of-date guide for gay travellers, came up with a telephone number for the local gay group. Adrella rang them up and we were told that the group met every other Tuesday over a Chinese restaurant on the outskirts of town. We dutifully arranged to meet on the appointed day and shuffled over to this restaurant. Instead of the hotbed of sin I was hoping for, I found myself nursing a warm whisky and Coke, the price of which would've been enough to pay the weekly grocery bill for a family of four, listening to a rather earnest but deadly boring young man droning on about gay rights above the Oriental soundtrack being played through the muzak system. The rest of the group comprised an angry young girl and a clinically obese man who propositioned Adrella in the toilet, receiving a flea in his ear for his trouble.

One night I got chatting to a bloke in a hotel bar that had a reputation for being popular with Tampere's seemingly non-existent gay community. He asked me if we'd care to come back and visit his family's summer house. It really was beautiful, situated on the side of a lake and painted in a soft duck-egg blue and white. We had a few drinks, fighting off his amorous advances since he was under the misapprehension that in the three of us he had a smorgasbord he could sample as the mood took him. Eventually he tired of chasing us around and suggested instead that we all take a sauna.

I didn't fancy this one iota, but Adrella and Ebony were instantly full of enthusiasm so I reluctantly agreed to join them in the sweat box. Once I'd become accustomed to the dry heat it was really very pleasant, especially as I got to beat our host with a bunch of birch twigs – hard.

The normal procedure after taking a sauna was to jump in the freezing cold lake, we were told, and after a large tot of whisky I took the plunge and leapt in. After the initial shock of the water temperature wore off, bobbing around in the still, cool waters of the lake just as the dawn was rising was a remarkable experience and the only one, apart from dropping condoms filled with water from the roof of the apartment on gangs of noisy drunks below, I can say I really enjoyed during my entire stay in Tampere.

*   *   *

I once met the late Eric Sykes on the branch line from York to Green Hammerton. He was off to play golf and I was on my way to the Hammerton Hotel for another three-night stint. My wig, in its usual mode of transport – a black bin-liner – sat next to me on the seat where I could keep an eye on it, until the train came to a sudden halt and sent it flying from the bin-bag and rolling down the aisle.

'What the . . .' Eric Sykes exclaimed at the sight of the Savage locks wedged under a seat. 'Is that a human head?'

We got talking and I was able to explain what I was doing with a huge white wig in a bin-bag.

'You know something?' he said. 'Comedy really is a funny thing. It's not a job, it's a vocation. You never stop, do you, looking for material to make a gag out of.'

I knew exactly what he meant. From that very first time I'd got a laugh from a gag I'd made up I was obsessed, constantly searching for the minutiae of life that would inspire me to come up with something funny.

I'd recently acquired two Persian kittens from a friend of ours, another act on the circuit named Billy St James, known to her chums as Madame Betty. Betty bred Persian cats and, unable to resist, I bought two beautiful kittens whom I called Lucy and Dolly. Lucy grew into a big blowsy moggy who I swore was the reincarnation of a prominent Nazi general as she had the habit of swaggering into a room and raising her right paw and growling something that sounded very like 'Heil Hitler!'. I got a lot of material out of those cats, as I did from Vera, who had temporarily moved in with me, having left the Black Cap in a hurry.

'I'll only be here for the weekend, Lily,' he said. Famous last words – he ended up staying six years.

As 81 Vicky Mansions was only a one-bedroom flat he had to sleep on the sofa cushions on the floor. Not that he minded as he was usually half pissed by the time his head hit the deck, as was I, as was everyone, it seemed.

When the hurricane of October '87 hit and great metal council bins took off down the South Lambeth Road and bounced off parked cars, and the hoarding next to the library was ripped apart by the sheer force of the wind and sent flying towards Victoria Mansions, breaking windows on its way, Vera slept soundly. Throughout the noise and the alarms and the gale-force wind blowing through the old sash windows that sent the Habitat blinds flying upwards and sticking to the ceiling, still he slept. He lay on his back on the sofa cushions with his mouth open, snoring at a volume that could compete with the raging storm outside. His face was jet black from a large soot fall in the fireplace next to him, like one of the Black and White Minstrels.

CHAPTER 10

I'VE GOT LOTS OF DIARIES, ALL OF THEM EMPTY APART from a few jottings here and there and the occasional rant against Murphy after we'd had another argument and I needed somewhere to vent my spleen. One entry states that if Edward Albee had really written *Who's Afraid of Virginia Woolf?* with two gay men in mind then Murphy and I would be ideal casting. All of my diaries start off the new year in the same way, with me getting up extremely late in the afternoon as a result of the previous night's celebrations.

Each and every year I open the pages of a brand new diary with good intentions, determined that this year I'm going to keep a comprehensive record of every day's events. I rarely get past January. The entry for 8 January 1988 states that after getting up late in the day following an evening in the Vauxhall that went on until 6 a.m. I had to go to work at Silks, a club in a shopping centre in Shepherd's Bush. Silks belonged to Tricky Dicky, a promoter and DJ who ran a lot of one-nighters and gave me a lot of work.

I normally didn't mind Silks that much and on this

night I was working with Hush as the Playgirls, which meant I didn't have to yak for half an hour on the mike, a blessing when I felt that I didn't have anything new to say. The diary records that on this night we 'had a fight with a couple of lairy queens'. Hush ended up punching one and I hit the other one, and the entire incident was captured on film by a BBC crew who were recording a documentary about life in Shepherd's Bush. Thankfully, to the best of my knowledge it has never seen the light of day.

There seems to be a lot of rough-housing in public houses throughout the pages of this book but I'm afraid that's how it was, and when the going got rough the rough got going. I've lost track of the times I've been involved in a punch-up in the Vauxhall or the times I've leapt from the stage to deal with those who I considered had stepped over the line, always safe in the knowledge that if it got out of hand Vera and Pat would be across that bar with the speed of a couple of Olympic pole-vaulters while Murphy, usually to be found at the other end of the room chatting someone up, would somehow be across the pub in seconds.

Paul, a friend of mine in Manchester who worked on a gay paper, introduced me to Bernard Jay, Divine's manager and friend. I'd been a devotee of the films of John Waters and of Divine since Doris Dale had first shown me the video and I got to meet Divine in the dressing room of the Hippodrome after the show. As was to be expected, he was nothing like his foul-mouthed alter ego who sat in a playpen at the end of his act and bit the heads off fish. Glenn Milstead, the man behind Divine, was a charming, friendly, smartly dressed gentleman whom I liked very much. He had a passion for marijuana, a substance he was experiencing trouble getting hold of in London. Chrissie soon remedied this problem by going back to the Mansions, returning with a bag of grass courtesy of our budgie-loving friendly neighbourhood dealer.

Bernard came to see me and Adrella work at the Black Cap and rang the next day to offer me a few dates in Fort Lauderdale. Murphy, who had been booking the acts into the Vauxhall for some time now, had also taken over the unenviable position as my manager as I hated having to deal with agents and pub landlords over the phone. Hopeless when it came to naming a fee, I often undercharged, but with Murphy now at the helm that burden was taken off my shoulders, leaving me free to deal with the job in hand.

Vera was now working behind the bar of the Vauxhall, thanks to me putting a word in for him with Pat. What with me appearing three times a week, Murphy booking the acts and Vera behind the bar, it was quite a family affair. 'I'll only stick it out for a month or so till I sort meself out,' Vera said, another case of famous last words as he ended up being a regular fixture. He stayed for over seven years as one of the team that *Time Out* magazine a little unfairly if not downright cruelly described as 'the ugliest bar staff in London'.

Bernard Jay told Murphy that he wanted to take just me on my own to work in the States, a suggestion that

I was totally opposed to as I wanted to go with either Adrella or Sandra and Doris. Despite my protestations, a deal was struck and so on a chilly March morning Paul, Murphy and I set off for sunny Florida. We stayed at the Marlin Inn Hotel, an old '50s beach hotel extremely popular with the gay crowd for its daily tea dances on the poop deck during the six weeks of spring break.

'Why don't you go down and join them?' Murphy asked as we watched the crowd of screaming, dancing, scantily clad tanned bodies below from the balcony.

'Cos I'd sooner join the Ku Klux Klan, that's why,' I answered. 'You know I hate anything like that.' I'd have felt like a grubby English sparrow among those birds of paradise cavorting around the pool and nothing would induce me to strip off among all that tanned American flesh to reveal my own blue-grey pallor. They all looked so healthy, sexy and glamorous and I was keeping well away.

'Well I'm going to have a look,' Murphy said, leaving me to try to do something with my wig which was less bouffant than usual, having travelled across the Atlantic hidden at the bottom of my case, rolled up in the leg of a pair of jeans in case customs asked too many questions. 'I'm not missing out on a party.'

Within five minutes he was back.

'Not to your liking then?' I asked, lifting the hair of the wig with a tailcomb and giving it a good blast from a can of lacquer.

'Well, there's gay and then there's very gay, and that down there is very, very, very gay' was the party boy's only comment.

319

The hair lacquer came in handy for killing the enormous palmetto bugs that scuttled across the floor with alarming regularity. One good squirt was enough to paralyse them, enabling me to squash them with the *Yellow Pages*. The covers of this makeshift instrument of death were soon splattered brown with the blood of my many victims.

During spring break Fort Lauderdale is heaving with teenagers and lying on the beach surrounded by thousands of the little monsters, each with a radio or ghetto blaster blaring out disco music, was hardly a relaxing experience. Every young male of the species took delight in hollering out, 'Pussy, pussy, hey puss-eee,' every time a desirable female came into sight even though he wouldn't know what to do with one if it were shoved in his face accompanied by a detailed instruction manual complete with torch and magnifying glass.

My first impressions of the country I'd wanted to visit since I was little weren't good, I'm afraid, and after my first night working the Copacabana Club I wanted to nuke the entire population of Florida.

They couldn't understand one single word I was saying. I might as well have been speaking in ancient Aramaic for all they knew, as my thick Birkenhead brogue was impossible for them to decipher. It didn't help matters much that I was gabbling from nerves and that the sound system, surprisingly for a club this size, was lousy, plus my microphone could've been the one that the Andrews Sisters used to entertain the troops during the war, it was so antiquated. In all it was a disaster and all I wanted to do was get straight on the first plane home, away from the chants of 'Pu-ssseee', non-stop partying, palmetto bugs and Americans.

I had a few days' stay of execution before my next gig, which was to take place in the disco of the hotel in lieu of payment for our rooms. I was dreading it, so we went to Disneyland for a couple of days, staying in the kind of run-down motel that I'd seen so often in the movies.

As a kid, my two goals in life were to go on holiday to a Butlin's Holiday Camp and Disneyland. My mother wouldn't even consider the former as she thought Butlin's 'common', and Disneyland was out of the question as it was way out of our price league.

'The only way you'll get to Disneyland, son, is if you join the merchant navy and go to sea,' I remember her saying as she ran a sheet through the mangle, 'or if your dad wins the pools and I don't hold out much hope on that one, seeing's how he couldn't win a bloody argument.'

Now here I was, standing at the gates of the Magic Kingdom and gazing upon Cinderella's Castle, gibbering ecstatically like a child, bursting at the seams to explore every single square inch of this promised land.

I tore around with the speed of a roadrunner, impatient to get on the rides and irritated with Paul and Murphy for not showing the same enthusiasm. I made poor, long-suffering Murphy go on the Peter Pan ride with me six times, oohing and aahing each time as our car, shaped like Captain Hook's galleon, flew over Tower Bridge. Either some pixie dust had fallen on him or he'd been temporarily lobotomized by the subliminal hammering he was taking from the Disney Corporation's brand of highly manufactured magic as he started to enjoy himself, even going so far as to ask me with glazed eyes and a rictus grin if I wanted to go on the Pinocchio ride again.

I'd like to take the opportunity to apologize here and now to the young woman who played Snow White, for I stalked her with the zeal of a *Star Trek* fanatic who'd been told that Mr Spock was in the vicinity. I'm surprised Disney didn't take a restraining order out on me, for every time Ms White turned round I was behind her, frantically waving at Murphy to take a photo.

I have to say it was a great day out; Disney certainly knows how to run a theme park. The staff fascinated me. Surely no one can be that cheerful? It wasn't natural. How did they do it? I'd have to be on heavy medication round the clock to keep that up and despite finding them slightly irritating and plastic I grudgingly admired them for their unwavering ability to never let the mask slip. They always managed to convey that Disneyland was the only place in the world they wanted to be, as they flashed that one-thousand-watt 'Zip-A-Dee-Doo-Dah' smile at everyone they ushered through the turnstile.

After nine hours of charging around Disneyland I lay on my bed in the motel, surrounded by a mountain of carrier bags containing an assortment of Disneyana gleaned from the shops on Main Street, exhausted but happy.

'I can't get this bloody tune out of my head,' Murphy moaned.

'Which tune?' I said, yawning.

'All of 'em, particularly that annoying La, la la la . . . shite.'

'You mean "It's A Small World"?' Paul piped up, starting to sing the damn thing.

'Don't!' Murphy and I chorused in unison, Murphy vanishing into the bathroom for a shower and me outside on the veranda for a fag.

The occupants of the room next door seemed to be checking out and I couldn't help noticing that they had a lot of luggage, including a set of lighting and camera equipment. I nodded and smiled to be polite and one of the men lugging a metal case out came over to me.

'Could I have one of those, buddy?' he asked, running his fingers through his shoulder-length hair. 'I sure as hell need one after a day in there.'

'You been shooting a film?' I asked offering him a Lambert & Butler.

'Yeah,' he said nonchalantly, accepting a light. 'We've been shooting a porno.'

'A porno? In the room? Don't the management mind?' I couldn't believe it.

'What? The management of this dump don't give a damn what goes on in these rooms as long as they get their money. How long are you staying here for?'

'We leave in the morning,' I said.

'Good thing, man, this place sucks, it's only fit for winos, hookers and people like us in the porn business. You wouldn't catch me getting into a dirty bed in this motel, oh no.'

Thanking me for the cigarette, he went back to his

colleagues and I wandered back into our room to tell the others what I'd just heard and to inspect the bedding for any suspicious stains.

I'd have done anything to get out of having to go on at the Marlin as I didn't want a repeat performance of my experience at the Copa. However, the audience at the Marlin were a different lot altogether. Whereas the Copa crowd were too cool for school, the patrons of the Marlin were a more down-to-earth bunch . . . a little rougher, shall we say, and far more my type of audience.

In the middle of 'Don't Tell Momma' a leather queen walked on to the dance floor and shoved ten dollars down the front of my basque. I thought he was sending me up until a young Latino sporting a vest that bore the slogan 'I love Florida', a sentiment I couldn't agree with, did the same thing, only this time he dropped his dollar bill down the top of my thigh-length patent boots.

I shouted to the DJ to stop the backing track as I wanted to enquire why these sons-of-bitches (an Americanism I'd picked up, but thankfully later dropped) were using me as a collecting box.

'It's a tip,' the leather queen shouted.

'A tip? I'm not a fuckin' cab driver,' I roared back to much merriment among the crowd.

'No,' he explained, 'over here if we like you, we tip you.'

'Really . . .'

I worked like a whore on a dock full of sailors on shore leave to get those tips, sending the crowd and the hotel up ruthlessly (the leather queen was a godsend) while talking about my experiences in Florida, real and fictional. I didn't really get mistaken for the Princess Aurora by gangs of adoring children in Disneyland, nor did I inadvertently land a starring role in a porn movie called *Lift My Veil and Kiss Me*, the torrid tale of a young nun's sexual awakening shot in a motel room with fourteen soldiers and an Alsatian.

I was simply doing what I did back home, only tailoring the material for an American audience and speaking a little slower to give them a chance to get used to my accent, and it paid off. The fire-eating brought them running with fistfuls of dollars, Skippy broke all box office records and by the time I got to the end of the rousing and slightly obscene parody (all right, downright filthy) of 'Que Sera, Sera' that I always finished with I resembled Ken Dodd's mattress with money sticking out all over the place, even from my wig.

By the time Murphy came back to the dressing room I'd offloaded my loot on to the make-up shelf and was busy counting it out.

'Five dollars, ten dollars, that's fifteen ... and another ten, twenty-five, and one dollar – what miserable bastard tipped a dollar?'

'They want you to do another couple of nights, Savage,' Murphy said, grinning like a Cheshire cat. 'They loved it.'

'I'll do the whole week at these prices,' I said, straightening out a crumpled twenty-dollar bill. 'I've made over three hundred bucks here. Look! Someone shoved a twenty down me drawers.'

'I'll have that,' Murphy said, snatching it out of my hand. 'Manager's perks.'

'Pimp,' I said, trying to snatch it back.

'If I'm a pimp, me little darlin',' he replied, 'then you know what that makes you, don't you? Now get changed and come out, the manager wants to buy you a drink.'

I did two extra nights and then flew to work the Copa in Key West, which turned out to be another enjoyable and highly profitable experience thanks to my new-found confidence and shameful hustling for tips.

'I must see if I can get the crowd at the Vauxhall into this tipping habit,' I said to Murphy on the way home.

'Try it,' he said, 'just try it.'

I did, and someone gave me 5p.

In April I marched with over thirty thousand others through London in a demonstration against Clause 28, an amendment to a government bill making it illegal to 'promote homosexuality in schools or the acceptability of homosexuality'. This bill came about after a Tory bigot named David Wilshire, who was later to be implicated in the MPs' expenses scandal, discovered an innocuous book entitled *Jenny Lives with Eric and Martin* in a teachers' resource centre. With the help of Dame Jill Knight, the Dolores Umbridge of politics, Wilshire was then able to introduce Clause 28.

'They'll be herding us into trucks and sending us to concentration camps next,' Murphy said grimly, echoing a lot of gay men and women's thoughts.

* * *

The comedian Simon Fanshawe and his partner Rick, always very much into the world of alternative comedy, asked if I'd like to compère a comedy show at the Glasgow Mayfest '88. I was a bit apprehensive at first about stepping out of my comfort zone but Murphy convinced me, saying it wouldn't do me any harm to get out and be seen by a wider audience. I'm glad he did as I had a ball.

The majority of the acts appearing at the Mayfest seemed to be staying in our hotel and each night after we'd all finished our respective shows the hotel bar became party central. Ian McKellen, still just a plain old CBE back then and not yet fully out of the closet although there were a few toes peeping out from under the door, was appearing in his play *Acting Shakespeare* at the Theatre Royal and he invited me and Murphy to go and see him. I was slightly in awe of Ian after watching him on stage as he'd managed to make Shakespeare, a playwright whose text was previously incomprehensible to me, suddenly make sense. He brought the words to life. It was a revelation, almost as if a magician had revealed the secret to a trick that had always had me puzzled, and I became both a fan of Ian's and a fan of Shakespeare. He gave me a book of Shakespeare's sonnets which I still have, my favourite starting with the lines

When forty winters shall besiege thy brow
And dig deep trenches in thy beauty's field

– mellifluous verse to describe the ageing process, which had Botox been invented in Mr S's day he probably wouldn't have written. Ian's a good man, generous of heart and mind, who knows how to have a good time, and we've remained firm friends ever since.

A mutual admiration society was set up between myself and Charabanc, a women's theatre group from Northern Ireland who were on just before me at the Mitchell Library. *Somewhere over the Balcony* was a dark comedy set in Belfast's infamous Divis Flats and written by Marie Jones, one of the trio of actors who later went on to write the hugely successful *Stones in Their Pockets*. I fell in love with these wild women who, like myself, enjoyed nothing more than a late night after a show spent drinking, singing and spinning a good yarn in the presence of lively company. Murphy sang 'Slievenamon', an Irish ballad that my father would've enjoyed and that had the Irish girls in tears and me heartlessly squirming.

Marie promised to put me in one of her plays if I agreed to perform it with them in the Divis Flats, which of course I did, so if you're reading this, Marie, I'm still bloody waiting.

Business was very good for the show at the Mitchell Library, which thankfully went extremely well. Despite my initial reticence at leaving the protective cocoon of the gay circuit for the uncharted territory of the Glasgow Mayfest I loved every minute of it, especially my glowing reviews in the broadsheets, which I pretended I hadn't seen as I'd already adopted the stance among actors that 'I never read them'.

I was nervous on the first night of the show, unable to sit still and chain-smoking to calm down.

'What's up with you?' Murphy said, annoyingly unruffled as I tried to hide my nerves in the dressing room I shared with the other comics. 'What are you getting nervous about? Don't forget, this lot out there have never seen you before, give 'em the old tried and true you've been doing down the Vauxhall.'

I had a little notebook in which I'd jotted down all manner of jokes and stories. I kept it hidden, embarrassed in case anyone saw it as I assumed that all comedy was supposed to be spontaneous. None of the other drag acts kept a 'joke book', or at least if they did I wasn't aware of it. Writing stuff down and preparing what you were going to say on stage I saw as slightly fraudulent.

Hattie Hayridge, a very funny comic on the bill who became our pal, sat down beside me and whipped a pad out, writing something at the top of the page.

'I always put down "Good Evening",' she said, pausing to think what was going to follow this greeting. 'Even though I never actually say it, it gets me started.'

'Do you always write out what you're going to say?' I asked her, agog that I'd found a kindred spirit who shared my guilty secret.

'Of course I do,' she said. 'I think everyone writes their set out, helps you to remember it.'

Another revelation, and from that day forth I no longer felt ashamed to consult my notebook in front of others.

I was loath to leave at the end of the week so Murphy suggested that we drive up to the Isle of Skye for a few days.

The four-hour drive from Glasgow to the Kyle of Lochalsh is one of the most beautiful in the world and the more I saw of Scotland the more I liked it. At the Kyle of Lochalsh we took the boat over to Skye, a more romantic way to get there but less practical than the yet-to-be-built controversial bridge.

The Isle of Skye. Even the name sounds magical and, compared to South Lambeth Road, it was. We checked into the Skeabost Country House Hotel, a former hunting lodge built by MacDonalds (the clan, not the fast food chain) on the edge of Loch Snizort. The view from our bedroom window was straight off the lid of a 1960s chocolate box, so beautiful it couldn't possibly be real. Not that stunning views are a rarity on Skye; everywhere you turn there's scenery to take your breath away.

Murphy went off to play golf while I took advantage of the bathroom and the giant bath just screaming to be filled with hot water and the bluebell bath oil that sat on a snowy white flannel on the bath rack. My bathroom at Vicky Mansions was still painted the same depressing chocolate-brown colour that the previous tenant had claimed made the room feel 'womb-like'. I couldn't be bothered to decorate it. I didn't know where to start as so much needed doing, including a new bath, sink and toilet. The fittings hadn't been changed since the day they were first installed just after the war.

Even John Haigh, the acid-bath murderer, would've come up with a different way of disposing of his victims faced with the prospect of my bath and bathroom.

* * *

Murphy was forever taking me on long hikes up mountains. I'd give out and moan every inch of the ascent, only to find when I got to the top and was finally allowed to sit, silent for once, and drink in the unbelievable glory of the panoramic view around us that I was glad I'd made the effort. When I wasn't walking and eating I was ensconced in the luxurious bathroom soaking in a bath reeking of bluebell soap and bath oil. I became addicted to the smell and craved it as an addict would cocaine, only instead of standing over the lavatory cistern snorting coke I was inhaling the complimentary bottles of all things bluebell.

Our supposed few days grew into a fortnight moving around the islands and staying in small hotels and I'd probably still be there now, I was so in love with the place, if we hadn't run out of money. I needed to get back to work.

The Royal Burlesk was billed as 'The Most Outrageous Show in Britain' when in actuality it was pretty tame stuff. It was a male strip show with me acting as compère and we appeared at the Wimbledon Theatre, the Theatre Royal, Hanley, and the Pavilion in Brighton. In spite of Brighton's racy reputation there was a rule about how much a stripper was allowed to take off and when the stage manager reminded everyone over the backstage tannoy just before the show went up that 'Strippers must leave their G-strings on or we'll be raided,' it was music to my ears – pure *Gypsy*. The expectant ladies in the audience weren't very pleased, however, if their repeated chant was anything to go by.

The only thing they seemed to want to see was 'dick'.

God bless the Tory councillor who accused the show of turning Brighton into the 'cesspit of Europe' and said we were 'promoting the most depraved filth to the younger generation', for no sooner had the *Brighton and Hove Leader* hit the newsagents' counters with its damning front-page editorial than the phones in the box office went mad, selling every ticket within half an hour. Such was the demand we could've run all through the summer with 'House Full' signs outside every night. It goes to prove, give the public what they want . . .

Despite having lots of offers to go and work in Liverpool I'd always turned them down as I reckoned I'd be slaughtered. You're never a prophet in your own town and as the majority of folk up there are wickedly funny I thought I didn't stand a chance. But after persistent phone requests from Tommy, the manager of Jody's club, and a pep talk from Murphy I conceded defeat and we set off for Liverpool. The tide was high and the room provided for me to get ready in downstairs was flooded and I had to get dressed standing in my case to avoid rising damp up my tights. It seemed the entire gay population had turned out for the homecoming of Lily Savage, each and every one a critic. I took more than a deep breath before I walked on to the dance floor in front of them – I necked a pint of cider.

'"How long are you in Liverpool for?" the bus conductor asked me,' I said. '"Do you come back home a lot then, girl?"

'"Well, it depends on how often our Vera sends me a

VO [visiting order],"' and with that I was off like a rat out of a trap.

It was wonderful working in Liverpool. We spoke the same language and I could joke about all the old characters who hung about Liverpool's gay bars, even daring to send up that sacred cow, Sadie, the formidable owner of Sadie's Bar Royale. Far from being offended, he appeared to be flattered, to the extent of allowing me to pull him up on to the dance floor at the end to take a bow, and stunning me and the audience by smiling graciously, the first time Sadie's lips had made such a movement in living memory.

We stayed in the Adelphi that night, the hotel that I'd walked past as a child, my mother telling me that it was 'too posh for us' when I asked her if we could go in. The Adelphi was once regarded as the most luxurious hotel outside of London and had played host in its day to such diverse characters as Winston Churchill and Roy Rogers and his horse, Trigger.

The magnificent public room was used as the interior of a liner for *Brideshead Revisited*, which is apt as the Adelphi was where all the wealthy transatlantic passengers stayed when waiting to take the boat to the States. The hotel has such wide corridors to enable the porters to stagger along under the weight of trolleys piled high and wide with steamer trunks. There used to be traces of the hotel's glory days in the rooms, particularly those with the huge walk-in wardrobes, the rows of glass-fronted drawers, each with a little brass plate bearing the name of the articles inside – evening gloves, wing collars, suspenders – memories of a bygone age slightly at odds with the avocado-green jacuzzi. I've got a soft spot for the Adelphi, having stayed there so many times over the years, and would love nothing more than for a trillionaire entrepreneur with a passion for the great liner hotels to restore her to her former glory.

I couldn't sneak into Liverpool and out again without visiting my mother first, so I rang her up and told her we were coming over.

'We?' she said, slightly panicked.

'Yes, me and a mate.' It seemed odd referring to Murphy as a mate but then I was hardly going to say he was my lover, was I? Not that I would've anyway. 'Lover' is too Lady Chatterley for me, 'boyfriend' is juvenile and 'partner' sounds far too formal, and as for introducing the paramour as 'This is me friend' . . . well.

'I hope you're not looking for something to eat,' she said, munching something, 'cos I've got nothing in.'

'Don't worry about food, see you in an hour.'

Before we checked out I rang Vera to tell him how the night had gone.

'Bernard Padden's been on the phone for you all morning. You've got to call him, it's urgent,' Vera said.

Bernard had written the plays I'd appeared in at the Latchmere and he'd recently set himself up as an agent, working from the front room of his north London flat. I'd signed up with him and he was bloody good as within three days he'd got me an interview for *The Bill*. I'd gone along to Barlby Road in west London to meet

Angela Grosvenor, the casting director, who told me that they were looking for someone to play a snout for one of the most popular characters, DS Ted Roach.

A snout is a police informant and this one just so happened to be a fully paid-up, card-carrying transvestite. At the meeting I discussed the part with the writer, Kevin Clarke, a fellow Birkonian, and the director, Brian Farnham, all of us coming to the same conclusion: that Roxanne, for that was this character's name, shouldn't be anything like Lily. She should be slightly pathetic, a raddled old alley cat, nervously chain-smoking as she delivered her information to Roach in some dark back alley or in a car parked in a side street of a run-down area of west London.

Kevin was one of the principal writers on *The Bill* and I ended up going back as Roxanne for three episodes as 'Personal Imports', my first episode, was considered one of the best ever written in the series so far. Kevin was a great writer. I took him down to the Elly to meet a couple of real-life Roxannes and I could see his mind clocking up overtime as he observed everything that was going on around him.

Even though my meeting went very well I couldn't help thinking on the bus home that in the end they'd probably settle on an experienced actor, and when I still hadn't heard anything after a week I reluctantly put it out of mind. Now here was Bernard telling me I'd got the job and would start filming on 22 August. I wanted to rush down Lime Street telling everyone I was going to be on *The Bill*. Everyone, that is, except my ma, who was still under the misapprehension that I was employed by Camden Council. She might just question this sudden transition from social services to acting. I was reticent about telling her as I wasn't sure how she'd react to seeing me trannied up. Also I didn't want her to worry. She was always wondering what I was up to and wouldn't understand why I'd given up a good job to go into a business that was notoriously competitive.

As we drove through the Mersey Tunnel I could imagine her frantically tidying up, plumping cushions and folding up the *Liverpool Echo* that was strewn across the sofa. She'd be 'throwing the Hoover around' before popping the teeth in, fluffing up her hair and patting her face with her Max Factor powder puff that was hard as a rock with age.

'So are you going to tell her about *The Bill*?' Murphy asked.

'I dunno,' I muttered.

'Does she watch it?'

'She loves it, so does Aunty Annie. They have lengthy discussions over the phone about it like they do after they've watched *Corrie*.'

'Well, you're scuppered then, aren't you, sugar? Why don't you just tell her? She'll more than likely be delighted.'

'But I'm in drag, Murphy,' I moaned.

'Who cares? She won't. Get over yourself, Savage, it's an acting job. Now shurrup and pass me some change out of the ashtray so I can pay the toll.'

* * *

My mother was instantly taken with Murphy's quiet reserve and completely bowled over when he paid her genuine compliments about her garden. I knew he'd really made the grade when I saw she'd got the best dishes out, the shiny orange ones with the translucent sheen that Uncle Harold had brought back from a trip to Hong Kong. Not many had that honour bestowed upon them.

'If me laddo had have given me fair warning you were coming I'd have got something in,' she apologized to Murphy, pressing him to sit down in front of a plate piled high with boiled ham and a salad made up of two lettuce leaves, a stick of celery, a spring onion, some slices of cucumber, half a hard-boiled egg and a tomato neatly arranged on the plate, followed by an apple pie and custard she'd knocked up in the time since I'd rung her.

'So why are you back up here then?' she asked, neglecting to add as she used to do that she hoped I didn't have the police on my tail. I told her we were visiting friends of Murphy's in Manchester, which was partly true as I was working there at Rockies that night and staying in Salford with pals of mine.

'You look like you need a good pan of scouse down you,' she said, eyeing me up. 'And when did you last have a good night's sleep? You've got circles under your eyes darker than a coal hole. I hope you're looking after yourself.'

It was true, I was showing all the hallmarks of too many late nights and was sporting what was known among the acts and fellow night owls as a nightclub tan. I'd been working for twenty-eight consecutive nights up and down the country, sometimes twice a night, and out of all those dates fifteen of them were unpaid benefits and fundraisers.

Although we didn't mind turning out to help raise a few bob, the majority of the acts, myself included, couldn't help feeling that we were being taken advantage of, especially when we found out that a couple of the pubs had pocketed the money instead of giving it to charity. From then on we vowed we'd only play benefits in pubs and clubs we knew and could trust.

Despite the enormous amount of funds raised by the drag acts, it rankled that we were still not allowed to perform on the main stage at the annual Lesbian and Gay Pride rally held in one of London's parks. Even though drag was the most popular form of entertainment with a lot of gay men and women on the pub circuit, the painfully politically correct crowd who ran the committee were totally opposed to anything as offensive as a drag queen on stage – unless of course you were American, when that was sexy and therefore totally acceptable. But a lowly British pub act? Get thee banished to a small tent somewhere out of the way, you shameful leper. It wasn't until 1990 that I was invited to step out of the cabaret tent and grace the main stage and that was only because I'd 'broken through the archetype and was received wonderfully as a social commentator'. In the face of such patronizing crap I should've told them to stuff it, but as I wanted to get up in front of thousands of people in the park on a very important day and be a part of it, unusually for me, I held my tongue.

I'd have liked to stay for a few days at my mother's. We had the car and could've taken her for 'little spins' to far-flung places that she loved like Parkgate and Bidston Hill, coming back with a boot full of leaf mould for her roses. Instead, as time was short we took her up to Landican Cemetery to visit my father's grave, taking the 'nice' route through the country lanes and quieter roads.

I watched her wipe my father's headstone down with a damp cloth she'd brought with her, wrapped in a carrier bag so it wouldn't leak in her handbag.

'Your name will be on here one day, son, I'm afraid,' she said, scraping furiously at a bit of bird shit with a nail file. 'Underneath mine.'

'It will not,' I said. 'I'm not having bottom billing and my name hidden behind a pot of chrysanths.'

'What do you want then? A bloody big neon sign with an arrow of flashing lights pointing to your name, saying here lies Paul O'Grady? You'll be wanting a one-armed bandit for a headstone next. It's Landican, not Las Vegas, you'll get what you're given, my lad, and be grateful you're not lying in a pauper's grave.'

After we'd dropped her off and said goodbye, Murphy said in the car on the way to Manchester, 'I see where you get it from now, you're like two peas in a pod – only with one difference.'

'What's that?' I asked.

'She's smart and you're dumb. Tell her about *The Bill*, she'll be over the moon. It's not her who's the prejudiced party here, it's you, so tell her and be done with it. She's going to find out anyway. Tell her.'

*   *   *

Each time I'd worked Nottingham it had been a disaster and I was beginning to believe that our association was jinxed. The first time I went up there to work for a promoter who was holding a one-nighter in a club, he failed to turn up, and after I'd stood outside the locked club for a couple of hours with the waiting crowd I gave up and went home. My return visit left me with a massive bill to have the car repaired. After we'd left it parked in the city centre someone had fancied a dance on the roof and the bonnet. And my third visit I'll never forget.

'If you're there, Paul, please give us a ring back as soon as poss. Ta. Oh, it's Neil by the way.'

When we got home there were a lot of messages on my answerphone from members of my family and I grew increasingly worried as I sat on the arm of the sofa listening to them.

'Paul, where are you? It's Mo, ring me, will you.'

Beep.

'Paul, it's Aunty Anne here, give us a ring as soon as you get this message, will you, love.'

Beep.

'Hiya, Paul. It's Sheila, we're still in Ireland, give us a ring.'

Despite it being three in the morning I rang my cousin Maureen, lighting a fag and bracing myself.

'I've got some bad news, love,' she said quietly. 'It's your mam. She passed away earlier this evening.'

Everything suddenly stopped still. It was as if the pause button on the video of my life had been pushed and I stood there motionless, my mouth open, unable to speak, the blood pounding in my ears as I held the receiver in my hand.

'Paul, are you there, love? Paul?' I could hear my cousin shouting at the other end of the line. 'Paul . . .'

Murphy drove me to Euston to catch the first train to Liverpool. I sat and stared out of the window through dead eyes as a rain-soaked London slowly came to life in the grey of the early morning. I felt detached from everything around me, an outsider looking in at a world I was no longer part of. My world was dark, a silent barren planet, drifting slowly in an orbit out of sync with everyone else's.

The man waiting at the traffic lights, pulling a face against the slight drizzle that had started to fall and looking at his watch impatiently, why was he in such a hurry? What was the point in rushing? We all get there in the end. Go home, go back to bed, enjoy your life, sod 'em, I wanted to shout, it can all wait.

On the train, which was mercifully almost empty, I went over the information Maureen had given me again and again in my head. Mam had felt unwell in the morning and despite her protestations, as is the family tradition, Aunty Annie had rung a doctor, who had wanted her to go into hospital. She refused, claiming there was nothing wrong with her and she'd be fine after a little sleep. In the late afternoon Aunty Anne lay on one bed in my nephew's room reading aloud from the *Liverpool Echo* to my mother, who was propped up on pillows in my other nephew's bed.

'It was a scented candle that caused that fire in Sarah Ferguson's house, Molly,' she said, raising her glasses and squinting at the print, the paper held almost at the tip of her nose. 'She's moved back in the royal lodge with Andrew, I wonder what's going on there?'

'That Fergie makes me bloody sick,' my mother replied, and on that note closed her eyes and went to sleep for ever.

I went to see her at the undertaker's to say goodbye. It had been less than six weeks since we'd stood at my father's grave and I'd watched her fussing over the headstone with a wet rag, and now here she was lying in a box in a pale pink bedjacket with a slight smile on her contented face, finally at peace.

At first I half expected her to open one eye and ask me what the bloody hell I thought I was up to, waking her up at this hour of the night. She really did look as if she was sleeping and it wasn't until I touched her hand and felt how cold it was that the message sank in.

We had a chat, or rather I did all the talking and she listened, which made a change. I told her all about Lily Savage and what I'd been up to these past few years, speaking freely and honestly as I should've done when I'd had the opportunity. She took it very well considering, but somewhere up in the heavens I could imagine her saying to my father, 'He's a dark horse, that one, Paddy, I knew he was bloody up to something.'

In the period leading up to the funeral I got Murphy to drive around Birkenhead and to places that were once important to me, taking pictures with a camera I'd bought in Grange Road. I found solace in revisiting my past, taking photographs of my old schools and all the places where I'd once worked and played, to capture them on film and take them back to London with me, clinging on to whatever took me back to when life was uncomplicated, to a time when the biggest decision I'd have to make was whether to wear the jeans or the flares for a night out on the tiles in Liverpool and if I'd be able to cadge the money off my mother to get there.

Now there'd be no more borrowing from the club books hidden under the cushions on the sofa or being asked what I wanted for my tea or told to get myself down to confession. Twenty-three Holly Grove was silent.

In the week preceding the funeral I had five dates booked in clubs around the north which I refused to cancel. Even though I was wandering around in a trance, I found that the hour on stage gave me temporary respite from the desolation I was feeling.

Pat and Breda came up for the funeral, as did Vera and Frank Clarke and Peter Turner. Old neighbours from the Lowther Street days surfaced in their black funeral coats and headscarves and the Union of Catholic Mothers turned out in force. Following the funeral tea at the Lauries Club, we moved on to my cousin John's house and sat in the garden silently drinking as Vera Lalley went through her entire repertoire of emotional ballads. To speak or, even worse, laugh during this impromptu recital would be tantamount to sacrilege. Vera would stop mid-flow and fix the offender with a glare that could peel paint before continuing where she'd left off once she was satisfied that they were suitably chastened. I was extremely fond of Vera and kept in touch with her by letter until her death, always sending her a 'couple of bob' at Christmas that, as she told me, she spent on boiled ham and a bottle of Bell's whisky.

Two days after the funeral I filmed my first scene on *The Bill* with Tony Scannell. All this was new to me and I didn't see the point in pretending I was a seasoned pro, familiar with working in front of a camera, so I wasn't shy about asking for advice. Everyone was extremely helpful and considerate. Tony was great to work with, as was Chris Ellison, who played the fearsome Burnside and was the complete opposite of his on-screen character.

Tony invited me to his dressing room to discuss the relationship between Roach and Roxanne. It was obvious from the script that the beaten-up tranny and the tough but damaged detective had known each other for years and that at one time their relationship might have been a bit more than just a professional one. We decided to play it along the same lines as Jimmy Cagney and his moll and this peculiar relationship between the cop and the tranny must have worked as I was asked back later in the year, the first guest player to repeat a role.

I didn't tell anyone that my mother had just died. People tend to pussyfoot around you if they know that you've recently had a bereavement and either overtly make a fuss of you or go out of their way to avoid you. *The Bill* came at the right time, allowing me to forget recent events while I was working on it.

Murphy collected me in the car after the first day's filming to drive me to Manchester to work the No. 1 Club, run by the irrepressible Jeff Bibby and one of Murphy's and my favourite venues. Jeff was very sympathetic and had got me a huge bunch of flowers which I gave to my sister, not telling her of course where they'd come from. We stayed at Holly Grove as I was working in Stoke-on-Trent the next night, followed by the New Penny in Leeds on the Sunday evening.

It seemed as if it were business as usual. I was gobby and lively on stage and managed to argue with Murphy with as much gusto as before, but inside I was numb. To describe oneself as feeling numb inside is a bit of a cliché, but it's only after experiencing it that you realize it's the perfect way to describe how you feel when you're sat alone in the silence of a darkened room, still wearing your outdoor clothes, incapable of thought or even motivating yourself to get up and put the lights on or make a cup of tea. I was to remain numb for some time.

I didn't want to leave Holly Grove or see it returned to the landlord. For all the years that they'd lived there, from that very first day when my dad had declared proudly to his young wife, 'Here it is, Moll, a home of our own and with an indoor lav and a bathroom as well,' it had never really been theirs. It was a rented property. At the letting agents in Liverpool I applied to take over the tenancy.

345

'Had your mother lived there long?' the understanding young lad behind the counter asked.

'Over forty years,' I replied flatly. I left with a new rent book. I was now the sole tenant of Holly Grove. The landlord offered to sell it to me for £9,000, a three-bedroom house with a garden and fabulous views over the Mersey. It was badly in need of complete renovation and it meant so much to me.

I didn't have nine grand. That was a fortune and I couldn't imagine getting my hands on it, as even though I was out working nearly every night I wasn't earning much and my overheads were high, particularly when it came to costumes. As Dolly Parton said, it costs a lot of money to look cheap. A loan from a bank was out of the question as I had and still have a mortal fear of debt.

I kept Holly Grove for a few months, using it as a base for when I was working the clubs in the north. It was strange to see Lily's wig defiantly sat on the kitchen table and I could hear my mother now . . .

'Paul, there's some big blonde woman's head on the table. What have you been up to this time? You haven't been decapitating prozzies, have you?'

My friend John Addy from the Gemini Club was throwing a party for his birthday at the beautiful Armathwaite Hall in the Lake District and he'd booked me as the surprise cabaret. Among the guests were Barbara Windsor, Su Pollard and Beryl Reid. After I'd done my bit in the drawing room, dragging Beryl up to sing a song with me, I stood chatting to one of the guests who seemed preoccupied and slightly agitated.

'Am I getting on your nerves?' I asked.

'No, not at all,' he replied, 'I'm grateful for the company. You see, my wife has just been found dead in the billiard room.'

'You're joking?'

'No,' he went on. 'She was found strangled with one of her own silk stockings, a bad show all round really.'

A bad show all round?

I went and sat next to Barbara in the bar. 'There's a fellah out there who says his wife's just been strangled in the billiard room.'

'That's two so far,' she said casually. 'There was a corpse on the main landing this afternoon.'

'Who was it?' She was taking this remarkably well, not seeming the least bit concerned that people were dropping like flies.

'I wonder who'll be next?' she said, giggling. 'It might be me, might even be you.'

This wasn't a birthday party, it was a ruse to get us all here and bump us off one by one, Agatha Christie style. Suddenly a strange woman stood up in the middle of the room and announced, 'I know who did it. I know who killed Mrs Potheringay.'

'Really, dear?' Beryl Reid said cheerily. 'Who?'

'It was—'

Before she could go any further a gunshot rang out and she dropped to the floor dead, and once everyone had recovered from the shock they started to cheer and applaud. The penny finally dropped: a group of actors had been hired to host a murder mystery weekend and very convincing they were too.

I sat next to Beryl at lunch the following day and she was very liberal with the brandy, applying a fresh coat of lipstick after each course until by the time the cheese and biscuits came it was up to her nostrils.

Not used to drinking in the afternoon, especially brandy, I felt courageous enough to tell the great lady gallantly, 'Beryl, you've got a gob to rival Bette Davis.'

'Have I, darling? Put it right for me, will you,' she said, handing me a napkin and sitting expectantly like a small child with jam around her mouth for me to wipe it off.

I went to visit her at her lovely little house on the Thames shaped like a honeypot. I spent a memorable hour, during which she recounted part of a sketch she'd performed as Marlene of the Midlands, a character I had loved as a child.

''Ave yoo met moi boifrind? He roides a mowtor boike. Id to tow in lither he is. We downt tayke 'im to the 'ospital if he cums off it, we 'ave 'im soled and heeled.'

'Why are you hanging on to your mother's house?' everyone kept asking me. The reason was simple. To let it go would be akin to an act of betrayal.

Harry on the end and Dot-Next-Door, two of the few original neighbours left, kept an eye on it for me when I wasn't there, which was often. Finally, reluctantly bowing to pressure from well-meaning friends and relatives who couldn't understand why I wanted to keep a property that would cost a lot of money to renovate and that I wouldn't be living in, I gave it back to the landlord.

My sister Sheila and her husband Peter, along with Aunty Annie and my cousin Tricia, came round to help me pack away what was left of my mother's belongings. Her clothes, beautifully cared for and most of them hardly ever worn, were divided up into bags for the charity shop and bags of stuff they wanted to keep. The selection of bizarre items that I wanted I crammed into a selection of carrier bags: plates, cutlery, a blue blanket that had been on her bed, a plastic statue of the Virgin Mary containing a murky liquid that had turned green with age, trivial items but ones that all had a history and were personal to me.

From my bedroom I took back to London all that was left of my childhood and teenage years: a papier-mâché money box in the shape of a hippy's head, an empty jar of French mustard that my mother had considered eccentric enough to put on the windowsill when she'd redecorated the room in the colours of Tara King of *The Avengers*' apartment to give it an air of authenticity, all my old books and school reports and two flannelette pillowcases that I'd slept on for as long as I could remember.

Aunty Anne and Sheila were quite tearful when the time came for them to say goodbye. 'When I think of the things that have gone in this house,' Aunty Anne said wistfully on the front doorstep, wiping her eyes and turning to take one last look, 'hard times and happy times. The only link with the old days, the times when everyone was all together.'

She blew her nose delicately and kissed me on the cheek.

'Ta-ra, son, don't be hanging around for too long in an empty house full of memories, it's not healthy. Get yourself back to London as quick as you can and get on with your life.'

She made her way slowly down the path, examining the roses for one last time.

'Let it go,' she said, pausing to sniff a peach rose that I remembered had started life as a cutting 'borrowed' from Lord Leverhulme's gardens on one of their many ambles around stately homes. 'Remember the past, but don't live in it.'

My train wasn't for another two hours, and as there was nothing to do since we'd cleaned the house from top to bottom and the electricity and gas had been cut off, I sat on the floor and waited. The rooms were empty, all the trappings that make a house a home, from the three-piece suite to the framed print of Polperro by Vernon Ward, bought in Boots on Grange Road by Aunty Chris for 7s. 6d. and that had hung proudly on the wall behind my dad's chair for as long as I could remember, had been split up and dispersed to charity shops and the rubbish tip.

I sat and stared at the wall, wondering how I was going to kill time until I could say goodbye and catch the 6.30 from Lime Street. Idly I leaned across to pick at a piece of the ubiquitous magnolia chip that was coming away from the wall – and before I knew it I'd pulled half of it off, exposing a section of the O'Gradys' very own Bayeux Tapestry. The next half-hour was spent scraping away furiously with a knife that had escaped Aunty Anne's eagle eye until the majority of the paper was off. Underneath it, drawn on the wall and perfectly preserved, was the family history. A drawing of Chad, a cartoon character older readers will remember from the war years, depicting a fellow peeping over a brick wall, his truncheon-shaped nose hanging halfway down it and 'Wot No Meat?' written underneath dominated the centre of the wall, with a half-decent drawing of Cruella de Vil executed by me as a boy in pencils and crayons given to me by a chambermaid in the Isle of Man. Steve Davis, my childhood friend who lived in the first house on the Grove, had written his name, as had my father, who had added his Air Force number and dated it 1947. Slightly faded was a poem written by my sister in a careful hand in red pencil and dated 1959:

I wish I was a little fish that swam beneath the ice
For when the girls came out to skate it would be
   rather nice.

My signature featured heavily, progressing from the childish scrawl of a five-year-old through to the neatly joined-up writing of my teens. My brother and cousins John and Mickey had drawn Spitfires in combat with Messerschmitts and an army of stick soldiers with rifles firing a broken line to represent bullets at the advancing enemy. In the corner by the pelmet it read 'Christine Savage plastered this wall' and underneath it some wag had written 'and she was plastered when she did it!, arf, arf' while in my mother's unmistakable

351

hand it said 'Cockies keep away please!', no doubt a reference to the plague of cockroaches that would scuttle around under the wallpaper, hungry for the homemade paste of flour and water. In the war years my mother had watched them, revolted, as she lay in bed with her two babies during the air raids.

How could I leave this behind? Why didn't I have a chisel or, even better, a bloody camera so I could record it for posterity?

I gathered up the shredded wallpaper from the freshly vacuumed carpet and carted it out to the bin, picking up the Vernon Ward that was propped against a bin-bag to take it home with me. We'd been through too much together to part now, I reasoned. We might as well finish the course.

The phone was still connected so I rang Reg.

'Prago?' he said, answering the phone in his inimitable style. 'Fong Towers, I'm afraid Her Imperial Highness is attending a rehearsal, this is her maid speaking. May I help you?'

I'd been offered a play called *A Vision of Love Revealed in Truth* by Neil Bartlett but in the end I'd reluctantly turned it down as it clashed with *The Bill* and Reg had taken over. I went to see the play when it opened at the Drill Hall and thought, like everyone else in London, that it was unlike anything I'd ever seen before. It was wonderful and so was Reg, who was much more suited to the part than I was, and in the end I didn't regret not doing it even though it would have been interesting.

'It's me,' I said, trying to inject a bit of cheer into my tone.

'Oh dear,' Reg said, dropping the maid act. 'Are you still in Liverpoolian?'

'Birkenhead.'

'Burke and Hare then, de-ar, whatever. How are you, dahling?'

I could tell he was high as a kite to be working in the legitimate 'Fah, Fah' again, his way of describing the theatre, and from how his career had suddenly picked up. He was hosting the Black Cap's talent nights. David Rosen, the DJ, had put together some tapes for him, silly things like the theme from *Skippy the Bush Kangaroo* and the typewriter song that the audience would join in with gusto. It was hilarious to watch a pub full of grown men and women singing along to 'A Windmill In Old Amsterdam' led by Regina, who was fast becoming a cult figure on the gay circuit.

'Come home, Miss Saveloy,' he said. 'Get yourself back to London, de-ar, on the next stream train out and make sure you don't talk to any strange men in the carriage. Keep your bonnet tilted, my de-ar, and remember what your mother told you . . . Oh, I'm sorry, dahling, that just popped out.'

How could I forget what my mother had told me? If only I'd listened to her on the odd occasion I might not have made such a mess of things, wasting my time going from job to job and not applying myself to studying for a career with good prospects, an excellent salary and the stability that she believed went with it.

'You're a drifter.' I could visualize her now, stood on

the kitchen step shaking her head. 'A bloody drifter. When are you going to settle down? Get a proper job, make something of yourself in the world?'

'Never, Mam, never,' I said aloud to the empty room. 'It's never going to happen.'

Taking one last quick look around the house I spotted her library ticket on the mantelpiece. One of the most poignant moments for me following her death was taking her library books back to the Birkenhead Central Library and closing the account that she'd had with them since she was a teenager.

Having spent at least one day a week in this library from as far back as I can remember, I knew every inch of the place and if I think about it now I can still smell that musty aroma from the long wooden boxes of index cards on the table and the noise from the date stamp as the librarian marked your book. The library ticket set me off into a violent bout of sobbing. How could such a small piece of light green cardboard be the key to so many potent memories?

'Hang on here, Paul, while I go and see if that new Georgette Heyer's in yet. She said she'd keep it for me . . .'

I felt better after a good cry. Pulling myself together and refusing to allow myself to wallow in any more potentially tear-jerking memories, I let myself out and without a backward glance struggled down the steep hill towards the station with my army of carrier bags and Vernon Ward's 'Misty Morning in Polperro' tucked under my arm. The sky was grey and overcast and a biting wind blowing up Sidney Road made my eyes stream, not that I needed any help from the icy breath of the Mersey as the tears ran freely again anyway.

I'd never felt so alone as I did at that moment, desolate at the realization that I'd just said goodbye for ever to my home, the place of safety that was always there, somewhere that I could go running back to, and frequently had, 'with my tail between my legs and no arse in my trousers' when I had nowhere else to go. Well, there was no going back now, my roots had been dug up and the ground concreted over. I was on my own. And, just as I'd wished, I was self-employed and self-sufficient and answerable to no one except myself, a person whom I considered unreliable and highly unpredictable.

How long would the Lily Savage act last? I'd given it a few years maximum before the audiences would tire of me and move on to a new fad and I was realistic enough to grasp the fact that if I were to rely on acting jobs as my sole source of income I'd be sat by a silent phone waiting for it to ring for the rest of my days. And what of Murphy? In my current pessimistic frame of mind with all the stops of misery pulled firmly out, particularly those marked self-pity, lack of self-worth and oh ye of absolutely little faith, I couldn't see our stormy but nevertheless loving relationship lasting past Christmas.

I'd be alone, I told myself pityingly, a self-employed orphaned drag queen on the wrong side of thirty with an uncertain future in showbiz. What was it Aunty Chrissie used to say to me when I was full of woe? What were those warm words of wisdom she'd impart after she'd listened to me bemoaning my lack of funds and pathetic situation?

'Get off the Cross for Christ's sake, will you, we need the wood.'

Yes, that was it, subtle but practical advice that perhaps it wouldn't do any harm to listen to. I might be down in my boots at the moment, unable to see any option other than to sentence myself to an indefinite term at the bottom of a dark well filled with misery, but at least I'd come out and told the family about my forthcoming appearance on *The Bill*. It had needed the fortification of whisky to loosen my tongue, and even so I hadn't been drunk or brave enough to mention the new woman in my life. I'd break them in gently about Lily Savage later on if the need arose, not that I thought it ever would as working mostly in gay bars and clubs I couldn't see how they'd possibly find out about my alter ego. I could hardly imagine my sister popping into the Vauxhall Tavern or Aunty Annie mixing with the clones in Rockies on a Friday night. No, my secret was safe and would remain that way for the time being.

'I wonder if Camden would have me back?' I said out loud to myself, turning to the wall to avoid a particularly cyclonic blast of air and scraping one of my Co-op carrier bags in the process. It split and sent the chip pan, complete with basket, bouncing down the hill towards the busy Old Chester Road.

'Bollocks,' I said, putting my collection of bags down and making an attempt to go after it before anyone else did and saw the condition it was in from years of active service on the back ring of the gas stove. It was heavily stained, with a permanent tidemark running along the inside from where the fat had lain idle and still in between sessions. This chip pan was nearly as old as me and we had a lot in common – we'd both done battle with Molly O'Grady née Savage and lost – and was this the time, like Holly Grove, to let this old trouper go?

I watched it bounce off the kerb, an action that would no doubt add another permanent impression to the many indentations it already bore, war wounds, a testament to the vigorous shakings and hammerings it had received from that Eleanor of Aquitaine with a chip pan, my mother, as she took out her angry frustration over one of my many misdemeanours. If there were a Dignitas for chip pans then this battle-scarred veteran, at the moment rolling perilously towards the busy traffic, should by rights have been sent to Switzerland with a one-way ticket years ago. Perhaps it would've been kinder to let it roll under the wheels of a 42 bus and join my mother in heaven, who'd no doubt be glad to be reunited with it as she could make chips for St Peter, served with corned beef and a tomato with a drop of Daddies sauce on the side.

I couldn't let it go. Like Vernon Ward and the rest of the paraphernalia I was lugging back to London with me, it was an old friend with, despite appearances, plenty of life left in it yet. Cursing, I picked up the carrier bags and struggled against the wind to save the chip pan. 'What Are We Going To Do With Uncle

Arthur?', the theme from *Upstairs, Downstairs*, was running inexplicably through my head.

'Here ya are, lad,' a woman shouted, running after me. 'Don't forget Our Lady.' She was holding the plastic statue of the Virgin Mary aloft like the Olympic torch. It must have fallen out of the split bag along with the pan.

'Thanks,' I said, shoving the Blessed Virgin unceremoniously into my coat pocket and trying to find room for the chip pan, saved from the jaws of death, in one of the carrier bags, which were already filled to capacity.

'Where are you off to then with all your bags in such a hurry?' she enquired.

'I'm going back to London,' I said, giving up on ever finding a space for the chip pan.

'And what are you going to do when you get there?' she asked.

And what was I going to do apart from wallow in this self-dug well of misery?

'I'm going on the telly,' I said, suddenly feeling brighter if not even a touch optimistic despite my determination to stay with my head buried in a cloud of perpetual gloom. 'Yes,' I went on, as if I were being interviewed on the red carpet about my forthcoming movie instead of standing at the bottom of Sidney Road with a chip pan in my hand, a plastic Our Lady peeping over the top of my coat pocket and talking to an old woman in a mac and slippers.

'I'm on *The Bill* next month, and then I'm going back in to shoot another ep in December.'

Shoot another ep, delicious words that rolled casually off the tongue as if I were accustomed to shooting eps every day of my life.

'Really?' she replied, obviously not quite clear as to what an ep was and why I was shooting the poor thing, but fascinated none the less by this unexpected encounter with someone off the telly on her way to the Crooked Billet for a bottle of Mackie's.

'You don't look like an actor,' she added doubtfully, eyeing up my carrier bags and my unshaven, unwashed and all-over general air of neglect. 'What would an actor be doing around here? There's a fellah in our block who was on *Granada Reports* but that's only because the police found thousands of pounds' worth of heroin in his flat. He got sent down at Chester Assizes last week. Good enough for him, the bloody swine, they should've hung him.

'Anyway,' she concluded, changing the subject, 'I'll watch you in the . . . erm . . .'

'*The Bill*,' I prompted.

'*The Bill* then,' she said none too convincingly, suddenly seizing her chance to dash across the road during a break in the traffic flow. 'What's your name then so I can look out for you?'

'Lily Savage,' I shouted after her.

'Who?' she shouted back with a puzzled frown.

'Lily Savage.'

But she never heard me as a passing bus drowned me out and anyway she'd vanished into the pub by then.

I wasn't sure why I'd said Lily Savage and not Paul. It just felt right. It was after all the name that I was building a reputation on and subconsciously I'd felt it was about time I acknowledged that fact. No one knew who Paul O'Grady was, even my professional name was Savage. Everyone called me either Lily, Lil or, as in Murphy's case, Savage. I was Paul to very few any more and a notion dawned on me, a fanciful if not slightly melodramatic one perhaps, that I'd left him behind in Holly Grove.

Lilian Maeve Veronica Savage, international sex kitten and riot consultant among other things, devoted mother to Bunty and Jason, sister to Vera and proud owner of a whippet called Queenie. Born to a lady wrestler and an unknown father – although her mother recalls him asking 'How much?' in an Irish accent – she was a woman of the streets, mined from the quarries of Lowther Street and Holly Grove and fired in the kilns of Birkenhead. At the moment she might be relatively unknown in her home town but she had fast become notorious in London and around the country's gay pubs and clubs.

Could there possibly be any mileage in such an act? Could it lead to anything bigger or would I continue doing the rounds until eventually I found myself aged seventy-five in a miniskirt and thigh-high boots, an anachronism, unloved and ignored, desperately hanging on in there out of financial necessity? Would I be grasping for something to say that would grab the attention of an audience old enough to be my great-grandchildren and far more interested in pursuing sex and drugs than listening to the pathetic geriatric in a tatty white wig rambling on to herself about her sister – even though once, according to those decrepit old queens still alive to tell the tale, she used to be something in her day?

At the moment I was glad to be making a living, content that I'd finally found a niche, no matter how temporary and precarious it felt. For the time being I'd hang on until something else came along.

As I walked down Green Lane towards the station for the very last time, the carrier bags hampering my progress made me stop for a moment to get my breath and redistribute the weight. For a brief moment I considered getting a portion of prawn curry and chips from the chippy by the monkey steps and going straight back to Holly Grove but the 'Uncle Arthur' soundtrack began playing in my head again exactly where it had left off, only this time it was final, as if it were playing out the last episode of a long-running series, my series, and there was no going back.

'Come on, you, chop, chop,' I could hear my mother saying as she always did when I was setting off on another venture or to one of my many job interviews. 'Opportunity doesn't come knocking regardless of what that Hughie Green says, and if you don't go looking for it then it'll never happen.'

I picked up my carrier bags, picture and chip pan and clanked my way to the train.

CHAPTER 11

2012

WHOA! I HEAR YOU SAY. WHAT HAPPENED AFTER YOU turned into Green Lane Station? What happened to the years between then and now? Well, as I explained at the top of the show, there simply isn't enough space in one book to jot it all down and do it justice. I could go the celeb/ghostwritten memoirs route and give you a quick rundown on my life and career, but that doesn't interest me. For the time being, unless otherwise invited, I'll stop at three volumes. There are a lot of deaths in this book, I know, but that's how it was I'm afraid and of all the people mentioned in these pages the majority are sadly now dead.

I've called this book *Still Standing* as I'm amazed that I still am. I've survived two heart attacks and a lifestyle that hasn't exactly been the healthiest but thankfully I'm still cooking with gas, even if it is on a slightly lower burner. I've grown more saturnine with age. The tongue is still sharp, unlike the memory, as I find I'm often questioning myself why I've just run up the stairs. What have I come up here for?

Ask me what I did last Tuesday and I would be unable to tell you without giving it a lot of thought, and yet I can remember the streets of the Birkenhead of my youth as clearly as if I had been there only yesterday. I can switch on the Google map in my mind and go travelling, recalling place names, dates, people, conversations and even bus routes that bear little resemblance to the Birkenhead of today.

The realization that I was old finally hit me in Waitrose when I found myself buying Steradent tablets and a packet of corn plasters. The latter were inconveniently placed on a bottom shelf near to the ground, forcing me to squat to examine the varieties of high-tech packaging that I hoped would contain something to give me temporary relief from the thing on the sole of my foot. I'm assuming it's a corn. It feels like I have a rosary bead trapped inside my sock when I walk, although when I sit on the loo and lift my leg up, nearly dislocating my knee in the process, to examine the sole of my foot I can't seem to see anything that could cause such discomfort.

I'm a virgin when it comes to buying the likes of corn plasters although they are extremely familiar to me. I grew up with packets of Carnation Corn Plasters dotted around the house as my mother was a 'martyr' to corns and bunions.

'Look at that poor thing,' she'd say, pointing to her little toe, misshapen and throbbing an angry shade of red thanks to a corn hanging on in there with the determination of a limpet on a rock. 'Chinese women who'd had their feet bound didn't have a toe like that,' she'd

add proudly, admiring the corn with something border-
ing on affection before attacking it with one of my dad's
Number 7 razor blades, her face a mask of concentration as she shaved this carbuncle with the skill
and dexterity of a master barber.

Unfortunately Waitrose don't seem to stock
Carnation Corn Plasters so I settled for a packet of
Scholl pads instead. (And when did they drop the
'doctor'?) As I attempted to stand up from my
ambitious squatting position I heard myself let out a
long, low involuntary moan.

'Gets you like that,' the woman standing next to me
said as she examined a pot of fish oils. 'I've got it in my
knees as well.'

I smiled at her, mumbling something non-committal
as I didn't feel qualified to enter into a lengthy
discussion of ailments.

As I moved on to the cold meats and dairy, a little old
man asked me if I'd mind passing him down a carton of
fruity yoghurt as he couldn't reach it.

'Full of sugar, this, you know,' I said, turning into
Jamie Oliver and handing him the yoghurt. 'You'd be
better off buying a pot of the plain live stuff and mixing
it with some fresh strawberries.'

'Do you work here then?' the little old man asked.

'No,' I replied, suddenly feeling foolish. 'It's just that
I read somewhere that those fruit yoghurts have loads
of sugar in them . . .' I heard my voice trailing off as I
realized I was now sounding like the nerd off *The Big
Bang Theory*.

'I think I'll stick to what I'm familiar with if you don't

mind,' he said politely after giving it some thought. 'I can't be messing about mashing up fruit at my age. I'm eighty-four, y'know.'

Those who have reached a remarkable age and are relatively hale and hearty with their faculties and mental agility still sharp as a pin feel a compulsion to tell every stranger that they encounter their age. And why not? Isn't it something to celebrate after all? Survival?

'Enjoy your yoghurt,' I said, smiling and meaning it, admiring this sprightly little octogenarian.

'I will,' he replied. 'I'm going to have it with my muesli for breakfast. Got to look after yourself, you know.'

At the grand old age of eighty-four here was a man determined to carry on living his life to the full, making sure that he remained independent by maintaining a healthy mind and body. He'd probably live for ever with that attitude.

How would I be at eighty-four, I wondered? Toothless without a doubt and poker-thin, gliding around the aisles hunched over the controls of a mobility scooter, mean of spirit and highly abusive. Not that you need worry, I told myself, you'll never make it to eighty-four. And with that I headed to the checkout, banishing all further gloomy thoughts.

As I started loading the contents of my trolley on to the belt the woman in front of me struck up a conversation.

'Fancy seeing you here,' she said in a voice that could be heard by the people on the bread counter.

'What are you doing in this neck of the woods then?'

I told her that I lived here and had done now for over thirteen years.

'Really?' she gasped as if I'd just admitted to living the life of a hermit deep in the woods. 'We've got a caravan in Dymchurch, been coming here for years. Lovely isn't it?'

I wholeheartedly agreed with her, adding that I had a traditional Romany caravan.

'Oh no,' she said, horrified, tucking a stray peroxide curl behind her ear. 'Ours is a nice static one on a site with all mod cons and everything to hand. I wouldn't fancy traipsing around the lanes in one of them things. I remember the gypsies when I used to come here hop-picking as a girl. I'm from the East End originally, the real East End.'

She was small and chubby with lots of gold jewellery, dressed in white slacks and a striped sun-top revealing flabby suntanned arms and an expanse of wrinkled décolletage of an unnaturally deep mahogany. She exuded sunshine both in manner and appearance and would no doubt have been described in her youth as 'a larky sort'.

'We don't stay here all the time though,' she went on as she carefully packed away the toilet rolls and All-Bran. 'The weather's too unreliable. No, we do a lot of cruising, my husband and I.'

I'm ambivalent when it comes to cruises. I've heard some horror stories about life on board a cruise ship, but even so, having never been on one, I'm still curious to give it a go. It's a dead cert that I'd enjoy a trip on the

Queen Mary, arriving in New York from Southampton and sailing majestically into harbour under the nose of the Statue of Liberty as my uncle and cousins had done so many times in the past on the great Cunard liners (not as passengers, no such luxury – they were merchant seamen). My uncle Harold in his trilby and smart suit was more 'New Yoik' than the New Yorkers.

But on the other hand, I know I'd hate a trip round the Bahamas on one of those top-heavy behemoths that have a tendency to tip over if more than one person flushes the toilet on the starboard side. Within ten seconds of setting my flip-flop-shod feet on deck it would suddenly dawn on me that I'd made a terrible mistake. Unable to do anything about it as by then the ship would have sailed, I'd either be forced to join in with the 'shipboard fun' or remain holed up for the entire trip in my cabin wishing everyone would just die or the captain would show some mercy and cast me adrift in a lifeboat.

The larky sort was aghast when I said as much.

'You'd love it,' she announced, shaking her head in disagreement. 'Cruises are wonderful if you sail with the right lot. There are some fabulous ones for people our age – you know, the over-fifties – and it's not all bingo and Ovaltine neither – although you can have those if you want them. No, there's fabulous shows and ball-room dancing and keep fit. Everyone's very lively, you wouldn't believe some of the carry-on – put the young ones to shame, they would.'

I don't know how old she thought I was but one thing was for sure, this lady would never see sixty-six again;

in fact the jury was out on the chances of her seeing seventy-five again, well preserved or not. The prospect of finding myself in the middle of the Med surrounded by elderly ravers fuelled by a deadly combination of HRT, Viagra and Seven Seas Tonic, who, when not keeping fit or ballroom dancing, were going at it hammer and tongs in their cabins, convinced me that a cruise was not for me.

As I was putting my shopping bags in the boot of the car one of them burst, as they inevitably do, torn to shreds by the corner of a carton of Lactofree milk. Environmentalists inform us that these plastic bags are most definitely non-biodegradable and virtually indestructible and I believe them, yet how come mine are in bits by the time I've reached the boot of the car?

Effing and blinding under my breath as it doesn't do to eff and blind out loud in Hythe, I bent to retrieve my spilt shopping. Mrs Larky Sort was loading up her shopping two cars away and came to help.

'Has your bag burst then?' she asked cheerfully.

'No,' I wanted to say, 'I just had the urge to throw a bag of King Eddy's and a punnet of strawberries around the car park,' but I didn't. Instead I just nodded and grinned inanely.

'Here,' she said, stooping down to retrieve something that had rolled out of sight under the car. 'You nearly lost your Steradent tablets and we can't be having that, can we?' She roared with laughter as she handed the tube over. 'How would you soak your teeth tonight?'

'They're not for me,' I muttered, aware that the young couple walking past had heard every word and were much amused. 'I'm doing my neighbour's shopping' (apologies to the neighbours now).

'Aren't you good,' she said as she drove off, making me feel guilty for lying. Bloody Steradent tablets. I never thought I'd see them on the side of my bathroom sink but the truth of the matter is I'm currently sporting a plate with a canine tooth on it. The tooth that it's temporarily replacing had to go. The poor little thing finally crumbled away to nothing, the damage irreparable after years of root canal work by an assortment of dentists with skills ranging from excellent to barbaric.

Before the titanium rods that would take the implants could be put in place I had to have a bone transplant in my jaw as well as having my sinuses moved. It sounds a lot worse than it was and hopefully by the time this goes to press I'll have a nice new tooth screwed into my jawbone.

While I'm waiting for all this intrusive and highly expensive procedure to begin I have to put up with this awful bloody denture and a pink plastic plate to cover the roof of my mouth that has to be glued in place and is driving me insane. Food is rendered tasteless and it's like talking with a piece of Lego in your mouth, so I only wear it if I'm on stage or the telly and prefer to go without it when no one, apart from close friends, is about. I never thought I'd hear myself emulating my mother by calling out, 'Has anyone seen my teeth?' after I've mislaid it. Once or twice I've forgotten that I haven't got it in and gone to the shop, to find myself forced to talk out of the corner of my mouth like a bad Humphrey Bogart impersonator.

The corn plasters are to ease the pressure of a corn I sustained during the rehearsals for the ill-fated *Coronation Street* musical, *Street of Dreams*. Oh, for a crystal ball and the powers of prophecy to forewarn me against getting involved in such projects.

I finished my second series of the ITV *Paul O'Grady Live!* (a title that had nowt to do with me, I hasten to add) and even though I was asked if I'd like to return in February 2012 I declined the offer for no other reason than that I wanted to try my hand at something different. Hosting a chat show was no longer a challenge. I felt that I was just another cog in the well-oiled publicity machine – plug the book, plug the film, plug the TV series. Nobody comes on to 'chat' any more, it's all about plugging the merchandise.

It had become far too easy and that was where the problem lay. I needed something entirely new that would give me that adrenalin rush again. I was bored with having to write out all the questions that I intended to ask the guests for approval from the network and their lawyers. The same rule applied to what I intended to say in the opening monologue, an obligatory five minutes employed by every chat show host in history that usually involves telling a few topical gags and hopefully warming the audience up in the process. This too had to be submitted to the lawyers and execs before I could be given the green light to utter a word of it, just in case anything I said could be taken as slander – which, in retrospect, I now see as a wise precaution on the network's part.

To give ITV their due, they didn't bat an eyelid the night I went into my rant live on air about the latest Tory cuts, venomously condemning them as 'Bastards who probably laughed when Bambi's mother got shot'. People thought I might get the sack or, even worse, be made to apologize live on air but ITV were very supportive and were in fact quite delighted with my temporary transformation into Dennis Skinner.

The competition for any A-listers (Hollywood stars or anyone with an American accent) who are coming to town is fierce among the many chat shows on offer and occasionally I had guests inflicted on me that I really didn't want but who the network insisted on. I'd moan and complain and kick off to no avail and in the end I'd resign myself to the fact that I'd have to get on with it and, to quote an old maxim frequently heard in show-biz circles, think of the money. I wouldn't have minded if these people were worth the fees they were paid but they frequently turned out to be disappointingly dull and, on occasion, complete prats. When I encountered these guests I'd grit my teeth, be dutifully courteous and affable, plug whatever needed plugging, do my job and then take the money and run, which is good for the bank balance but bad for the soul.

Luckily there were very few guests that I really couldn't stomach. In fact, more often than not, a guest I wasn't looking forward to meeting would charm the pants off me and convert me into one of their adoring fans for life. In the eight years I interviewed the famous, there were only nine individuals who I really took exception to and loathed and six who made me extremely nervous, as they'd obviously had a little pharmaceutical help before the show. Their erratic behaviour during the interview had me on tenterhooks, making me self-mutilate under the desk in case they swore or came out with something completely untoward, particularly at five o'clock.

As for all the rest, well, I consider myself very lucky to have been able to spend some time in the company of these remarkable people. I'd be beside myself with glee at the realization that I was chatting away happily with the stars who were my idols as comfortably as if we were old friends.

At Lauren Bacall's book launch the lady herself greeted me warmly, introducing me to the group gathered around her as 'my good friend Paul'. For me it was an encounter tinged with regret that those old movie-loving friends and family members weren't alive any more to witness Humphrey Bogart's widow referring to me as her 'good friend'.

Now and then I had to take up arms and fight for a guest that I desperately wanted on the show, particularly if this person was perhaps a little more obscure than the usual run from the light entertainment stable. This would automatically disqualify them as a suitable candidate for the couch, the common cry being 'because the viewers won't know who they are'. I had to adopt a degree of low cunning and learn to sound impartial when mentioning the name of my choice. Too much enthusiasm was fatal. It was far wiser to sound vaguely uninterested, in a 'just thought I'd mention them while I'm here' sort of way, until eventually Chad, our celebrity booker, was given the go-ahead to ring the agent and book 'em.

It's not arrogance to say that I was positive the viewers would love these guests and thankfully I was proven right when they invariably went down a storm.

Leslie Jordan, the diminutive star of *Will and Grace* and *Sordid Lives*, had the studio audience eating out of his hand. He enchanted the crowd with his self-deprecating honesty and Southern charm, as did Caroline Rhea, the Canadian stand-up comedian and actor probably best known in the UK for playing *Sabrina the Teenage Witch*'s Aunt Hilda. We'd booked Caroline for the Halloween show and she was incredibly warm and very, very funny and within seconds of her sitting on the sofa every single member of the audience and crew had fallen in love with her.

Nadine Coyle of Girls Aloud was on that show as well, proving herself a real trouper by singing live 'I Put A Spell On You', a song that she wasn't familiar with and only got to rehearse a couple of times before going on air. While she sang I supposedly accompanied her on a white grand piano behind her that rose off the floor as the number progressed, slowly turning a full circle before returning to its original position. It was a very clever trick and I'm not going to reveal how it's done but I will say that it was bloody painful. To stay seated, I had to push down hard with my feet and up with my thighs against the underside of the piano to support myself. Nadine never missed a beat throughout all of this lunacy. She just carried on singing as if she were totally oblivious to the chaos going on behind her, wowing the audience in the process and gaining respect for masterfully pulling off what is a difficult song to sing.

Barbara Knox, the woman who gave life to *Corrie*'s Rita Tanner (she'll always be Littlewood to me), is a true television legend, the Garbo of Weatherfield, notorious for fiercely guarding her privacy and for hardly ever agreeing to an interview. I'd tried to get her for years until eventually, to everyone's surprise including her own, she agreed to appear. When the much-anticipated day arrived it was like a visitation from royalty, which in television terms she is.

Barbara is a charming, unassuming lady who was genuinely humbled by the fuss the team had made of her. They'd gone to town, filling the dressing room with flowers and little gifts that we knew she'd like, making sure that she had everything she needed. Barbara is a real pro, yet backstage she confessed to being extremely nervous before she went on as she'd never been on a live chat show before. She needn't have worried for as soon as she appeared at the top of that staircase the studio audience did their collective nut, giving her a standing ovation. Miss Knox, genuinely overwhelmed and every inch the star, showed not a trace of nerves.

Perched elegantly on the end of the sofa wearing a fur hat that had once belonged to her mother, she exuded the old-style glamour that's so often missing today. She was relaxed and I could've easily chatted to her for the full hour. At the conclusion of the interview the audience gave her another standing ovation and as she stood there thanking them it was apparent that she couldn't quite believe that the warmth and affection in that studio was all for her. I told her afterwards that the last time I heard applause like that was on a Marlene Dietrich LP. We had quite a late one in the green room that night, I seem to recall; it was gone 3 a.m. when Barbara, the boys from McFly and I eventually left the premises and a bloody good time was had by all.

I've had lots of late ones drinking in the green room after the show. Tom Jones is very good company, always up for a few bevvies and a laugh, and loves to compare notes about the clubs we've worked in the past. Bette Midler is another one who enjoys trading stories about the early days and some of the places we found ourselves working in. 'I wasn't called Bathhouse Bette for nothing,' she said when we were chatting in her dressing room after the Christmas Eve show and I was secretly over the moon when she wryly referred to us both as 'a pair of old troupers doing the rounds'.

I'd hit it off instantly with Lady Gaga when she first appeared on the C4 teatime show. Apart from being a brilliant musician, she is a very interesting and captivating young woman indeed. Hearing that I was back on air, she interrupted her tour to fly to London on her only day off to do the show. We gave her the whole hour and it was funny to see all the mums and dads sat with Gaga's 'Little Monsters' in the audience. Gaga was great value and a good sport and the show did very well in the ratings. I gave her a pair of skull cufflinks that had once belonged to Fats Waller and a very nice Burleigh Ware teacup and saucer I got off eBay.

I confess to being one of Gaga's greatest admirers. She

does extraordinary work campaigning for human rights and Aids awareness and is a thoroughly decent human being, and if she wants to go out wearing a frock made out of three lamb chops and a quarter of corned beef with two pickled onions for earrings then that's her affair.

As soon as the show ended I took off for China and Tibet with André, my partner of the last six years. (There's a book here.) Our first port of call was Shanghai and I was amazed at how much the city had changed since I was last here in the nineties. (Another book.) From our hotel on the Bund we could see across the Huangpu River to the east side and Pudong, the skyline now dominated by a mass of brilliantly illuminated and highly elaborate skyscrapers that hadn't been there before. Impressive as this mighty vista was, I still sought out the old Shanghai and with the help of an excellent guide we managed to catch a few glimpses into the past. My favourite was the Astor House Hotel, once the grandest of all hostelries in Shanghai but sadly run-down and allowed to fall into rack and ruin. The old place is now being sensitively renovated and visiting it one hot sticky morning, stepping off the noisy, dusty street and into the cool of the oak-panelled lobby, I knew I'd be back one day to stay there. André was horrified when I mentioned this, considering the Astor one step up from a dosshouse, but for me it reeked of the Shanghai that I was constantly seeking.

Standing alone in what was once the ballroom, I turned my iPod on and listened to Paul Whiteman and his orchestra, who were once resident here. I tried to picture this room in its heyday, in an era of tea dances when it was host to Shanghai society both high and low. Ignoring the jumble of tables covered in red-paper tablecloths and little vases that contained the type of plastic flowers you find in pound shops, I allowed my imagination to run riot and for a brief moment I was transported back to a sepia age of jazz and cocktails and opium and White Russian taxi dancers.

'I'm definitely going to stay here one day,' I said to André dramatically. 'I'm going to soak up the atmosphere and write a novel about Shanghai.'

'Don't talk sheete,' he responded in his Brazilian accent. 'I give you one night in here.'

Lhasa in Tibet bore no resemblance to the city of *Lost Horizon* that I'd imagined. It was dirty, noisy and, if it hadn't been for the presence of heavily armed Chinese military on every street corner and rooftop and of course the temples, Lhasa could've passed for the tallest and grittiest 1960s council estate in the world. It also seemed de rigueur in Lhasa for every motorist to sound their horn continuously day and night and I found it very disappointing.

As in Shanghai, we had a guide who picked us up each morning from the hotel and spent the day taking us around every temple in the Lhasa area. Apart from the street market, there didn't seem to be anything else to do. Call me a philistine but unless you are a devoted Buddhist on a pilgrimage or have a keen interest in ancient Tibetan temples and all the paraphernalia that goes with them, I think you can be excused if, like me, you begin to feel a little jaded at the sight of your seventy-ninth statue of Buddha, regardless of how mystical and ancient it is – especially if it involves a heart-attack-inducing climb up thousands of the steepest steps ever cut into the side of a building to see it. After a while they all began to look like Jim Broadbent and I was quite relieved when I came down with altitude sickness and was confined to my bed for the rest of my stay.

The altitude sickness miraculously vanished as soon as the plane took off for Hong Kong from Lhasa Airport, possibly the most chaotic in the world, and it was good to be able to breathe again instead of gasping for air like a goldfish out of its bowl. Hong Kong felt like a different planet after Lhasa and it was a relief to check into the familiar surroundings of the Mandarin Oriental, a hotel that I've stayed in many times before. (Sorry, here's another book . . .) Apart from it being very lovely, it's one of the few hotels in hermetically sealed Hong Kong to have a balcony and windows that open.

As I always do when I'm in HK, I took a day trip over to Kowloon on the Star Ferry. I like to sit on the top deck and remember all the different people I've taken this trip with over the years. The evocative smell of diesel mixed with the odours of the harbour awakens the parts of the memory that have become dulled over the years and allows me to recall conversations and those pressing concerns that seemed oh so important at the time but appear ridiculous and trivial in the cold light of the present day.

* * *

While I was waiting for a script for *Street of Dreams* to materialize I went off and did a play for ten dates in October 2011 at the Finborough, a fifty-seater fringe venue in Earls Court that I was informed is very prestigious, sort of the Royal Court of fringe theatre, having won lots of awards for the work they produce there.

I remember back in the eighties when the Finborough was a gay bar with a bit of a racy reputation. It used to do 'stay-behinds' and consequently was popular with a lot of the drag acts who fancied a bevvy after work. I slipped in the toilets one night, somehow wedging myself between the wall and the toilet pan, unable to move as I'd twisted my dicky knee. Eventually one of the more mature drag queens, attired in a peach wig and a lurid tangerine kaftan with a cleavage that would put a well-upholstered prima donna to shame, came to my assistance.

The legendary Stanley Baxter had suggested to writer and actor Fidelis Morgan that it was about time a charming Irish comedy called *Drama at Inish* was revived in London and within months *Inish* was financed, cast and into rehearsal with Fidelis in the director's chair. Actors, I've discovered, get things done: they don't sit about wasting time, they make things happen.

I know Fidelis well, having been introduced to her by Celia Imrie who, like me, is a big fan of Fidelis's brilliant Countess Ashby de la Zouche books. In fact we liked them so much we bought the rights between us, set up a company and are currently trying to get a series commissioned. It would make excellent Sunday night viewing (BBC take note). There was a tiny part for me in *Inish*, a character called Mr Slattery who lives with 'an owld termagant of an aunt' and is inspired, after witnessing a drama performed by a troupe of travelling players, to try to purchase weedkiller to hasten the demise of his penny-pinching relative.

The Finborough may have won countless awards but I bet there wasn't one in there for the dressing room. Thirteen of us were crammed into a not particularly large space we had to share with another show that appeared on alternate nights.

They'd stuck huge signs up over their props and costumes saying DO NOT TOUCH, which slightly rankled with us and lots of cries of 'cheek' and 'as if' echoed around the dressing room. We also got the impression that 'the other lot' considered us a bit Light Ent as their play was a heavy Irish drama and ours was a comedy, and apart from being polite on the stairs we didn't mix.

I borrowed a shoulder-length ginger wig of rat's tails off Vanessa, my make-up artist, and flung a suitable outfit together, complete with a pair of wire-rimmed specs with lenses as thick as beer-bottle bottoms off eBay that made me look like a sex offender. Greg, the wardrobe master, got me an overcoat and a pair of hobnail boots. Veronica, the assistant director, drilled me relentlessly until I had a passable Irish accent and off I went.

I can honestly say that I've never worked anywhere so

small before or to such a tiny audience. It was comparable to performing in a large front room; the front row were almost on stage with us. You could not only see the whites of their eyes but the fillings in their back teeth as well and I found it claustrophobic at first.

But I really enjoyed my time with *Inish*. I earned bugger all but then you rarely earn anything in fringe theatre; you don't go into the job with the intention of coming away with any money and I wasn't disappointed. I had a wonderful time working with first-rate actors headed by Celia Imrie, who I'd crawl over a bed of broken glass for twice nightly with a matinee on Saturday if required to do so. As with any theatrical production I've been involved in, we availed ourselves of the bar downstairs after the show and on more than the odd occasion at my instigation ventured 'up west'. They were a great bunch of people and we've remained friends since.

The Christmas date for *Street of Dreams* was, to nobody's surprise, postponed as the show 'wasn't quite ready' and instead new dates were set for March. What show? Apart from the songs, we still didn't have a show. Although more than a little relieved that we now had more time to get this epic together, I was also annoyed that we hadn't been given more notice of this foreseeable cancellation as I and a lot of others had turned down lucrative offers of work over Christmas.

With time on my hands I prepared for Christmas with all the gusto of Santa's elves, even though I err on the side of the Grinch. Plonking myself in front of the telly one evening, brain dead and numb from a laborious session of writing out hundreds of Christmas cards and then ringing round to try to find the addresses of the recipients of my seasonal sodding greetings, I found I was totally absorbed in what Kirsty Allsop was up to on the telly.

Instead of trying to find a suitable property for a couple who were incapable of making a decision as to whether they wanted tea or coffee, let alone if they wanted to live in a converted oasthouse in Kent or a loft apartment in Soho, she was doing something fascinating with twigs and pine cones. It would, she said, give your home an original festive feel and be the envy of your friends and neighbours and it wouldn't cost very much, after the initial outlay for industrial staple guns, wire, glue, sequins, spray paint, etc.

Fired up by Kirsty's passion and the relative ease with which she made these decorations, I spent a good deal of time and money on Amazon gathering together the basics for the masterpiece I was about to create. A stream of parcels began to arrive daily and I set about decorating the banisters with artificial but highly realistic (or so the packaging claimed) pine garlands, endless strands of fairy lights and enough orna-mentation, ranging from gingerbread men and striped candied canes to hundreds of glass balls and a goblin I'd bought in Venice, to make the Christmas electric parade at Disneyland look like a single torchlight in the dark. My banisters outshone the cheesiest of Norman Rockwell's illustrations depicting the American Christmas Dream, and each time we went upstairs to fetch something we'd invariably forget what it was we were going up there for as we spent so much time oohing and ahhing at the display on the staircase.

Decorating the banisters took up all of November and most of December. It was high maintenance and I watched over my creation with a protective eye. God help any poor soul who used the banisters to haul their tired carcass up the stairs to bed. I'd go for the throat.

On the day I was recording my Radio 2 Christmas show I took a taxi bike over to Barnes to visit Sue Carroll, the columnist with the *Daily Mirror*, who had been diagnosed with pancreatic cancer. Refusing to let this terminal disease destroy her, she was still alive and kicking long after the life expectancy the doctors had given her. This gutsy woman, whom I'd known for some time and had enjoyed many a boozy night out with over the years, was now very seriously ill. Confined to a state-of-the-art bed in her comfortable sitting room, she was propped up on a multitude of pillows with an oxygen mask in one hand and a Benson and Hedges in the other, taking intermittent whiffs from both of them as she greeted me.

It had been a while since I'd seen her and apart from her hair, still thick and glossy blonde, her appearance had seriously deteriorated. I wasn't shocked, I'd seen so many friends in this emaciated condition down the years that I'd come to accept it, and we sat and chatted together openly and honestly for a short while as I drank my tea and we shared a ciggy. She was still interested to hear what was going on and I filled her in on the *Street of Dreams* saga.

'I wouldn't have anything to do with it,' she said in between coughing fits, filling the oxygen mask with smoke in the process. 'D'you want me to do a story on it? Ring me after Christmas with all the details.' Typical Sue, always the journalist and optimistic till the bitter end. Her body might have given up on her but her resolve to survive was stronger than ever.

'Are you doing anything about the hacking?' she asked, referring to my discovery that my mobile had been hacked. 'Or are you still going to let it go?'

When Scotland Yard had rung to advise me to make an appointment with the officers in charge of Operation Weeting and take a solicitor with me, my initial reaction was to panic and ask, 'Why? What have I done?'

There was evidence that Glenn Mulcaire, the private detective working for the *News of the World* who had been arrested and imprisoned for hacking, had been a busy boy, as my name and mobile number as well as those of some of my friends and relatives had been found among his notes. There was also evidence that someone had been hacking into my phone.

I certainly didn't feel 'violated' by this intrusion. Violation is a word best applied to the suffering of a victim of a sexual assault. I felt disappointed.

I had always been as honest as I think is necessary with the press, sometimes to my own detriment, and I was usually happy to give interviews when asked, so I really felt cheated to think that someone wasn't satisfied with this and was taking the liberty of listening to my voicemails in the vain hope that he'd discover some salacious news worthy of his mistress, the Witch of Wapping, and the rag that was the *News of the Screws*.

Despite pressure to sue, I chose to ignore the whole affair. I wasn't interested in compensation and as no real harm was done apart from eavesdropping on messages left by Cilla Black – 'It's Cilla 'ere, d'ya want to go to Vera Lynn's birthday party?', a request I never thought I'd hear, or 'It's me, ring us' from my Vera – I didn't really feel I could enter the media circus and stand up alongside Milly Dowler's parents, people who have a genuine reason to be taking the *NOTW* to task, and moan about something I considered extremely trivial in comparison.

'Perhaps you're right,' Sue said after I'd explained this to her. 'It's certainly a more dignified response.'

Seeing that she was growing tired I said goodbye, promising to come and see her in the New Year.

'Next time you come we'll have a glass of champagne,' she said as I was leaving. 'Be careful on the back of that motorbike.'

Sue died as the credits rolled on the Christmas Day *Downton Abbey*. She was a big *Downton* fan while I sort of sit on the fence, undecided as to whether I am a fan or not. I'm mad for the devious Miss O'Brien, woefully underused in the last series, and I'm concerned about the cook who was, if you recall – that's assuming you watch the show, if not then disregard this bit – going slowly blind, groping around for her utensils and confusing salt for sugar and a well-hung haunch of venison for the chauffeur until the master sent her off to see someone high up in all things ocular.

This learned gentleman was obviously a genius, an early pioneer of the contact lens or perhaps even laser surgery, as come series two our cook is prancing around the kitchen, not a bother on her nor a pair of spectacles either as she reads the small print on packets and manages quite nicely to distinguish between a paring knife and a fish kettle. This poor half-blind woman who previously could only get about the kitchen by feeling her way along the walls was now delicately removing the tiny bones from a fresh salmon she was filleting. Incredible.

I had intended to relay all this to Sue when I next spoke to her as she enjoyed listening to a good rant, but instead I found myself on Boxing Day writing a tribute to her for the *Daily Mirror*. I never got to go to her funeral as my face was so swollen from the bone implant in the jaw and the rehoming of my sinuses that I couldn't even open my eyes, let alone speak, added to which I was sporting a pair of lips that looked as if I'd had ten tons of collagen injected into them. An appearance in this state at a celebrity funeral would only have resulted in my ending up in the tabloids and those ubiquitous celeb-obsessed mags and being accused of having had all manner of plastic surgery.

Apart from my physical appearance I felt like I'd been hit, *Tom and Jerry*-style, by a cast-iron frying pan in the face. The only relief I got from the throbbing was to lie down with a bag of frozen peas on my face, which I did, and I thought about life and how quickly it can be taken from you.

*   *   *

2012 started badly. As most of the usual suspects were out of town, my New Year's Eve was an extremely sedate affair with just Moira, our friend who minds my dogs and consequently virtually lives here in Kent with me, and Vera and I gathered around the kitchen table listening to music and chatting. To liven up the proceedings I got the absinthe out and suddenly, instead of retiring after the midnight chimes as planned, we ended up progressing well into the morning, dancing and singing.

I gave a demonstration of my Gladiator Ballet, playing my trumpet while bumping and grinding although not quite as energetically or indeed with as much puff as in previous years, but after a sit-down and a swig of something fairly strong I was up again executing a quick jive with Vera (Vera leading). He was in no fit condition to stand up, let alone whirl around among the dog bowls on the kitchen floor like a dervish to the energetic strains of Mr Bill Haley and his Comets.

At around 3 a.m. Vera asked if he'd taken his sleeping pill. He couldn't remember if he had or not and although both Moira and I protested that he couldn't possibly need one after drinking so much and with the hour so late he insisted that without his pill he'd never get a wink of sleep. Just to be on the safe side he took another one.

Getting him up the stairs and trying to keep him away from the banisters was fun. I thought I'd succeeded until during one unguarded moment he managed to bring down half a dozen baubles, a string of fairy lights and

Cinderella's coach. As he stood on the landing flailing about and discarding an artificial pine garland that had caught around his wrist, he momentarily put me in mind of the bit in the movie when King Kong goes on the rampage through New York, dragging a train off the track and tossing it casually aside as Vera had done with my beautiful pine garland.

Normally if somebody has taken a strong sleeping pill, possibly two with booze, I might be concerned, but in Vera's case there's no need to worry as he has the capacity to swallow an entire pharmacy with very little effect. A few years ago I started to study herbology seriously, a subject I'd been fascinated with ever since buying a book published in the thirties by a woman called Mrs M. Grieve entitled *A Modern Herbal*. It's a tome that looks like it means business and it became my bible. Since my discovery of Mrs Grieve and the tutorial that good woman has given me, I've developed an extensive knowledge of herbs and their usage, growing a wide variety both medicinal and culinary and all strictly legit at home on my allotment.

Normally when I take up a hobby I'm wildly enthusiastic at the start and throw myself into it whole-heartedly, whether it be calligraphy, painting, fishing or making soap, but once I've mastered the basics my interest wanes and I quickly move on to something else. With herbs it has been different. I'm a firm believer in the power of these remarkable plants that we take for granted and if you complain of an ailment then I'll have a cure for it somewhere in the garden. No matter how much you protest, you will be made to take it as it's for your own good.

There's no room for cissies in my dispensary and after an initial fear of poisoning, my friends have come to trust my potions and remedies, grudgingly admitting that they work even if they have had them forced down their throat by me in the manner of a strict Edwardian nanny. A few leaves from the feverfew plant, eaten between small slices of bread to disguise the bitter taste, will get rid of a migraine. An infusion made from the root of the marshmallow plant will miraculously cure heartburn and if you can't sleep in our house you'll be packed off to bed with a cup of valerian tea.

Valerian is a powerful soporific and to test the potency of the grated root of this plant I found a willing guinea pig in Vera. When I brewed up a pot of the stuff he drank a hefty mugful, sweetened with a teaspoon of honey, and was still asleep two hours later, sitting bolt upright on the sofa with his mouth open like a ventriloquist's doll in a dressing room. Eventually and to my great relief he came out of this coma, fully refreshed and claiming no side-effects. Even so, I learned from this that less is more and weakened the dosage so that it no longer packs a punch with the potency of a Mickey Finn.

I certainly wouldn't recommend that anyone reading this book rush out to the woods and hedgerows and start self-medicating without consulting their GP first, providing they can get an appointment that is, or having some knowledge of what they are about to swallow and the possible side-effects. Herbs can be very beneficial but there are some that should never be taken at the same time as a prescribed medication as that's asking for trouble.

Living in the countryside I often come across interesting fungi in the woods and fields and though I'm tempted to pick them I never do as I don't trust myself. I don't have the knowledge or the skill to identify the edible from the deadly.

Once I came across a clump of shaggy ink caps that appeared from nowhere in the shade of a long-dead cherry tree. Recognizing these little beauties from a book on the subject, I made a creamy mushroom soup and served up a big bowlful to Joan, who runs both me and the office with frightening efficiency. She was by now wearing the same expression and adopting the sort of body language I should imagine an enemy of the Borgias displayed on being offered a drink.

Even though I kept telling Joan to 'stop being so daft and get it down yer', I drank mine with my fingers crossed. Moreish as we both agreed the delicate nutty flavour of the soup was, I surreptitiously watched Joan over my bowl as she swallowed each spoonful with nervous trepidation, half expecting her to keel over at any minute and flatten the dog. Thankfully we didn't end up in A and E or with me in a police cell and Joan in a body bag. Even so, I've never made anything from mushrooms I've picked in the wild again as eating them is just too bloody stressful, a bit like playing Russian roulette.

In parts of France you can waltz into a chemist with a basket of wild mushrooms you've picked and the chemist will tell you which ones are edible and which, if any, are poisonous. Imagine doing that here in Boots. They'd call security and have you chucked out.

The big favourite of all my concoctions that everyone swears by is Four Thieves Vinegar. The origins of this cure-all stem from the days of the plague. Four thieves, having finally been caught and convicted after a long and successful crime spree looting the homes and businesses of plague victims, were offered the option of having their sentences commuted from being burned at the stake to hanging if they would reveal the secret that had prevented them from catching the disease. Even though they'd constantly been exposed to it they had somehow managed to evade infection themselves. The answer was Four Thieves Vinegar. It's easy to make and variations on the recipe exist on the internet but the real recipe, the original one that was concocted in a thieves' garret, requires a little more than the basic ingredients of herbs, garlic and vinegar. For maximum potency a little witchery pokery needs to be employed and that is where the true secret of Four Thieves Vinegar lies. Much as I'd like to tell you, dear reader, again I'm afraid that if I did I'd have to kill you.

I certainly felt like killing Vera as I watched him bouncing off the walls as he made his way towards the bathroom leaving a trail of pine garland and a long strand of fairy lights, still winking despite the mauling they'd had. I switched the lights off and went to bed or at least I made an attempt to as Bullseye, one of my dogs, who never normally shows any interest in getting on the bed, had obviously made a New Year's resolution to fully occupy my side in 2012. After a wasted struggle and a few half-hearted attempts at a masterful command to shift the dead and deaf weight my dog had become, I settled down on the three inches of mattress that was left and, clinging on with fingers and toes, I tried to sleep.

It dawned on me after about half an hour of dozing that Vera was still in the bathroom, probably rabbiting on to someone on his mobile. Eventually I went to investigate, only to find that he was having an intense conversation in the dark with the bathroom wall.

'Who are you talking to?' I hissed, not wanting to wake Moira.

'These three soldiers,' he answered incredulously, implying that I needed to get myself down to Specsavers. Given Vera's alcohol and possible pill consumption, I wasn't the least bit surprised by this response.

'Three soldiers?' I asked, just to be sure that I hadn't misheard as I was a little fuzzy with drink myself.

'I'm sorry about that,' Vera said, dismissing me and turning back to the wall. 'I didn't think we'd be interrupted in here . . .' He paused, waiting for me to go back to bed.

'Yes?' he said irritably, annoyed that I was still there. 'I'm trying to have a conversation here if you don't mind.'

'What are you talking about?' I asked, beginning to wonder if perhaps there really were three soldiers in there with him, hidden behind the bathroom door.

'Never you mind.'

'Oh go on, Vera, tell us.'

'We're planning a siege,' he said, as if stating the obvious.

'Did he say he's planting a seed?' Moira, still awake, piped up from her bedroom.

This prompted Vera to forsake his army comrades and launch himself from the bathroom into her room instead, holding on to the door frame to steady himself as he delivered an incomprehensible lecture.

Seeing that Moira was surrounded by dogs, he demanded to have one on his bed as well and eventually, after I'd given up and gone back to bed, Moira gave him Louis, thinking that they'd make compatible cellmates as they both snore like mountain trolls.

We'd been back in our beds less than five minutes when a shrill yelp from Louis and a moan from Vera shattered the silence. Rushing to his room we found an outraged Louis and Vera giving a realistic performance of *The Phantom of the Opera*. By that statement I don't mean he was sitting in a gondola in the middle of the bedroom belting out 'The Music Of The Night': it was a different tune that rent the still of the early morning. Vera, perched on the edge of a bed that resembled an abattoir, was clutching his cheek, blood oozing through his fingers, howling, 'Me face, me face!'

Louis, normally a loving little character who had never bitten anyone before, was in some discomfort from an ulcer on his eye and Vera had obviously leaned on him, causing the dog to attack out of pain and fear.

We sobered up quickly, at least Moira and I did. Vera,

having clearly taken two sleeping pills, was thankfully anaesthetized. His piles could've been removed, if he'd had any, with a pencil sharpener and he wouldn't have felt a thing.

I had the good sense to spray the sizeable area of his face that had been savaged with a can of antiseptic which unfortunately turned his face bright orange and made his injuries look even worse than they already were. However, I came to the conclusion that it was better to look like he'd been the victim of an over-enthusiastic TOWIE in a tanning salon than risk infection so I carried on regardless.

In the morning he had no recollection of the night's events until he saw his face in the mirror. By now it was heavily swollen and showed all the signs of being infected. He really ought to have gone to the local hospital but who wants to sit in a long queue of casualties in an understaffed A and E on New Year's Day? So he left it until he got back to London the next day, when the staff at St Thomas's considered putting him on a drip and keeping him in overnight as his face was so heavily infected.

Three days later I had the operation on my jaw to prepare me for the implants. Returning home still under the effects of the sedation, I was able to empathize with Vera as I couldn't recall how I'd got back or indeed what had happened to me. We sat at the kitchen table, Vera's battered face swathed in bandages, mine black and blue and as swollen as a hamster with mumps.

'Happy New Year, Vera,' I groaned with bitter irony

as I attempted to drink tea through oedematous lips that had developed a will of their own.

'And the same to you,' he muttered, wincing in pain as he spoke. 'A right bloody pair, aren't we?'

Indeed we were.

Sandi Toksvig had interviewed me at the Hay Literary Festival and if Stephen Fry is reputed to have a brain the size of Kent then Sandi's is bigger than the entire British Isles. She's extremely erudite with a dry sense of humour and the interview, conducted in front of an audience, went very well thanks to her easy interviewing style. I like Sandi and afterwards in the hospitality tent she suggested that I write a screenplay for myself and Sheila Hancock as part of a series of plays that Sky Arts had commissioned. I didn't think I was up to the job but Sandi was having none of it and arranged a meeting between the three of us at Sheila's house overlooking the Thames.

Now Sheila Hancock has always been one of my big favourites. She's an extremely versatile actor with enviable comic timing and the prospect of working alongside the woman who had given Bette Davis a run for her money in *The Anniversary* was more than slightly daunting.

I'd interviewed Sheila a few times on the teatime show to talk about her books, *Just Me* and *The Two of Us: My Life with John Thaw*, in which she dealt with widowhood and adapting to life on her own. The books are beautifully written without a shred of self-pity, which is typically Sheila, and a pure joy to read.

Over a lunch prepared by Sandi as Sheila doesn't cook, sensible woman, we hatched out a plot line. Sandi came up with the title *Nellie and Melba* and slowly the characters began to evolve. It was to be set in the late seventies in Hoylake on the Wirral. Sheila's character, Melba, was an ex-chorus girl who had found herself up the duff after a liaison with a ne'er-do-well during the run of a panto at the Floral Pavilion before the war. She was a true blue southerner who hated living in the north, constantly lamenting her lost youth and theatrical career as she taught ballroom dancing in her conservatory to gentlemen with two left feet. Her son, Neville, in his fifties and still living at home with his mum, worked for the Department of Social Security while secretly harbouring a desire to go on the stage like the idols of the musical theatre that he worshipped. He kept a vast collection of LPs of musicals in a bedroom still very much unchanged since he was a boy.

Eventually, after a drunken night observing a talent show in a gay pub, he is inspired to enter himself, coercing his friend Maureen from work to join him in a double act. Originally we'd thought Neville would perform in drag singing 'One Fine Day' from *Madame Butterfly* and, unbeknown to him, his mother would join him wearing an identical costume. However, I wasn't over-keen on this idea as it meant dragging up again, something I was anxious to avoid as it seemed a bit predictable, and so instead I had them doing Al Jolson's 'Sonny Boy' with Neville as a ventriloquist's dummy. In the story Maureen was supposed to act as the ventriloquist but come the night she loses her bottle and flees, allowing Melba to step in and save the day.

After that meeting with Sheila and Sandi I rushed home, fired with enthusiasm, and hammered away on the laptop in my bedroom until I had turned out a screenplay that was longer than Bergman's uncut version of *Fanny and Alexander*. Sandi carefully edited it down, adding more dialogue, and by the end of it we had a good workable script. I must say that during the entire process Sandi was a tower of strength, supportive, encouraging, considerate and full of sound advice. She helped me consistently throughout the making of *Nellie and Melba*.

Writing *Nellie and Melba* was extremely enjoyable and the more I delved into all the characters involved the more I became aware that the underlying theme was loneliness and the sadness and regret of a life un-fulfilled. Melba's career upon the wicked stage was cut short by an unplanned pregnancy that condemned her instead to a life scraping a living as a single mother at a time when such things were frowned upon and in a part of the country she loathed.

Dull, ordinary Neville earned his living being abused by the claimants he interviewed for the Social Security before going home to Mum at the end of a long day, when he'd sit down to a tea of tinned peas, boiled ham and chips followed by a solitary session listening to show tunes in his bedroom while Melba washed and ironed his pyjamas downstairs. Neville's mate, Maureen from work, beautifully played by Rosie Cavaliero, who lived with her sick father and shared Neville's obsession with musicals, was also a lonely character, secretly carrying a torch for Neville, a love left unrequited as I saw Neville as asexual, unable to express any emotions for a man or woman for fear of being exposed to rejection and ridicule. Even the drag queen, Patty O'Rose, was not your typical screen portrayal. Drag queens are normally written and played as bitchy predators, while Patty was tough but warm-hearted, showing her caring side as she gently admonished the elderly fire-eater, Flamin' Nora, about the dangers of wearing polyester when performing. The actor who played Patty, Jonathan D. Ellis, did her proud.

Filming began in late January, during what must have been the coldest spell of the year, on location in a studio in Chertsey. The snow lay thick on the ground as Sheila and I sat wearing nightclothes in a room of a long-deserted unheated house, miraculously transformed into Melba's 1970s kitchen by the highly creative team. As I was up at five every morning it had seemed practical to stay in a hotel near to the location to cut down on the travelling, so Joan had booked me into a hotel in Egham called Great Fosters, an outrageously beautiful former royal hunting lodge built in the 1500s. No doubt every American tourist who crosses the ancient threshold is overwhelmed to find themselves staying in an original royal residence.

I was put in the vast and majestic splendour of the tapestry room, sleeping in a bed the size of a front garden among beautiful furnishings and with a fireplace you could park a van in. Unfortunately, gratifying to the eye as this room was, it was also extremely cold but once those logs in that fireplace were lit, I thought, the room would be toasty in no time. I looked forward to lying in bed in the dark, watching the flames cast shadows among the ornate plaster carvings that adorned the ceiling. Health and safety put paid to that dream, declaring the fireplace that had warmed the room for centuries without burning the house down unsafe, thus leaving guests with a central heating system unable to cope with the extreme weather and with an inadequate fan heater.

I couldn't get warm on that shoot, none of us could. I seemed to be permanently cold, a condition not helped by the blood-thinning medication I take that reduces the blood to the consistency of skimmed milk, leaving me chillier than Jack Frost on a holiday in Alaska.

The weather by now had turned incredibly bitter and the bathroom at the hotel was akin to the temperature that I imagine is found in the bathrooms of those private boys' schools in the wilds of Scotland that the royal family sent their kids to, so I gave a bath before bed a miss and made do with the fan heater and a hot-water bottle thoughtfully provided by an apologetic management. It wasn't their fault, you can't double-glaze grade 1-listed windows and the expense of ripping out walls and tearing up the floors would probably bankrupt the place. Regardless of my chilly stay, I intend to go back when the weather improves, to explore the gardens and enjoy the beauty of this magnificent building. It might have helped if I'd worn the long johns provided by the wardrobe department, but they itched, and anyway I'm far too vain to wear long johns. They make my skinny pins look like pipes that have been lagged for winter and the idea of having an accident, being rushed to hospital and being caught out wearing a pair in front of a posse of doctors and nurses is unthinkable.

The cabaret scene in which Neville and Melba enter the talent show was shot in my old alma mater, the Royal Vauxhall Tavern. It was nice to be back and I felt comfortable, if not a little strange, being up on that stage and sat on a trunk with Sheila Hancock's hand up the back of my jumper.

During a break in filming I stood on the stage and looked around the room, recalling the years I'd spent in this pub, able to evoke the memory of those long-dead men and women I'd worked with, drunk with, fought with, made friends with and even fallen in love with. All of them came vividly back to mind as I drank in the atmosphere and knew that the Vauxhall was part and parcel of me, a place as familiar as Holly Grove. This old boozer was cemented firmly into my psyche and preserved intact for ever.

Nellie and Melba received excellent reviews and was the second-most-watched programme of all time on Sky Arts, according to an industry paper. I enjoyed making and writing it and I'm currently having a go at writing a series as I believe there's a lot of mileage in the characters that's worth developing. It seems a shame to waste the chemistry between Sheila and me, besides which I'd very much like to work with her again.

At last a read-through with the entire cast for *Street of Dreams* was announced, to be held at the Dominion

Theatre. Former cast members Julie Goodyear, Brian Capron and Kevin Kennedy were sat around the enormous table along with Kym Marsh and Katy Kavanagh who plays Julie Carp. Katy was going to be the Angel of Death in a short scene I'd written as a comedy device to get Martha bloody Longhurst off.

I hadn't even taken my coat off before Kieran Roberts, *Corrie*'s executive producer, and Tony Warren, the original creator of the show and a telly legend, pounced on me, unhappy about the opening monologue and insisting ever so nicely that I changed it.

I couldn't understand the fuss, it was all about the *Street* after all. Instead of the sanctimonious drivel about broken hearts and strong women that previous scripts whined on about, in my opening I pointed out that *Street of Dreams* was perhaps the wrong title for a place that had more serial killers per square inch than Broadmoor and where the majority of the residents have eaten their fair share of porridge at one time or another. It's just as well that Weatherfield has the most lenient judicial system in the world as even if you do get sent down for life, as in the case of murderer Tracy Barlow, you can guarantee you'll be out and back on the street on a technicality in the time it takes for your roots to grow out.

The Barlows are the Borgias of the *Street*. Ken Barlow, a man incapable of keeping his pecker in his pocket, would nail anything with a pulse while his wife Deirdre would let any passing stranger take her up the ginnel without even a second glance to see if the nets were twitching. In fact they really are a highly promiscuous lot on the *Street*, and up for it at the drop of a hat with just about anyone regardless of age or sex.

I've been a fan of the *Street* for as long as I can remember and they'd obviously misread my opening. I'd written it as an affectionate send-up, not meant with any malice, but the horrified ITV execs were claiming that I was agreeing with their detractors and adding fuel to the protests that *Corrie* was no longer the show it used to be. They thought I meant it had been trans-formed into a latter-day Sodom and Gomorrah by producers callously resorting to gratuitous sex and violence to win ratings.

My script was too strong a taste for the palate of the *Corrie* execs and to avoid a fuss I scrapped it, vowing that never again would I offer to contribute so much as a comma towards the script for this show.

Predictably the performances planned for the *Street of Dreams* in March were postponed, so I started work on a series about Battersea Dogs and Cats Home for ITV with an enthusiasm that surprised everyone except me. I'd always wanted to do a show based around animals and after years of my pleas falling on deaf ears my wish had finally been granted and I was determined to enjoy every minute.

The crew were great, with Kate Jackson, the pro-ducer, and Jill Worsley, the director, working miracles on a shoestring budget. I was only contracted to work for six days but you couldn't keep me away from the place, I loved it so much, and in the end I stayed six months. Battersea Dogs and Cats Home has been taking in the abused, unwanted strays of London since 1860. Apart from a little local government funding, the home relies solely on the generosity of the public and within a couple of days of filming there I was so overwhelmed by the amount of loving care and attention that's lavished upon every cat and dog during their stay that I changed my will.

Those who work at Battersea certainly don't do it for the salary, which as you can imagine is hardly going to make a City trader choke with envy. The hardworking staff and volunteers do it because every one of them is mad about dogs or cats and is a hundred per cent committed to the animals in their care.

One of the worst cases of animal cruelty that Battersea has ever seen was when a young Staffie bitch was brought in. She had been found by a member of the public in a park, dumped inside a suitcase. This scared little dog, who was christened Sparkles, was so emaciated that every single bone in her body was visible. She looked like a skeleton of a dog with a wet dishcloth thrown over it.

What I found so heartbreaking was that this beautiful dog was still trusting and affectionate despite the abuse she'd suffered at the hands of her previous owner, who had used her as a puppy machine and starved her to near death. In the nineteenth century, Sir John Bowring wrote, 'I cannot understand that morality which excludes animals from human sympathy, or releases man from the debt and obligation he owes to them.' Neither can I but personally if I ever got my hands on the person who did that to Sparkles I'd nail them upside down, naked, to the barn door, smear their vile bodies with a solution of sugar syrup, tip the hive over and set the bees on them. Sometimes I think I missed my vocation: my being born too late is the Spanish Inquisition's loss.

If you want to know what happened to Sparkles you'll have to watch the series.

Far from being depressed or traumatized, I always felt good about life after a day in Battersea, particularly if I'd helped rehome a dog. It became quite an obsession of mine and I'd hang around the courtyard and pounce on unsuspecting passers-by, asking them if they were looking for a dog, because if they were there was a nice bitch upstairs, a lovely old girl, in the manner of a canine pimp.

My friend Amanda Mealing came down with her sons Milo and Otis and left with a pretty little white Staffordshire bull terrier they christened Nancy who's now living the life of Riley in the countryside. I've grown very fond of Staffies since I got to know the breed at Battersea. Originally they were known as the nanny dog as they are so trustworthy with children, but time and tabloid plus a plethora of gob-shite owners who shouldn't be allowed near any living organism have maligned the reputation of this magnificent breed.

It's a crying shame that the subspecies of society have adopted the Staffie as their breed of choice for no other reason than that it makes them look 'ard. They train them to be vicious fighting dogs, parade them around public parks without a lead or muzzle and find it great sport when they attack responsible dog owners' pets. Good owners make good dogs. A case in point is Frank, an ex-Battersea dog who was adopted by one of the staff, who trained Frank to do every trick in the book. He can even sing. I proudly entered Frank for the agility course at Crufts and to my eternal surprise we won, possibly because I'd threatened to sleep with the judges if we lost.

I'd said that I wanted it written into my contract that I was not allowed, under any circumstances, to adopt a Battersea dog. I fell in love every day with just about every mutt in the pound but my big passion was a boxer called Carmine. How I adored Carmine! Ignoring the fact that he slobbered, drooled, moulted and would never win a beauty competition, I was seriously considering adopting him. He was gorgeous, and would take great delight in sitting on my knee and gazing lovingly into my eyes, even though he was the size of a small donkey. Oh, I was hooked, he had me in the pad of his paw and if I hadn't believed that I'd be away for quite a while on tour with *Street of Dreams* he'd be sat next to me right this very minute.

Moira, who minds my dogs when I'm away, already has two of her own and it would be unfair to saddle her with a dirty great boxer who I just know my dogs would resent bitterly. Oh my lordy, why did I meet this bloody dog? Eventually a decision was made for me when a very nice young couple who were clearly as infatuated with him as I was took him home with them.

As Carmine lurched out of the gate with his new owners he turned and gave me a look, not a look of reproach but one that said 'See ya around, kid', before loping off into the sunset. I could've wept buckets but as I was on camera I didn't as I think there's enough bloody people willing to weep on telly at the drop of a cheque without me swelling the ranks. In true British tradition I kept my upper lip as stiff as a board.

I did, however, to my eternal shame, crack at the end of the shoot. All the staff and volunteers turned out and I had a guard of honour made up of dogs with Claire Horton, the chief exec of the home, making a speech that made me squirm as I hate praise. She concluded by asking if I'd consider becoming an ambassador for Battersea, an honour that I was more than proud to accept.

Despite all this love and affection my eyes remained bone dry and it wasn't until I was led through the crowd to be presented with something else that the floodgates opened.

There he was, immortalized in bronze, an exact replica of my lovely old boy Buster on a plinth with a little bronze plaque underneath that read 'Buster Elvis Savage, the greatest canine star since Lassie'. (Another book, quite a thick one at that.) I was a gibbering mess and there wasn't a dry eye in the house, and it was the perfect end to what had been a glorious time spent at Battersea.

Oh and by the way, just in case you're wondering, I didn't leave empty-handed in the end – but then I knew I wouldn't, as did everyone who knows me. I've now got a Jack Russell/ chihuahua cross called Eddy, the size of a newborn kitten and as tough as a marine, the offspring of

Bourbon, a neglected little chihuahua who was found abandoned and heavily pregnant tied to the gate of Battersea Dogs Home. My dogs might have refused to accept Carmine but I knew they'd be fine with a puppy, particularly Olga who mothers him.

That's four dogs now and if the show is successful and runs for a few more series then I'm going to end up on Channel 4, the subject of one of those programmes about people who are compulsive hoarders, sat on the sofa buried under a mound of dogs.

Adrella (Peter), a friend of over thirty years, had, like Sue, been diagnosed with cancer. Peter had cancer of the throat which, had it been diagnosed earlier, would more than likely have been treatable. At first we all thought that he'd beaten it, but he was now deteriorating by the day and the cancer had spread to major organs. I asked him if he'd like to come and stay with me in Kent for a bit of fuss and country air, at the same time enabling me to spend some time with him before his condition worsened and to say a private goodbye while we still could.

For the first few days he lay on the sofa alternating between watching repeats of *Bullseye* on the telly and playing Sudoku, chain-smoking up to sixty fags a day, reasoning that as he now had terminal lung cancer it didn't really matter any more, a sad fact I couldn't argue with. Even if I had I would've been shot down in flames as there was no arguing with Peter once he'd set his mind to something.

However, after waking up one morning barely able to

breathe and with a throat that felt like he'd been sucking pear drops made of cut glass he never smoked again, calmly getting on with his Sudoku and his telly. Then one day he discovered he had neither the energy nor the enthusiasm and Sudoku and *Bullseye* along with the ciggies were permanently abandoned.

Apart from energy drinks, he could no longer take any nourishment orally. Instead he fed himself with some concoction in a bottle via a tube in his stomach, pointing out that he was the ideal house guest as apart from keeping him supplied with endless cups of tea I needn't worry myself about catering.

He came downstairs very late one afternoon after a particularly bad night, a combination of pain plus the horrors of what the future held, had kept him awake. Pale and drawn, he looked at me with dead eyes and asked in all seriousness if I could make up a potion that would assist his demise.

'I don't want to end up rotting away in a hospice, waiting to die,' he explained calmly, staring out of the kitchen window, 'and as you're the herbalist in the family there must be something you can brew up from that herb garden of yours that would help me on my way.'

I stopped what I was doing and looked at him incredulously. 'Are you seriously asking me to pop you off?'

'Well, not in so many words,' he replied, still gazing out of the window. 'But if you could just point me towards some deadly plant or weed I could help myself and, well . . . Oh, don't be so bloody difficult.'

'I'd end up in the dock of the Old Bailey charged with murder,' I pointed out as he turned to face me. 'And then what?'

'Well, you could do "We Both Reached For The Gun" from *Chicago*,' he said deadpan, 'or "Roxie" with a chorus line of inmates behind you as backing dancers.'

Despite the underlying gravity of the situation we both laughed, setting Peter off on a prolonged coughing bout that left him physically exhausted.

'I give in,' he said quietly when the bout had finally subsided, lowering himself slowly into a chair and sitting for a while staring into space, deep in thought. Eventually he gave a long breath, a drawn-out sigh that seemed to have a calming effect on him but one that signalled the dawning that here was an enemy he'd fought every inch of the way but the time had now come to face the end of the journey.

'Of course you haven't given in,' I said, putting on a brave face and acting as if I were talking about a failed driving test. 'You never give in. Belligerence is your middle name.'

He sighed again. He no longer looked like the Peter that I knew. I watched him now, slumped wearily in the chair, his tartan dressing gown covered in cat hairs and fag ash, with two pairs of dirty glasses, way beyond repair and held together by goodwill and Sellotape, perched on the end of his nose. He seemed to be shrinking before my eyes as if he were a balloon slowly deflating, the air gradually slipping away from him until all that was left was that bloody dressing gown hanging off the chair.

'I'll put the kettle on,' I said as millions do in times of stress, 'and make a cup of tea. D'ya want one? I'll give it a good lacing with hemlock.'

'Ooh goody,' he said, suddenly brightening up. 'You can bring it up to me in bed and poison me there.'

Peter was no quitter. He had a resolve of iron and was admirable in the way he always stuck to his guns, right or wrong, at whatever cost. This brief and uncharacteristic lapse into desperation was the only time he considered throwing in the towel and I don't believe for one minute he wanted me to supply him with the means to the end. It was just his way of conveying to me how bleak dealing with cancer can be, particularly when you can't sleep in those wee small hours of the morning and your darkest thoughts come out of the shadows to plague you.

I only saw him a few times after he left. He was admitted to hospital shortly after returning to his little flat in Dean Street and after visiting him in the rare moments I got between filming in Battersea Dogs Home and attempting to rehearse *Street of Dreams* as he lapsed in and out of consciousness, I said my final goodbye.

I've sat through too many round-the-clock bedside vigils in hospital wards waiting for loved ones to expire, each time vowing that I'd never put myself through this most harrowing of experiences again. Now, for the sake of sanity and self-preservation, I prefer to slip away and remember my loved ones as I always knew them and not as an emaciated shell with tubes to sustain life hanging out of every orifice.

* * *

After I'd left the ward I sat quietly in one of the little shelters in the square outside for a while, my mind blank, unable to assimilate any information, preferring instead to switch off and to go with the numbing sensation that was slowly creeping over me, allowing it to take control.

'You're that fellah off the telly,' an elderly man in pyjamas and a dressing gown said as he passed. 'What are you doing here?'

'I've just been to see a friend for the very last time,' I answered him bluntly, unable and unwilling to put the act on for him.

'Is that so, my friend,' he said, the beaming smile on his face suddenly switching to one of concern. 'Old friends are valuable and losing one is a great loss. I'm very sorry to hear that, very sorry indeed.'

I muttered a thank you as he sat down beside me.

'You known this friend a long time?' he asked, ignoring the no smoking sign and offering me a cigarette.

'Over thirty years,' I replied, comfortable in this stranger's company. 'We used to do a double act many moons ago.'

'Really?' he said, turning on the lighthouse beam of a smile again. 'You must have had some good times.'

'We certainly did.'

'And now you've got some good memories.'

'We certainly went through a lot.'

'Then why the long face?' he laughed.

'Because I feel like the last of a dying race,' I moaned.

411

'Almost every act I've worked with has died, there's hardly any of us left.'

'Well there you go,' he exclaimed. 'The reason you are still standing.'

'Why?'

'To fly the flag and keep us all going, that's why you're still standing. Now haven't you got work to go to?'

'More than enough, thank you very much,' I said, suddenly overcome with a surge of sickening optimism that kick-started me back into life again.

'Then go and enjoy it,' he said, 'and good luck.'

'Does the sister on the ward know you're out?' I asked, getting up to leave. 'Don't they mind you coming out in your pyjamas?'

'I don't tell them,' he said. 'I won't be in for much longer anyway. I'm going on holiday when I get out of here.'

'Anywhere nice?'

'Trinidad, I'm going home to see some of my old friends,' he said, grinning at me. 'Sit in the sun and drink and enjoy the good conversation.'

As I crossed the road a woman stopped me and said that she hoped her father hadn't been making a nuisance of himself. Her father was obviously the man in the shelter and I was able to answer sincerely that I'd enjoyed his company and our chat.

'He comes out for a smoke,' she said, nodding at him in the shelter and smiling, suddenly resembling her father, 'even though he shouldn't in his condition.'

'Well, he seems healthy enough,' I chipped in, eagerly

defending my new friend, 'and it can't do him any harm.'

'He has inoperable cancer,' she replied quietly, unable to look me in the eye. 'He hasn't got long, less than a month, they said. He's talking about going back to Trinidad but the journey alone would kill him.'

'You wouldn't think there was anything wrong with him,' I said, 'he's so full of beans. It's just not fair, is it?'

'No, I don't suppose it is, but that's life, isn't it? And that's my father so thank you for talking to him. He gets lonely in the hospital surrounded by all those sick people.'

I watched her join her indefatigable father who was busy telling her excitedly that I was that fellah with the dog off the telly. Giving him a final wave which he didn't notice, I set off to find a taxi to take me to Battersea Dogs Home.

Peter died peacefully and with dignity. I got out the black tie and much as I'd rather not have had to I got up during the funeral service and delivered my version of a eulogy. I've done this so many times now over the years at Golders Green Crematorium that I'm surprised I haven't been offered a residency.

After the service we congregated outside. There were a lot of old friends and faces that I hadn't seen in years and I really wanted to join them at the Vauxhall Tavern afterwards for the reception. I'm a firm believer in observing certain rituals: not eating meat on Good Friday, not looking at the full moon through glass and seeing the deceased off with a boiled ham butty and a couple of large whiskies after a funeral.

Instead I got on the back of a taxi bike and went to rehearsals at Shepperton Studios for *Street of Dreams*. Eventually we opened at the Manchester Arena. One day I'll tell the tale but for the moment I have to stay silent for legal reasons.

Living in rural Kent is just glorious when the weather is fine but because of the recent appalling weather my passion for the bucolic life is beginning to wane. Standing as I have at the window each morning staring out at a grey, bleak vista, almost obscured by a combination of rain and fog, I've felt as if I've been trapped in a particularly grim Ingmar Bergman film. My allotment, usually bursting with fruit and veg, is barren, the root vegetables rotten in the ground and the soft fruits and lettuce devoured by a plague of Spanish slugs. I can hear the bastards out there now, moaning about the euro and munching on my bloody lettuces.

Our summers are going to remain sodden and miserable for the next twenty years, according to one expert I was listening to on the radio, and if this is true then I'm going to have to consider warmer climes as I couldn't bear to live in a perpetual state of winter. After all, I didn't sign up to dwell in bloody Narnia, did I? Fortunately the weather has changed and my mood with it and, with the warm sunshine on my back as I roam around the fields, I'm reminded why I chose to live in this beautiful corner of the world.

My lovely old pig, Blanche, had to be put to sleep

earlier this year and once she'd ascended to that pigsty in the sky I vowed that that was it – no more pigs. Famous last words as usual, for at the last count I have two adult pigs, Tom and Holly, and eight piglets, nine chickens, four dogs, two very old goats, one with arthritis, Minnie my barn owl, her beau Icarus and their two chicks, Percy, short for Perseus, and Andromeda, Andy to her friends, eight sheep including Winston, an incredibly friendly sheep who started life being stolen from a field and dumped in a wheelie bin in Manchester before ending up here with me.

I can't just pack up and descend on the Venice Lido, the only place in the world I could contemplate living in besides here or London, with a menagerie like mine, can I? And anyway, as property on the Lido is among the most expensive in Europe all I'd be able to afford is a tin hut down an alley that would make living conditions intolerable.

I'm talking rubbish as I'd be unable to give any of them away even if I could find good homes for them, so it looks as if I'll be dividing my time between London and Kent for the time being. On reflection, that's not a bad prospect.

Apart from a nice house by the beach on the Venice Lido, I've never wanted to live abroad as I love this country, even though I worry about the society I live in and the way those in positions of great responsibility conduct their affairs on our behalf. I feel I can no longer trust the police, the Church, not that I have since childhood, bankers (apart from my own reputable bank), corrupt politicians and a press who feel they are entitled to know every last intimate detail of your life and are happy to tap into your phone to find out about it. And they wonder why people riot. If it seems that those we are supposed to respect are allowed to help themselves and get away with it, then why can't the man in the street?

You won't be surprised to hear that I've nothing but contempt for our current government, my suspicions growing when I learn that during the Leveson Inquiry the phrases 'I don't remember' and 'I don't recall' were used by this prime minister we've found ourselves landed with forty-nine times in total. Maybe he needs to see someone about this loss of short-term memory, a complaint usually associated with long-term drug abusers. Not that I'm suggesting for one minute that Mr Cameron spliffs up in the garden of Number 10, it's just that his memory seems to be deteriorating rapidly. After all, he did leave the kid behind in the pub, didn't he? A scarf or a glove you can understand, but your daughter? Let's hope the voters forget him just as quickly during the next election, leaving him free to tour holiday camps and care homes as a 'memory act' with his old pal the Dark Lord of News International, billed under the name Dandelion and Murdoch.

'Enjoy your youth while you've got it,' my auntie Annie used to say. 'You'll be old soon enough.'

I never took any notice of her at the time, preferring to believe that I would remain forever young and that old age was unimaginable. Well, it's time to pay the piper, kid. I've become what my mother would have described as 'an old nit', a cross between Victor Meldrew and Catherine Tate's Nan character. I no longer suffer fools and absolutely refuse to tolerate ignorance, lousy service or blind authority without questioning it first. I'm civil to children and old people, providing the former aren't 'ard-faced and I'm not stuck behind the latter when they are driving at ten miles an hour, and I'll always defend and speak up for the underdog. As for homophobic remarks, be my guest but you won't be going home with your teeth intact.

The other afternoon when the sun came out briefly to remind us of what she looked like I sat in the rocking chair on the porch of my summer house listening to the radio with Eddy on my knee, watching my two grandchildren playing on the lawn, and wondered how in God's name did I ever arrive here? My daughter is in the house packing for the trip to Disneyland Paris that she and her husband, Phil, are taking the kids on tomorrow. I'm wisely staying at home for the sake of everyone involved.

And what of Lily? Well, I've agreed to unleash her for the very last time in *Aladdin* at the O2 in London this Christmas and then it really is goodbye. The Walker Art Gallery in Liverpool held an exhibition of Lily's costumes and going back to open it I felt very proud of the old girl who had started out in a south London pub and had achieved the impossible, making her way to the London Palladium and prime-time entertainment. Now she was a museum piece up there among one of the finest collections of art and sculpture in Europe.

What would my mother have made of it all, I often wonder? And what would the lad sat in his bedroom listening to Laurie Johnson on his record player and dreaming of a life in London as a spy with a cool apartment and an even cooler car say, if the old me could go back in time for a brief moment to tell him that the unattainable will one day come true?

In 2011 Chichester University threw open their doors to celebrate fifty years of *The Avengers* and the moment I got wind of this forthcoming slice of heaven on earth I was on the phone offering my services. Those beautiful, wonderful organizers allowed me to host it and for an entire weekend the old nit became a boy again.

I was to interview Linda Thorson and Honor Blackman and to celebrate this red-letter day I decided to hire a helicopter to take Linda and me to Chichester, Honor having sadly gone down the day before by car. It was a beautiful June morning when the helicopter landed on the rugby pitch of the university and as there had been a fire alarm everyone had evacuated the building and was outside to greet us.

The *Avenger* fans went crazy. Here she was in the flesh, Tara King herself, and arriving by what else? A shiny white helicopter, as befitting a secret agent of her stature, with me by her side dressed in a bespoke suit of grey complete with velvet collar à la Steed. The little boy pinched himself with glee.

It was a wonderful weekend and great to be among like-minded people with a common bond. I felt that I'd found my tribe. The students who previously had never even heard of *The Avengers* had pulled out all the stops, re-creating *Avenger*-land in the grounds of the university with a giant chessboard, umbrellas hanging from trees and even Mother's headquarters in the shape of a London Routemaster bus.

I've interviewed Honor many times now. She's an incredible lady and it was a treat to talk to her for over an hour. Linda was also good value as she always is and later on in the evening we hosted the auction in the Hellfire Club – me slightly pissed and both of us extremely leery. We've known each other for some time now and have become close friends and if anyone has a bestselling autobiography in her then it's Linda.

After the interview with Linda we left the lecture theatre and walked straight on to the waiting helicopter that was taking us home to Kent.

'This is the only way to travel,' Vera said, bewitched, softly caressing the side of the helicopter as if it were a thoroughbred horse. 'You'll have to get one, Lily.'

Vera had never been in a helicopter before and had cadged a lift home with us – well, it wouldn't be a show without Punch, would it? – and he was beside himself at the prospect of his inaugural flight.

We sat in the comfortable white leather seats drinking chilled champagne and admiring the magnificent view as the helicopter flew low over the south coast and towards the meadow outside my back door in time for dinner. It was pure *Avengers* and if I can ever get the Tardis, a prop from the teatime show and currently parked outside my garage, to function as it should then that *Avenger*-crazy lad in Holly Grove is in for one hell of a shock when I go back and tell him what's in store.

Never mind be careful what you wish for – go ahead

and wish all you want as you may be surprised at the result.

I've never considered myself to be an ambitious sort, nor have I ever had what you could call a game plan. I never expected the amount of success that I've achieved and am constantly amazed that I've got where I have – as indeed, no doubt, are a lot of people.

I can never sit back on my laurels and relax as I'm convinced that the wolf, if not actually at the door, is still lurking somewhere nearby, ready to pounce and take it all away.

I get called a workaholic and I suppose I am, finding it virtually impossible to just sit and read a book or watch a film. My mind is permanently preoccupied and I frequently find myself not knowing where to begin when it comes to dealing with the various irons I have in the fire.

On occasions, when feeling particularly harassed, I find myself contemplating the supposed joys of retirement, only to quickly scotch any such fantasies by sharply reminding myself of Bran, an elderly Border collie that my dad brought home to Birkenhead from the farm in Ireland.

Bran had been a working sheepdog all of his life and the peaceful retirement in Holly Grove that my father envisioned for him eventually drove him mad. Left without anything to do, he began rounding up local children, herding them into a corner and terrifying them in the process. And, unaccustomed to traffic, he'd frantically chase cars and bikes up and down Sidney Road.

Poor old Bran became very ill and to everyone's regret had to be put to sleep.

'Died of a broken heart, that dog,' my mother often said years later. He was used to working, not the sort of dog to lie in front of the fire. Without any purpose left in his once active life, I think he just gave up.

I've no intention of giving up just yet and will continue to work for as long as someone will employ me. I'm starting work on a new series for the BBC next week and there's a 'little cracker' that I've written for Sky to film with Alison Steadman playing my mum, then there's Lily's final call in panto . . . I'm hoping it will be a pleasant and calamity-free ending to what started out as a disastrous year, although I doubt it. What was the biblical phrase that a Christian Brother used to describe me? 'Born to trouble, as the sparks fly upwards'? You can bloody well say that again!

INDEX